Prisoners of Ho
A Tale of Colonial V

Mary Johnston

Alpha Editions

This edition published in 2024

ISBN 9789362518903

Design and Setting By
Alpha Editions
www.alphaedis.com
Email - info@alphaedis.com

Contents

CHAPTER I	- 1 -
CHAPTER II	- 10 -
CHAPTER III	- 18 -
CHAPTER IV	- 26 -
CHAPTER V	- 33 -
CHAPTER VI	- 40 -
CHAPTER VII	- 48 -
CHAPTER VIII	- 58 -
CHAPTER IX	- 62 -
CHAPTER X	- 68 -
CHAPTER XI	- 73 -
CHAPTER XII	- 80 -
CHAPTER XIII	- 88 -
CHAPTER XIV	- 94 -
CHAPTER XV	- 103 -
CHAPTER XVI	- 111 -
CHAPTER XVII	- 118 -
CHAPTER XVIII	- 126 -
CHAPTER XIX	- 131 -
CHAPTER XX	- 139 -
CHAPTER XXI	- 148 -
CHAPTER XXII	- 153 -
CHAPTER XXIII	- 162 -
CHAPTER XXIV	- 167 -

CHAPTER XXV	- 170 -
CHAPTER XXVI	- 180 -
CHAPTER XXVII	- 184 -
CHAPTER XXVIII	- 190 -
CHAPTER XXIX	- 198 -
CHAPTER XXX	- 205 -
CHAPTER XXXI	- 211 -
CHAPTER XXXII	- 218 -
CHAPTER XXXIII	- 224 -
CHAPTER XXXIV	- 229 -
CHAPTER XXXV	- 233 -
CHAPTER XXXVI	- 238 -
CHAPTER XXXVII	- 246 -

CHAPTER I

A SLOOP COMES IN

"She will reach the wharf in half an hour."

The speaker shaded her eyes with a great fan of carved ivory and painted silk. They were beautiful eyes; large, brown, perfect in shape and expression, and set in a lovely, imperious, laughing face. The divinity to whom they belonged was clad in a gown of green dimity, flowered with pink roses, and trimmed about the neck and half sleeves with a fall of yellow lace. The gown was made according to the latest Paris mode, as described in a year-old letter from the court of Charles the Second, and its wearer gazed from under her fan towards the waters of the great bay of Chesapeake, in his Majesty's most loyal and well beloved dominion of Virginia.

The object of her attention was a large sloop that had left the bay and was sailing up a wide inlet or creek that pierced the land, cork-screw fashion, until it vanished from sight amidst innumerable green marshes. The channel, indicated by a deeper blue in the midst of an expanse of shoal water, was narrow, and wound like a gleaming snake in and out among the interminable succession of marsh islets. The vessel, following its curves, tacked continually, its great sail intensely white against the blue of inlet, bay and sky, and the shadeless green of the marshes, zigzagging from side to side with provoking leisureliness. The girl who had spoken watched it eagerly, a color in her cheeks, and one little foot in its square-toed, rosetted shoe tapping impatiently upon the floor of the wide porch in which she stood.

Her companion, lounging upon the wooden steps, with his back to a pillar, looked up with an amused light in his blue eyes.

"Why are you so eager, cousin?" he drawled. "You cannot be pining for your father when 'tis scarce five days since he went to Jamestown. Do the Virginia ladies watch for the arrival of a new batch of slaves with such impatience?"

"The slaves! No, indeed! But, sir, in that boat there are three cases from England."

"Ah, that accounts for it! And what may these wonderful cases contain?"

"One contains the dress in which I shall dance with you at the party at Green Spring which the governor is to give in your honor—if you ask me, sir. Oh, I take it for granted that you will, so spare us your protestations. 'Tis to have a petticoat of blue tabby and an overdress of white satin trimmed with yards and yards of Venice point. The stockings are blue silk, and come from the French house in Covent Garden, as doth the scarf of striped gauze and the shoes, gallooned with silver. Then there are my combs, gloves, a laced waistcoat, a red satin bodice, a scarlet taffetas mantle, a plumed hat, a pair of clasped garters, a riding mask, a string of pearls, and the latest romances."

"A pretty list! Is that all?"

"There are things for aunt Lettice, petticoats and ribbons, a gilt stomacher and a China monster, and for my father, lace ruffles and bands, a pair of French laced boots, a periwig, a new scabbard for his rapier, and so on."

The young man laughed. "'Tis a curious life you Virginians lead," he said. "The embroidered suits and ruffles, the cosmetics and perfumes of Whitehall in the midst of oyster beds and tobacco fields, savage Indians and negro slaves."

The girl put on a charming look of mock offense. "We *are* a little bit of England set down here in the wilderness. Why should we not clothe ourselves like gentlefolk as well as our kindred and friends at home? And sure both England and Virginia have had enough of sad colored raiment. Better go like a peacock than like a horrid Roundhead."

Her companion laughed musically and sang a stave of a cavalier love song. He was a slender, well-made man, dressed in the extreme of the mode of the year of grace sixteen hundred and sixty-three, in a richly laced suit of camlet with points of blue ribbon, and the great scented periwig then newly come into fashion. The close curled rings of hair descending far over his cravat of finest Holland framed a handsome, lazily insolent face, with large steel-blue eyes and beautifully cut, mocking lips. A rapier with a jeweled hilt hung at his side, and one white hand, half buried in snowy ruffles, held a beribboned cane with which, as he talked, he ruthlessly decapitated the pink and white morning-glories with which the porch was trellised.

The house to which the porch belonged was long and low, built of wood, with many small windows, and at either end a great brick chimney. From the porch to the water, a hundred yards away, stretched a walk of crushed shells bisecting an expanse of green turf dotted with noble trees—the cedar and the cypress predominating. Diverging from this central walk were two narrower paths which, winding in and out in eccentric figures, led, on the one hand, to a rustic summer-house overgrown with honeysuckle and trumpet-vine, and on the other to a tiny grotto constructed of shells and set in a tangle of periwinkle. Along one side of the house, and protected by a stout locust paling overrun with grape-vines, lay the garden, where flowers and vegetables flourished contentedly side by side, the hollyhocks and tall white lilies, the hundred-leaved roses and scarlet poppies showing like gilded officers amidst the rank and file of sober esculents. Behind the house were clustered various offices, then came an orchard where the June apples and the great red cherries were ripening in the hot sunshine, then on the shore of a second and narrower creek rose the quarters for the plantation servants, white and black—a long double row of cabins, dominated by the overseer's house and shaded by ragged yellow pines. Along one shore of this inlet was planted the Indian corn prescribed by law, and from the other gleamed the soft yellow of ripening wheat, but beyond the water and away to the westward stretched acre after acre of tobacco, a sea of vivid green, broken only by an occasional shed or drying house, and merging at last into the darker hue of the forest. Over all the fair scene, the flashing water, the velvet marshes, the smiling fields, the fringe of dark and mysterious woodland, hung a Virginia heaven, a cloudless blue, soft, pure, intense. The air was full of subdued sound—the distant hum of voices from the fields of maize and tobacco, the faint clink of iron from the smithy, the wash and lap of the water, the drone of bees from the hives beneath the eaves of the house. Great bronze butterflies fluttered in the sunshine, brilliant humming-birds plunged deep into the long trumpet-flowers; from the topmost bough of a locust, heavy with bloom, came the liquid trill of a mock-bird.

It was a fair domain, and a wealthy. The Englishman thought of certain appalling sums lost to Sedley and Roscommon, and there flitted through his brain a swift little calculation as to the number of hogsheads of Orenoko or sweet-scented it would take to wipe off the score. And the girl beside him was beautiful enough to take Whitehall by storm, to be berhymed by Waller, and to give to Lely a subject above all flattery. He set his lips with the air of a man who has made up his mind, and turned to his companion, who was absorbed in watching the white sail grow slowly larger.

"How long, now, cousin?"

"But a few minutes unless the wind should fail."

"And then you will have your treasures. But, madam, when you have assumed all the panoply your sex relies on to increase its charms 'twill be but to 'gild refined gold or paint the lily.' The Aphrodite of this western ocean needs no adornment."

The girl looked at him with laughter in her eyes. "You make me too many pretty speeches, cousin," she said demurely. "We know the value of the fine things you court gallants are perpetually saying."

"Upon my soul, madam, I swear—"

"Do you know the amount of the fine for swearing, Sir Charles? See how large the sail has grown! When the boat rounds the long marsh she will come more quickly. We will soon be able to see my father wave his handkerchief."

The young man bit his lip. "You are pleased to be cruel to-day, madam, but I am your slave and I obey. We will look together for Colonel Verney's handkerchief. How many black slaves does he bring you?"

She laughed. "But half a dozen blacks, but there will be several redemptioners if you prefer to be numbered with them."

"Redemptioners! Ah, yes! the English servants who are sold for their passage money. I thank you, madam, but *my* servitude is for life."

"The men my father will bring may not be the ordinary servants who come here to better their condition. He may have obtained them from a batch of felons from Newgate who have been kept in gaol in Jamestown until word could be got to the planters around. I am sure I wish the ship captains and the traders would stop bringing in the wretches. It is different with the negroes: we can make allowance for the poor silly things that are scarce more than animals, and they grow attached to us and we to them, and the simple indented servants are well enough too. There are among them many honest and intelligent men. But these gaol birds are dreadful. It sickens me to look at them. Thieves and murderers every one!"

"I should not think the colony served by their importation."

"It is not indeed, and we have hopes that it will cease. I beg my father not to buy them, but he says that one man cannot stop an abuse—that as long as his fellow-planters use them he might as well do so too."

Sir Charles Carew delicately smothered a yawn. "The ship that brought me over a fortnight ago," he said lazily, "had a consignment of such rascals. It was amusing to watch their antics, crowded together as they were in the hold. There were two wild Irishmen whom we used to have on deck to dance for us. Gad! what figures they cut! The captain and I had a standing wager of five of the new guineas as to which of the rascals could hold out longest, promising a measure of rum to the victorious votary of Terpsichore. When I had lost a score of guineas I found that the captain was in the habit of priming his man before he came upon deck. Naturally, being filled with Dutch courage, he won."

"Poor Sir Charles! What did you do?"

"Sent the captain a cartel and fought him on his own deck. There was one man in the villainous company whom, I protest, I almost pitied, though of course the rogue had but his deserts."

"What was he?"

"A man of about thirty. A fellow with a handsome face and a lithe well-made figure which he managed with some grace. He had the air of one who had seen better days. I remember, one day when the captain was bestowing upon him some especially choice oaths, seeing him clap his hand to his side as though he expected to touch a rapier hilt. He was cleanly too; kept his rags of clothing as decent as circumstances allowed, and looked less like a wild beast in a litter of foul straw than did his fellows. But he was an ill-conditioned dog. We had some passages together, he and I. He took it upon himself to defend what he was pleased to call the honor of one of his precious company. It was vastly amusing.... After that I fell into the habit of watching him through the open hatches. A little thing provides entertainment at sea, Mistress Patricia. He would sit or stand for hours looking past me with a perfectly still face. The other wretches were quick to crowd up, whining to me to pitch them half pence or tobacco, but try as I would, I could not get word or look from him. Sink me! if he didn't have the impudence to resent my being there!"

"It was cruel to stare at misery."

"Lard, madam! such vermin are used to being stared at. In London, Newgate and Bridewell are theatres as well as the Cockpit or the King's House, and the world of *mode* flock to the one spectacle as often as to the other. But see! the sloop has passed the marsh and has a clean sweep of water between her and the wharf."

"Yes, she is coming fast now."

"What is coming?" asked a voice from the doorway.

"The Flying Patty, Aunt Lettice," the girl answered over her shoulder. "Get your hood and come with us to the wharf."

Mistress Lettice Verney emerged from the hall, two red spots burning in her withered cheeks, and her tall thin figure quivering with excitement.

"I am all ready, child," she quavered. "But, mark my words, Patricia, there will be something wrong with my paduasoy petticoat, or Charette will not have sent the proper tale of green stockings or Holland smocks. Did you not hear the screech owl last night?"

"No, Aunt Lettice."

"It remained beneath my window the entire night. I did not sleep a wink. And this morning Chloe upset the salt cellar, and the salt fell towards me." Mistress Lettice rolled her eyes heavenward and sighed lugubriously. Patricia laughed.

"I dreamed of flowers last night, Aunt Lettice; miles and miles of them, waxen and cold and sweet, like those they strew over the dead."

Mistress Lettice groaned. "'Tis a dreadful sign. Captain Norton's wife (she that was Polly Wilson) dreamed of flowers the night before the massacre of 'forty-four. The only thing the poor soul said when the war-whoop wakened them in the dead of the night and the door came crashing in, was, 'I told you so.' They were her last words. Then Martha Westall dreamed of flowers, and two days later her son James stepped on a stingray over at Dale's Gift. And I myself dreamed of roses the week before those horrid Roundhead commissioners with the rebel Claiborne at their head and a whole fleet at their back, compelled us to surrender to their odious Commonwealth."

"At least that evil is past," said the girl with a gay laugh. "And ill fortune will never come to me aboard the Flying Patty, so I shall go down to the wharf to see her in. Darkeih! my scarf!"

A negress appeared in the doorway with a veil of tissue in her hand. Sir Charles took it from her and flung it over Patricia's golden head, then offered his arm to Mistress Lettice.

The wharf was but a stone's throw from the wooden gates, and they were soon treading the long stretch of gray, weather-beaten boards. Others were before them, for the news that the sloop was coming in had drawn a small crowd to the wharf to welcome the master.

The dozen or so of boatmen, white and black, who had been tinkering about in the various barges, shallops and canoes tied to the mossy piles, left their employments and scrambled up upon the platform, and a trio of youthful darkies, fishing for crabs with a string and a piece of salt pork, allowed their lines to fall slack and their intended victims to walk coolly off with the meat, so intense was their interest in the oncoming sail. A knot of negro women had left the great house kitchen and stood, hands on hips, chatting volubly with a contingent from the quarters, their red and yellow turbans nodding up and down like grotesque Dutch tulips. The company was made up by an overseer with a broadleafed palmetto hat pulled down over his eyes and a clay pipe stuck between his teeth, a pale young man who acted as secretary to the master of the plantation, and by three or four small land-owners and tenants for whom Colonel Verney had graciously undertaken various commissions in Jamestown, and who were on hand to make their acknowledgments to the great man.

They all made deferential way for the two ladies and Sir Charles Carew. Mistress Lettice commenced a condescending conversation with one of the tenants, Darkeih added a white tulip to the red and yellow ones, and Patricia, followed by Sir Charles, walked to the edge of the wharf, and leaning upon the rude railing looked down the glassy reaches of the water to the approaching boat.

The wind had sunk into a fitful breeze and the white sail moved very slowly. The tide was in, and the water lapped with a cooling sound against the dark green piles. In the distance the blue of the bay melted into the blue of the sky, while the nearer waters mirrored every passing gull, the masts of the fishing boats, the tall marsh grass, the dead twigs marking oyster beds—each object had its double. On a point of marshy ground stood a line of cranes, motionless as soldiers on parade, until, taking fright as the great sail glided past, they whirred off, uttering discordant cries and with their legs sticking out like tail feathers. Slowly, and keeping to the middle of the channel, the boat came on. Upon the long low deck men were preparing to lower the sail, and a portly gentleman standing in the bow was vigorously waving his handkerchief. The sail came down with a rush, the anchor swung overboard, and half a dozen canoes and dugouts shot from under the shadow of the wharf and across the strip of water between it and the sloop. The gentleman with the handkerchief, followed by a man plainly dressed in brown, sprang into the foremost; the others waited for their lading of merchandise.

Before the boat had touched the steps the master of the plantation began to call out greetings to his expectant family.

"Patricia, my darling, are you in health? Charles, I am happy to see you again! Sister Lettice, Mr. Frederick Jones sends you his humble services."

"La, brother! and how is the dear man?" screamed Mistress Lettice.

"As well as 'tis in nature to be, with his heart at Verney Manor and his body at Flowerdieu Hundred."

The boat jarred against the piles and the planter stepped out, grasping Sir Charles's extended hand.

"Again, I am happy to see you, Charles," he cried in a round and jovial voice. "I have been telling my up-river good friends that I have the most topping fellow in all London for my guest, and you will have company enough anon."

Sir Charles smiled and bowed. "I hope, sir, that you were successful in the business that took you to Jamestown?"

"Fairly so, fairly so. Haines here," with a wave of the hand towards the man in brown, "had a lot picked out for me to choose from. I have six negroes and three of those blackguards from Newgate—mighty poor policy to shoulder ourselves with such gaol sweepings. I doubt we'll repent it some day. The blacks come by way of Boston, which means that they will have to be cockered up considerably before they are fit for work. Is that you, Woodson? How have things gone on?"

The overseer took his pipe from between his teeth and made an awkward bow.

"Glad to see your Honor back," he said deferentially. "Everything's all right, sir. The last rain helped the corn amazingly, and the tobacco's prime. The lightning struck a shed, but we got the flames out before they reached the hogsheads. The Nancy got caught in a squall; lost both masts and ran aground on Gull Marsh. The tide will take her off at the full of the moon. Sambo 's been playing 'possum again. Said he'd cut his foot with his hoe so badly that he couldn't stand upon it. Said I could see that by the blood on the rag that tied it up. I made him take off the rag and wash the foot, and there wa'n't no cut there. The blood was puccoon. If he'd waited a bit he could 'a' had all he wanted to paint with, for I gave him the rope's end, lively, until Mistress Patricia heard him yelling and made me stop."

"All right, Woodson. I reckon the plantation knows by this time that what Mistress Patricia says is law. Here come the boats with the boxes. Tell the men to be careful how they handle them."

After a hearty word or two to tenants and land owners the worthy Colonel joined his daughter and sister; and together with Sir Charles Carew they watched the precious boxes conveyed up the slippery steps, the overseer shouting directions, plentifully sprinkled with selected, unfinable oaths to the panting boatmen. When all were safely piled upon the wharf ready to be wheeled to the great house, the empty boats swung off to make room for others, laden with the colonel's Jamestown purchases.

One by one the articles climbed the stairs, each as it reached the level being claimed by the overseer and told off into a lengthening line. Six were negroes, gaunt and hollow-eyed, but smiling widely. They gazed around them, at the heap of clams and oysters piled upon the wharf, at the marshes, alive with wild fowl, at the distant green of waving corn, the flower-embowered great house, the white quarters from which arose many little spirals of savory smoke, and a bland and childlike content took possession of their souls. With eager and obsequious "Yes, Mas'rs" they obeyed the overseer's objurgatory indications as to their disposition.

There next arose above the landing the head of a white man—a countenance of sullen ferocity, with a great scar running across it, and framed in elf locks of staring red. The body belonging to this prepossessing face was swollen and unshapely, and its owner moved with a limp and a muttered curse towards the place assigned him. He was followed by a sallow-faced, long-nosed man, with black oily hair and an affected smirk which twitched the corners of his thin lips. Singling out his master's family with a furtive glance from a pair of sinister greenish eyes, he made a low bow and stepped jauntily into line.

The third man rose above the landing. Sir Charles, standing by Patricia, laughed.

"This world is a place of fantastic meetings, cousin," he said, airily. "Now who would suppose that I would ever again see that chipping from a London gaol I told you of—my shipmate of cleanly habit and unsocial nature. Yet there he is."

CHAPTER II

ITS CARGO

The afternoon sunshine lay hot upon the house and garden of Verney Manor—the leaves drooped motionless, the glare of the white paths hurt the eye, the flowers seemed all to be red. The odor of rose and honeysuckle was drowned in the heavy cloying sweetness of the pendant masses of locust bloom. Down in the garden the bees droned in the vines, and on the steps the flies buzzed undisturbed about the sleeping hounds. Above the long, deserted wharf and the green velvet of the marshes quivered the heated air, while to look upon the water was like gazing too closely at blue flame. From the tobacco fields floated the notes of a monotonous many-versed chant, and a soft, uninterrupted cooing came from the dove cot. Heat and fragrance and drowsy sound combined to give a pleasant somnolence to the wide sunny scene.

Deep in the cavernous shade of the porch lounged the master of the plantation, his body in one chair, his legs in another, and a silver tankard of sack standing upon a third, over the back of which had been flung his great peruke and his riding coat of green cloth, discarded because of the heat. Thin, blue clouds curled up from his long pipe, and obscured his ruddy countenance.

His shrewd gray eyes under their tufts of grizzled hair were half closed in a lazy contentment, born of the hour, the pipe, and the drink. The world went very well just then in Colonel Verney's estimation. His crop of the preceding year had been a large and profitable one; this year it bid fair to be still more satisfactory. During the past few months he had acquired a number of servants and slaves, and his head rights would add a goodly number of acres to his already enormous holdings; land, land, always more land! being the ambition and the necessity of the seventeenth century Virginia planter. Trader, planter, magistrate, member of the council of state, soldier, author on occasion, and fine gentleman all rolled into one, after the fashion of the times; Cavalier of the Cavaliers, hand in glove with Governor Berkeley, and possessed of a beautiful daughter, for whose favor one half of the young gentlemen of the counties of York and Gloucester were ready to draw rapier on the other half,—Colonel Verney's world was a fair and stirring one, and gave him plentiful food for meditation on a fine afternoon.

Opposite him sat his kinsman and guest, Sir Charles Carew. He was similarly equipped with pipe and sack, but there the resemblance to his host ended, Sir Charles Carew being a man who made it a point of honor to be clad like the lilies of the field on every possible occasion in life, from the carrying a breach to the ogling a milkmaid. The sultry afternoon had no power to affect the scrupulous elegance of his attire, or to alter the careful repose of his manner. In his hand he held a volume of "Hudibras," but his thoughts were not upon the book, wandering instead, with those of his kinsman, over the fertile fields of Verney Manor.

"You have a princely estate, sir, in this fair, new world," he said at last, in a sweetly languid voice.

The planter roused himself from considering at what point of his newly acquired land he should begin the attack upon the forest. "It's a fair enough home for a man to end his days in," he said with complacence.

"We of the court have very erroneous ideas as to Virginia. I confess that my expectation of finding a courteous and loving kinsman," a gracious smile and inclination of the head towards the older man, "is the only one in which I have not been disappointed. I thought to see a rude wilderness, and I find, to borrow the language of our Roundhead friends, a very land of Beulah."

"Ay, ay. D' ye remember what old Drayton sings?

'Virginia!

Earth's only paradise!'

And a paradise it is, with mighty few drawbacks, now that the King has come to his own again, if you except these d—d canting Quakers and Anabaptists, and those yelling red devils on the frontier, and the danger of a servant insurrection, and the fact that his Majesty (God bless him!) and the Privy Council fleece us more mercilessly than did old Noll himself. I verily think they believe our tobacco plants made of gold like those they say Pizarro saw in Peru. But 'tis a sweet land! Why, look around you!" he cried, warming to his subject. "The waters swarm with fish, the marshes with wild fowl. In the winter the air rings with the *cohonk! cohonk!* of the wild geese. They darken the air when they come and go. There in the forest stand the deer, waiting for your bullet; badgers and foxes, bears, wolves, and catamounts are more plentiful than are hares in England. You taste pleasure indeed when you ride full tilt through the frosty moonlight, down the ringing glades of the forest, and hear the hounds in full cry, and see before you, black against the silver snow, a pack of yelling wolves. Then in summer the woods are full of singing birds and of such flowers as you in England only dream of. Strawberries make the ground red, and there are wild melons and grapes and mulberries, and more nuts than squirrels, which is saying much for the nuts. Everything grows here. 'Tis the garden of the world. And what is there fairer than the green of the tobacco and the golden corn tassels? And the noble rivers, whose head waters no man has ever found, hidden by the Lord in the Blue Mountains near to the South Sea! Sir, Virginia is God's country!"

"You in these lowlands have no trouble with the Indians?"

"None to speak of since 'forty-four, when Opechancanough came down upon us. The brush with the Ricahecrians seven years ago was nothing. They are utterly broken, both here and in Accomac. Further up the rivers the devil still holds his own, we hearing doleful tales of the butchery of pioneers with their wives and children; and above the falls of the far west, in the Monacan country, and towards the Blue Mountains, is his stronghold and capitol; but here in the lowlands all's safe enough. There is no fear of the savages. Would we could say as much of the servants!"

"Why, what do you fear from them?"

"It's hard to say; but an uneasy feeling has prevailed for a year or more. It's this d—d Oliverian element among them. You see, ever since his Majesty's blessed restoration, gang after gang of rebels have been sent us—Independents, Muggletonians, Fifth Monarchy men, dour Scotch Whigamores—dangerous fanatics all! Many are Naseby or Worcester rogues, Ironsides who worship the memory of that devil's lieutenant, Oliver. All have the gift of the gab. We disperse them as much as possible, not allowing above five or six to any one plantation, we of the Council realizing that they form a dangerous leaven. Should there be trouble, which heaven forbid! they would be the instigators, restless mischief-makers and overturners of the established order of things that they are! Then there are their fellow criminals, the highwaymen, forgers, cutpurses and bullies of whom we relieve his Majesty's government. They are few in number, but each is a very plague spot, infecting honester men. The slaves, always excepting the Portuguese and Spanish mulattoes from the Indies, who are devils incarnate, have not brain enough to conspire. But in the actual event of a rising they would be fiends unchained."

"A pleasant state of affairs!"

"Oh, it is not so serious! We who govern the Colony have to take all possibilities, however unpleasant, into consideration. I myself do not think the danger imminent, and many in the Council and among the Burgesses, and well-nigh all outside will not allow that there is danger at all. We passed more stringent servant laws last year, and we depend upon them, and upon the great body of indented servants, who are, for the most part, honest and amenable and know upon which side their bread is buttered, to repress the unruly element."

"What will you do with the convicts you brought with you this morning?"

"Use them in the tobacco fields just now when all hands are needed to weed and sucker the plants, and afterwards put them to hewing down the forest. I told Woodson to bring them around to me this afternoon when they had been decently clothed. I always give the scoundrels a piece of my mind to begin with. It saves trouble."

"Do they give you much trouble?"

"Not on this plantation. Woodson and Haines are excellent overseers."

The planter refilled his pipe, struck a light with his flint and steel, and leaning back amidst the fragrant clouds, allowed his eyelids to droop and his mind to wander over a pleasant sunshiny tract of nothing in particular.

Sir Charles tasted his sack, adjusted his ruffles, and resumed his reading. But even the delectable adventures of the Presbyterian knight, over whom all London was laughing, palled on such an afternoon, and the young gentleman, after listlessly turning a page or two, laid the book across his knee, and with closed eyes commenced the construction of an air castle of his own.

He was roused by the sound of approaching footsteps upon the shell path leading to the back of the house, and by the harsh voice of the overseer.

"Here come your hopeful purchases, sir," he said lazily.

The overseer turned the corner of the house and came forward with the three convicts at his heels. He doffed his hat to the two gentlemen, then turned to his charges. "Fall into line, you dogs, and salute his Honor!"

The first man, he of the long nose and the twitching lip, smiled sweetly, and bent so low that his fell of greasy hair well-nigh swept the steps; the second, with a brow like a thunder cloud, gave a vicious nod; the third, with as impassive a countenance as Sir Charles's own, bowed gravely, and stood with folded arms and a quietly attentive mien.

The planter gathered himself up from his chair and came forward to the top of the steps, his tall, corpulent figure towering above the men below much as his fortunes towered above theirs.

"Now, men," he said, speaking sternly and with slow emphasis. "I have just one word to say to you. Listen well to it. I am your master; you are my servants. I reckon myself a good master, it not being my way to treat those belonging to me, whether white or black, like dumb beasts. Give me obedience and the faithful work of your hands, and you shall find me kind. But if you are stubborn or rebellious, by the Lord, you will rue the day you left Newgate! Whipping-post and branding-irons are at hand, and death is something closer to a felon in Virginia than in England. Be careful! Now, Woodson, what have you put these men to?"

"They'll go into the three-mile field to-morrow morning, your honor, unless you wish other disposition made of them."

"No, that will do. Take them away."

The overseer faced about and was marching off with the recruits for the three-mile field when his master's voice arrested him.

"Take those two in front on with you, Woodson, and send me back the brown-haired one."

The "brown-haired one" turned as his companions disappeared around a hedge of privet and came slowly back to the steps.

"You wished to speak to me, sir?" he said quietly.

"Yes. You are the man who was tolerably helpful in the squall last night?"

"I was so fortunate as to be of some small service, sir."

"You understand the handling of a boat?"

"Yes, sir."

"Hum. I will tell Woodson to try you with a sloop when the press of work in the fields is past. What is your name?"

"Godfrey Landless."

"Chevalier d'Industrie and frequenter of the Newgate Ordinary," put in Sir Charles lazily. "Of the Roundhead persuasion too, if I mistake not,—from robbery in the large, descended to thievery in the small; from the murder of a King to knives and a black alley mouth. Commend me to these grave rogues for real knaves! Pray inform us to what little mishap we owe the honor of your company. Did you mercifully incline to relieve weary travelers over Hounslow Heath by disburdening them of their heavy purses? Or did you mistake your own handwriting for that of some one else? Or did you woo a mercer's wife a thought too roughly? Or perhaps—"

The man shot a fiery upward glance at the slim, elegant figure and mocking lips of his tormentor, but kept silence. Colonel Verney, who had returned to his pipe, interposed. "What is all this, Charles? What are you saying to the man?"

"Oh, nothing, sir! This gentleman and I were shipmates, and I did but ask after his health since the voyage."

"Sir Charles Carew is very good," the man said proudly. "I assure him that the object of his solicitude is well, and only desires an opportunity to repay, with interest, those little attentions shown him by his courteous fellow voyager."

The planter looked puzzled; Sir Charles laughed.

"Our liking is mutual, I see," he said coolly. "I—but what is this, Colonel Verney! Venus descending from Olympus?"

Out of the doorway fluttered a brilliant vision, all blue and white like the great butterflies hovering over the clove pinks. Behind it appeared the faded countenance of Mrs. Lettice, and a group of turbaned heads peered, grinning, from out the cool darkness of the hall.

"Papa!" cried the vision. "I want to show you my new dress! Cousin Charles, you are to tell me if it is all as it should be!"

Sir Charles bowed, with his hand upon his heart. "Alas, madam! I could as soon play critic to the choir of angels. My eyes are dazzled."

"Stand out, child," said her father gazing at her with eyes of love and pride, "and let us see your finery. D' ye know what the extravagant minx has upon her back, Charles? Just five hogsheads of prime tobacco!"

Mistress Lettice struck in: "Well, I'm sure, brother, 'tis much the prettiest use to put tobacco to, to turn it into lace and brocade and jewels,—much better, say I, than to be forever using it to accumulate filthy slaves."

Patricia floated to the centre of the porch and stood sunning herself in a stray shaft of light, like a very bird of paradise. The "tempestuous petticoat," sky-blue and laced with silver, swelled proudly outwards, the gleaming satin bodice slipped low over the snowy shoulders and the heaving bosom, and the sleeves, trimmed with magnificent lace and looped with pearls, showed the rounded arms to perfection. Around the slender throat was wound a double row of pearls, and the golden ringlets were partially confined by a snood of blue velvet. She unfurled a wonderful fan, and lifted her skirts to show the tiny white and silver shoes and the silken silver-clocked ankles. Her eyes shone like stars, faint wild roses bloomed in her cheeks, charming half smiles chased each other across her dainty mouth. Such a picture of radiant youth and loveliness did she present that the Englishman's pulses quickened, and he swore under his breath. "Surely," he muttered, "this is the most beautiful woman in the world, and my lucky stars have sent me to this No Man's Land to win her."

"How do you like me?" she cried gayly. "Is 't not worth the five hogsheads?"

Her father drew her to him and kissed the smooth forehead.

"You look just as your mother did, child, the day that we were betrothed. I could not give you higher praise than that, sweetheart."

"And does it really lack nothing, cousin?" she cried anxiously. "Is it in truth such a dress as they wear at Court?"

"Not at Whitehall, madam, nor at Brussels, nor even at St. Germains have I seen anything more point device than the dress,—nor as beautiful as the wearer," he added in a lower voice and with a killing look.

The girl's face dimpled with pleasure and innocent, gratified vanity. She swept him a magnificent courtesy, and he bent low over the slender fingers she gave him. Suddenly he felt them stiffen in his clasp, and looking up, saw a curious expression of fear and aversion pass like a shadow across her face. She spoke abruptly. "That man! I did not see him! What does he here?"

Sir Charles wheeled. The convict, forgotten by the two gentlemen, had been left standing at the foot of the steps, and his sombre eyes were now fixed upon the girl in a look so strange and intent as fully to explain her perturbation. Through his parted lips the breath came hurriedly, in his eyes was a mournful exaltation as of one who looks from a desert into Paradise. He stood absorbed, unconscious of aught save the splendid vision above him. For a moment she stared at him in return, her eyes, held by his, slowly widening and the color quite gone from her face. With a slow, involuntary movement one white arm rose, and stiffened before her in a gesture of repulsion. The fan fell from her hand upon the floor with a click of breaking tortoise shell. The sound broke the spell, and with a strong shudder she turned her eyes away. "Make him go," she said in a trembling voice. "He frightens me."

Sir Charles sprang forward with an oath. "Curse you, you dog! Take your ill-omened eyes from the lady! Colonel Verney, do you not see that the fellow is annoying your daughter?"

The planter had fallen into a reverie born of recollections of the Patricia of his youth, long laid in her grave, but he roused himself at the words of his guest.

"What's that?" he cried. "Annoying Patricia!" He walked to the head of the steps and raised his cane threateningly.

"Hark ye, sirrah! The servants of Verney Manor, white or black, felon or indented, need all their eyesight for their work. They have none to waste in idle gazing at their betters. Begone to your mates!"

The man who, at Sir Charles's intervention, had started as from a dream, colored deeply and compressed his lips, then glanced from one to the other of the group above him. There was pain, humiliation, almost supplication in the look which he directed to the girl who had brought this rating upon him. He glanced at his master with a countenance studiously devoid of expression, at Mistress Lettice with indifference, at Sir Charles Carew with chill defiance. Then, with a grave inclination of his head, he turned, and a moment later had disappeared behind the hedge.

CHAPTER III

A COLONIAL DINNER PARTY

Three days later the master of Verney Manor gave a dinner party.

At Jamestown, twenty miles away, the Assembly had just adjourned after a busy session. A law debarring that "turbulent people" the Quakers from further admittance into the colony, and providing cold comfort for those already within its doors, was passed with acclamation, as was another against Anabaptists, and a third concerning the hue and cry for absconding servants and slaves. The selling rates for wines and strong waters were fixed, a proper penalty attached to the planting of tobacco contrary to the statute, a regulation for the mending of the highways adopted, a fine imposed for non-attendance at church, the Navigation Act formally protested against, the trainbands strengthened, an appropriation made for the erection of new whipping-posts and pillories, a cruel mistress deprived of the slave she had mistreated, a harborer of schismatics publicly reproved, and a conciliatory message and present sent to the up-river Indians—when the Assembly adjourned with the consciousness of having nobly done its duty. The only measure upon which there was not unanimity of opinion was one proposing the erection of school-houses at convenient cross-roads, and the Governor's weight being thrown into the balance against it, it was promptly quashed.

The burgesses from the fourteen counties filled the twenty houses that constituted the town to suffocation. Up-river planters, too, had come in, choosing the time the Assembly was in session to attend to their interests in the "city." Several ships were in harbor, and their captains, professing themselves tired of salt water, threw themselves upon the hospitality of their friends ashore. The crowded population overflowed into the houses of the neighboring planters, who, after the manner of their kind, entertained profusely, giving jovial welcome and good liquor to all comers. There was a constant jingling of reins along the bridle paths, a constant passing of white-sailed sloops upon the river, as gentlemen in riding coats and jack boots, or in laced coats and silk stockings, fared to and fro between plantation and town. In the intervals of business the worthy burgesses and their fellow planters made merry. They were good times—for king's men—and it behooved every loyal subject to follow (at a respectful distance) his Majesty's example, and get all possible enjoyment from a laughing world. So there were horse-races and cock-fights and bear-baitings, as well as dinners and suppers, at which much sack and aqua vitæ was drunk to king, church, and reigning beauties. And if a quarrel sprung, full armed, from the heated brains of young gallants, crossed rapiers did but add a piquancy, a dash of cayenne, to life.

Popular with the elder gentlemen because of his excellent Madeira, quick wit, jovial soul, and friendship with the Governor, and with the younger by virtue of being father to Mistress Patricia Verney, Colonel Richard Verney had no difficulty in securing a score of guests for a day's entertainment at Verney Manor.

About ten in the morning of the appointed day the guests began to arrive, some by water, some on horseback, Colonel Verney meeting each arrival with a stately bow and a high-flown speech of welcome, and handing him on to the hall where stood Sir Charles Carew and the ladies of the household.

Upon a pillion behind her father, Major Miles Carrington, Surveyor-General to the Colony, came Mistress Betty Carrington, bosom friend to Mistress Patricia Verney. Her sweetly serious face, pensive eyes, and smooth, dark hair, with her dress of sober silk and kerchief of finest lawn, demurely crossed over her bosom, contrasted finely with Patricia's radiant beauty, decked in shimmering satin and rich lace, and heightened by a tinge of vermilion upon the smooth cheek, and a long black patch beneath the left temple. The two met like friends whom weary years have parted, and indeed they had not seen each other for nearly a week.

All the guests, save one, had arrived. Colonel Verney fidgeted, sent a servant wench to look at the kitchen clock, and dispatched his secretary to an upstairs window, whence was visible a long stretch of what courtesy called the highroad.

The secretary returned and whispered his master. "God be thanked!" exclaimed the latter. "I feared that his machine had mired in the Two-Mile Swamp, or had toppled into a gully coming through the Devil's Strip. Gentlemen, the Governor's coach is in sight. Shall we adjourn to the porch and there await his Excellency?"

A mighty straining, jingling and lumbering came with the breeze down the road and proceeded from a pillar of dust which was approaching the house with reasonable rapidity. Presently the road changed from a trough of dust into a ribbon of greensward. The cloud dissipated itself, streaming away like the tail of a comet, and a ponderous and much begilt coach, drawn by six horses, their manes and tails tied with red ribbons, and outriders in gorgeous livery at the heads of each pair, rolled, or rather bumped into sight. With a seasick motion it undulated over the green acclivities of the road, and finally drew up beside the great horse-block at the gate.

Two lackeys sprang from their perch behind the vehicle, flung open the door, and lowered a short flight of steps. A very stately gentleman, richly dressed, with a handkerchief of point in one hand and a jeweled snuff-box in the other, descended the steps, placing one shapely leg in its maroon-colored stocking before the other with the mannered grace of the leader of a Coranto.

Colonel Verney met him with a low bow and smiling face, after which the two embraced, for they were old friends.

"My dear Governor!"

"My dear Colonel!"

"I am charmed to welcome your Excellency to my poor house."

"My dear Colonel, I am charmed to be here. Gad! the possession of the only chariot in the Colony is a burdensome honor! I thought dinner would be over, and the stirrup cup in order while I was creeping, like a snail with his house on his back, over these 'fair and pleasant roads'—as I call them in my book, eh, Dick! But you have a goodly company, I see; Ludwell, Fitzhugh, Carey, Anthony Nash, mine ancient enemy Lawrence, Wormeley, Carrington our Puritan convert and his pretty daughter, young Peyton, and that pretty fellow, your nephew or cousin, is he? Odzooks! he is much what I was at his age, begotten of Delilah and Lucifer, hand of iron in glove of velvet, eh, Dick! I hear he is hail-fellow-well-met with the King and with Buckingham and Killigrew and their wild set. Ah, boys will be boys! 'We have heard the chimes at midnight,' eh, Dick?"

And the Governor in high good humor skipped up the steps with the agility of youth, bent low with sugared compliments over the hands of his hostesses and of Mistress Betty Carrington, and gave courteous greeting to the assembled gentlemen, after which the company flowed back into the grateful twilight of hall and "great room," where the weather, the state of the crops, and the last horse-race engaged them until the announcement of dinner.

With a flourish of his costly handkerchief, the Governor offered his arm to the young mistress of the house, and led the way to the dining-room, where old Humfrey, the butler, marshaled the guests to their seats. Mistress Betty Carrington had for her cavalier Sir Charles Carew, to whose honeyed words she listened with a species of awe, wondering in her innocent soul if all the wild tales they told of this very fine, smooth-tongued, handsome gentleman could be true.

Doctor Anthony Nash made a long and fluent grace wherein much latinity was aired, a neat allusion made to the *jus divinum*, and an anathema hurled against those "who break down the carved work of the sanctuary." Then was uncovered the mighty saddle of mutton, reposing in the dish of honor, the roast pig, the haunch of venison, the sirloin of beef, the breast of veal, the powdered goose, the noble dish of sheepshead and bluefish, and the pasty in which was entombed a whole flock of pigeons. These *pièces de resistance* were flanked by bowls of oysters, by rows of wild fowl skewered together, by mince pies and a grand salad, while upon the outskirts of the damask plain were stationed trenchers piled with wheat bread, platters of pease and smoking potatoes, cauliflower and asparagus, and a concoction of rice and prunes, seasoned with mace and cinnamon and a pinch of assafœtida. A great silver salt-cellar stood in the centre of the table, and smaller receptacles of the same metal held pepper and spices. Silver flagons of cider and ale were placed at intervals, the Madeira, Fayal and Rhenish awaiting upon the sideboard the moment when, the cloth drawn and the ladies gone, a gentlemanly carousal should be inaugurated.

The company drew their Russian leather chairs closer to the table, spread over their silken knees the fringed damask napkins, and for a space little was to be heard but the sound of knife and spoon (forks there were none), for the morning ride had sharpened appetites. The servants passed from chair to chair; the master, seconded by his daughter and sister, pricked his guests on to fresh attacks, pressing a third slice of mutton on one, a fresh helping of capon upon another, protesting that a third ate as though it were a fast day, and that a fourth drank as though the October were sea-water.

When the cloth was drawn and the banquet put on, tongues were loosened. The Governor quoted passages from his "Lost Lady" to Patricia, lifting her lovely flushed face from the carving of a tart with wonderfully constructed towering walls. Behind a second turreted marvel of pastry, Mistress Lettice and Mr. Frederick Jones sighed and ogled with antique grace. Sir Charles Carew, fingering his cherries, told a piquant little court anecdote to Mistress Betty Carrington, and was lazily amused at the blush and veiled eyelids with which the young lady received it. Young Mr. Peyton, on her other side, looked very black.

The wine was put on and the toast to King and Church drunk standing, after which the ladies dipped their white fingers into the basin of perfumed water, dried them on the silver-fringed napkin, and sailed to the door, through which, after the profoundest of courtesies on the one side and the lowest of bows upon the other, they vanished, leaving the gentlemen to wine and wassail.

Colonel Verney drank to the Governor; the Governor to Colonel Verney; Sir Charles to the author of the "Lost Lady" and the "Discourse and View of Virginia," so tickling the Governor's vanity thereby that he became altogether charming. Mr. Peyton toasted Mistress Betty Carrington, and Mr. Frederick Jones, Mistress Lettice Verney, "fairest and most discreet of ladies." They drank to Captain Laramore's next voyage, to Mr. Wormeley's success in vine planting, to Major Carrington's conversion. They drank confusion to Quakers, Independents, Baptists and infidels, to the heathen on the frontier and the Papists in Maryland, the Dutch on the Hudson and the French on the St. Lawrence,—"Quebec in exchange for Dunkirk!" In short, there were few things in heaven or earth but justified draughts of Madeira.

The room filled with a blue and fragrant mist proceeding from twenty pipe-bowls. Mr. Peyton sang a pretty song of his own composing. The company applauded. Sir Charles Carew, in a richly plaintive tenor voice, sang a lyric of Rochester's. Several of the gentlemen looked askance (the clergyman had left the room with the ladies), but on the Governor's crying out "Excellent!" they considered themselves over-squeamish, and clapped loudly.

Sir Charles, being dry after his song, drank to Hospitality,—"A duty," he said, smiling, "that you gentlemen make so paramount that you must wonder at the omission of 'Thou shalt be hospitable' from the Decalogue."

"Faith, sir!" cried Mr. Peyton, "God is too good a Virginian not to consider such a commandment superfluous."

The Governor commenced a story which all present, but one, had heard a dozen times. It mattered the less, as it was a good one. Sir Charles capped it with a better. The Governor told a weird tale of Lunsford's men, the "babe-eating" regiment. Sir Charles recounted a little adventure of His Grace of Buckingham with a quack astrologer, a Court lady, and an orange girl, which made the company die of laughter.

"Rat me! but you tell a story well, sir!" said the Governor, wiping his eyes.

"I serve King Charles the Second, your Excellency."

"And so have to live by your wit, eh, sir?"

"Precisely, your Excellency."

"Emigrate to Virginia, man! to the land of good eating, good drinking, good fighting, stout men, and pretty women—who make angelic wives." And the Governor, who loved his own wife with chivalric devotion, kissed a locket which he wore at his neck. "Come to Virginia where we need loyal men and true. Lord! we all thought the millennium was come with the king, but damme! if it doesn't seem as far off as ever! Not that his Majesty is to blame," he added quickly, as though fearing that his words might be taken as an aspersion upon Charles's ability to conduct the millennium single-handed. "The naughty spirit of the age sets itself against the Lord's Anointed. The Puritan snake is but scotched, not killed. It's the old prate of freedom of conscience, government by the people, and the like disgusting stuff (no offense to you, Major Carrington) that makes the trouble of the times both here and at home. I sigh for the good old days when, for eleven sweet years, no Parliament sat to meddle in affairs of state, when Wentworth kept down faction and the saintly Laud built up the Church which he adorned." And the Governor buried his woes in the Rhenish.

"Sir William Berkeley's loyalty is proverbial," said Sir Charles suavely. "The King knows that while he is at the helm in Virginia, the colony is on the high road to that era of peace and prosperity which his majesty so ardently desires—for his tax-paying people. And I have thought more than once of late that I might do worse than to dispose of my majority in the 'Blues,' bid the Court adieu, and obtaining from his Majesty a grant of land, retire here to Virginia to pass my days on my own land and amid a little court of my own, in the patriarchal fashion you gentlemen affect. Under certain circumstances it is a course I might possibly pursue." He glanced at his kinsman, whose countenance showed high approval of a plan which dovetailed nicely with one of his own making.

"Can you guess the 'certain circumstances' which are to give us the pleasure of his confounded company?" whispered Mr. Peyton to Mr. Carey.

"An easy riddle, Jack. Damn the insolent, smooth-spoken knave of hearts, and confound the women! They all drop to a court card."

"Not Mistress Betty Carrington. *She* looks below the surface."

"Humph! What does she see below thine? An empty gourd with a few madrigals and sonnets, and fine images, conned from the 'Grand Cyrus,' rattling about like dried seeds?"

"Hush, thou green persimmon! the Governor is speaking."

The governor rose with care to his feet. His wig was awry, his cravat of fine mechlin under one ear. Benevolent smiles played like summer lightning across his flushed face. He raised his tankard slowly and with attentive steadiness. "Gentlemen," he said in a high voice, "we have eaten and we have drunken. Dick Verney's wine is as old as the hills and as mellow as sunlight. It groweth late, gentlemen, and some of you have miles to travel, and it takes cool heads to ride the 'planter's pace.' For William Berkeley, gentlemen, Governor of Virginia by the grace of God and his Majesty, King Charles the Second, it takes more than Dick Verney's wine to fluster him. I call a final toast. I drink again to our loving friend and host, the worshipful Colonel Richard Verney, to his beauteous daughter and sister, to his man-servant and his maid-servant, his ox and his ass, and the stranger which is within his gates." He smiled benignly at a reflection of Sir Charles in a distant mirror. "Gentlemen, the devil, you see, can quote scripture. Let the cup go roun', go roun', go roun'."

The toast was drunk with fervor, and the party broke up.

The Governor, with Colonel Ludlow and Captain Laramore, was to sleep at Verney Manor, and Mistress Betty Carrington was left by her father to bear Patricia company for a day or two. One by one the remainder of the company rode or sailed away, those who had an even keel beneath them being in much better case than their brethren on horseback.

When the last sail showed a white speck in the distance, Patricia and Betty came out upon the porch and sat them down, one on either side of the Governor, with whom they were great favorites. Colonel Ludlow and Captain Laramore were at dice at a table within the hall, and Colonel Verney had excused himself in order to hear the evening report from his overseers. Sir Charles Carew, very idle and purposeless-looking, lounged in a great chair, and studied the miniature upon his snuff-box. The Governor, whom the wine had mellowed into a genial softness, a kind of sunset glow, alternately puffed wide rings of smoke into the air, and paid compliments to the young ladies. The evening breeze had sprung up, rustling the leaves of the trees, and bringing with it the sound of the water. In the western sky crimson islets forever shifted shapes in a sea of gold. A rosy light suffused the earth. In it the water turned to the pink of a shell, the marshes became ethereal and far away, earth and sky seemed one. The flashing wings of gull and curlew were like fairy sails faring to and fro.

"If I had wings," said Patricia dreamily, her hands clasped over her knees, "I would fly straight to that highest island of cloud. The one, Betty, that looks like a field of daffodils, with those beautiful peaks rising from it, and the violet light in the hollows. I would set up my standard there, Sir William, and the island should be mine, and I would rule the fairies that must inhabit it, with a rod of iron—as you rule Virginia," she ended with a laugh.

The Governor laughed with her. "You would have no such stiff-necked folk to deal with, my love, as have I."

"No, they should all be good Cavaliers and Churchmen—no Roundheads, no servants—and if Indians on neighboring isles threatened we would pray for a wind and sail away from them, around and around the bright blue sky."

"And when you are gone to take possession of your castle in the air what will poor Virginia do?" gallantly demanded the governor.

"Oh, she would still exist! But I am not going to-night. The princess of the castle in the air is engaged to his Excellency the Governor of Virginia for a game of chess. In the mean time here comes my father, who shall entertain your Excellency while Betty and I go for a walk. Come, Lady-bird."

The two graceful figures twined arms and moved off down the walk. Sir Charles looked after them a moment, then, with a "Permit me, sir," to the Governor, he snapped the lid of his snuff-box and started down the steps. The Governor laughed. "We will excuse you, sir," he said graciously. "Dick," to Colonel Verney, as the young gentleman hastened after the ladies, "that fine spark is to be your son-in-law, eh?"

"It is the wish of my heart, William."

"Humph!"

"He has birth and breeding. His father was my good friend and kinsman, and as loyal a Cavalier as ever gave life and lands for the blessed Martyr. He died in my arms at Marston Moor, and with his last breath commended his son to me. My dear wife was then expecting the birth of our child, of Patricia. I can see him now as he smiled up at me (he was ever gay) and said, 'If it's a girl, Dick, marry her to my boy.' Well! he died, and his brother took the boy, and my wife and I came over seas, and I never saw the lad from that day to this, when he comes at my invitation to visit us."

"Well, he is a very pretty fellow! And what does Patricia say to him?"

"Patricia is a good daughter," said the Colonel sedately, "and is possessed of sense beyond the average of womenkind. She knows the advantages this match offers. Sir Charles Carew can give her a title, and a name that's as old as her own. He is a man of parts and distinction, has served the King, is familiar with the courts of Europe. I do not pin my faith to the tales that are told of him. His father was a gallant gentleman, and I am not the man to believe ill of his son. Moreover, if, as he hath half promised, he will come to Virginia, he will throw off here the vices of the Court, the faults of youth, and become an honest Virginia gentleman, God-fearing, law-abiding, reverencing the King, but not copying him too closely—such an one as thou or I, William. The king should give him large grants of land, and so, with what Patricia will have when I am gone, there will be laid the foundation of a great and noble estate, which, please God, will belong in the fair future of this fair land to a great and noble family sprung from the union of Verney and Carew. Patricia, trust me, sees all this with my eyes."

"Humph!" said the Governor again.

CHAPTER IV

THE BREAKING HEART

Sir Charles was up with the two girls before they reached the garden; and they passed together through the gate and into the spicy wilderness. The dew was falling, and as they sauntered through the narrow paths, Betty held back her skirts that the damp leaves of sage and marjoram might not brush them; but Patricia, gathering larkspur and sweet-william, was heedless of her finery. At the further end of the garden was a wicket leading into a grove of mulberries. The three walked on beneath the spreading branches and the broad, heart-shaped leaves, until they came to a tree of extraordinary height and girth whose roots bulged out into great, smooth excrescences like inverted bowls. Patricia stopped. "Betty is tired," she said kindly, "and she shall sit here and rest. Betty is a windflower, Sir Charles, a little tender timid flower, frail and sweet—are you not, Betty?" She sat down upon one of the bowls, and pulled her friend down beside her. Sir Charles leaned against the trunk of the tree. "Betty is a little Puritan," continued Patricia; "she would not wear the set of ribbons I had for her; and that hurt me very much."

"O Patricia!" cried Betty, with tears in her eyes. "If I thought you really cared! But even then I could not wear them!"

"No, you little martyr," said the other, with a kiss. "You would go to the stake any day for what you call your 'principles.' And I honor you for it, you know I do. Cousin Charles, do you know that Betty thinks it wrong to hold slaves?"

Sir Charles laughed, and Betty's delicate face flushed.

"O Patricia!" she cried. "I did not say that! I only said that we would not like it ourselves."

"'Pon my soul, I don't suppose we would," said Sir Charles coolly. "But, Mistress Betty, the negroes have neither thin skins nor nice feelings."

"I know that," said Betty bravely; "and I know that our divines and learned men cannot yet decide whether or not they have souls. And, of course, if they have not, they are as well treated as other animals; but all the same I am sorry for them, and I am sorry for the servants too."

"For the servants!" cried Patricia, arching her brows.

"Yes," said Betty, standing to her guns. "I am sorry for the servants, for those who must work seven years for another before they can do aught for themselves. And often when their time is out they are bowed and broken; and those whom they love at home, and would bring over, are dead; and often before the seven years have passed they die themselves. And I am sorry for those whom you call rebels, for the Oliverians; and for the convicts, despised and outcast. And for the Indians about us, dispossessed and broken, and—yes, I am sorry for the Quakers."

"I waste no pity on the under dog," said Sir Charles. "Keep him down—and with a heavy hand—or he will fly at your throat."

"Hark!" said Patricia.

Some one in the distance was singing:—

"Gentle herdsman, tell to me

Of courtesy I thee pray,

Unto the town of Walsingham,

Which is the right and ready way?

"Unto the town of Walsingham

The way is hard for to be gone,

And very crooked are those paths

For you to find out all alone."

The notes were wild and plaintive, and sounded sadly through the gathering dusk. A figure flitted towards them between the shadowy tree trunks.

"It is Mad Margery," said Patricia.

"And who is Mad Margery?" asked Sir Charles.

"No one knows, cousin. She does not know herself. Ten years ago a ship came in with servants, and she was on it. She was mad then. The captain could give no account of her, save that when, the day after sailing, he came to count the servants, he found one more than there should have been, and that one a woman, stupid from drugs. She had been spirited on board the ship, that was all he could say. It's a common occurrence, as you know. She never came to herself,—has always been what she is now. She was sold to a small planter, and cruelly treated by him. After a time my father heard her story and bought her from her master. She has been with us ever since. Her term of service is long out; but there is nothing that could drive her from this plantation. She wanders about as she pleases, and has a cabin in the woods yonder; for she will not live in the quarters. They say that she is a white witch; and the Indians, who reverence the mad, lay maize and venison at her door."

The voice, shrill and sweet, rang out close at hand.

"Thy years are young, thy face is fair,

Thy wits are weak, thy thoughts are green,

Time hath not given thee leave as yet,

For to commit so great a sin."

"Margery!" called Patricia softly.

The woman came towards them with a peculiar gliding step, swift and stealthy. Within a pace or two of them she stopped, and asked, "Who called me?" in a voice that seemed to come from far away. She was not old, and might once have been beautiful.

"I called you, Margery," said Patricia gently. "Sit down beside us, and tell us what you have been doing."

The woman came and sat herself down at Patricia's feet. She carried a stick, or light pole, wound with thick strings of wild hops, which she laid on the ground. Taking one of the wreaths from around it, she dropped the pale green mass into Patricia's lap.

"Take it," she said. "They are flowers I gathered in Paradise, long ago. They wither in this air; but if you fan them with your sighs, and water them with your tears, they will revive.... Paradise is a long way from here. I have been seeking the road all day; but I have not found it yet. I think it must lie near Bristol Town, Bristol Town, Bristol Town."

Her voice died away in a long sigh, and she sat plucking at the fragrant blooms.

Patricia said softly, "She talks much of Bristol Town, and she is always seeking the road to Paradise. I think that once some one must have said to her, 'We will meet in Paradise.'"

"I know little of Paradise, Margery," said Sir Charles, good-naturedly; "but Bristol Town is many leagues from here, across the great ocean."

"Yes, I know. It lieth in the rising of the sun. I have never seen it except in my dreams. But it is a beautiful place—not like this world of trees. The church bells are ever ringing there, ... and the children sing in the streets. It is all fair, and smiling and beautiful, all but one spot, one black, black, black spot. I will tell you." She sunk her voice to a whisper and looked fearfully around. "The mouth of the Pit is there, the Bottomless Pit that the Preacher tells about. It is a small room, dark, dark, ... and there is a heavy smell in the air, ... and there are fiends with black cloth over their faces. They hold a draught of hell to your mouth, and they make you drink it; ... it burns, burns. And then you go down, down, down, into everlasting blackness." She broke off, and shuddered violently, then burst into eldritch laughter.

"Shall I tell you what I found just now while I was looking for Paradise?"

"Yes," said Patricia.

"A breaking heart."

"A breaking heart!"

Margery nodded. "Yes," she said. "I thought it would surprise you. I find many things, looking for Paradise. The other day I found a brown pixie sitting beneath a mushroom, and he told me curious things. But a breaking heart is different. I know all about it, for once upon a time my heart broke; but mine was soft and easy to break. It was as soft and weak as a baby's wrist, a little, tender, helpless thing, you know, that melts under your kisses. But this heart that I found will take a long time to break. Proud anger will strengthen it at first; but one string will snap, and then another, and another, until, at last—" she swept her arms abroad with a wild and desolate gesture.

"What does she mean?" asked Sir Charles.

"I do not know," answered Patricia.

Margery rose and took up her leafy staff.

"Come," she said. "Come and see the breaking heart."

"O Patricia!" cried Betty, "do not go with her!"

"Why not?" asked Patricia resolutely. "Come, cousin, let us find out what she means. We will go with you, Margery; but you must not take us far. It grows late."

Margery laughed weirdly. "It is never late for Margery. There is a star far up in heaven that is sorry for Margery, and it shines for her, bright, bright, all night long, that she may not miss the road to Paradise."

She glided in front of them, and moved rapidly down the dim alley of trees, her feet seeming scarce to touch the short grass, and the long green wreaths, stirred by the wind, coiling and uncoiling around her staff like serpents. Patricia, with Betty and Sir Charles, followed her closely. She led them out of the mulberry grove, through a small vineyard, and into a patch of corn, beyond which could be seen the gleam of water, faintly pink from the faded sunset.

"She is taking us towards the quarters!" exclaimed Patricia. "Margery! Margery!"

But Margery held on, moving swiftly through the waist-deep corn. Betty looked down with a little sigh at her dainty shoes, which were suffering by their contact with the dew-laden leaves of pumpkins and macocks. Sir Charles put aside the long corn blades with his cane, and so made a way for the girls. He felt mildly curious and somewhat bored.

Suddenly they emerged upon the banks of the inlet, within a hundred yards of the quarters. Patricia would have spoken, but Margery put her finger to her lips and flitted on towards the row of cabins.

Before them stretched a long, narrow lane, sandy and barren, with a pine-tree rising here and there. Rude cabins, windowless and with mud chimneys, faced each other across the lane. Half way down was an open space, or small square, in the centre of which stood a dead tree with a board nailed across its trunk at about a man's height from the ground. In either end of the board was cut a round hole big enough for a man's hand to be squeezed through, and above hung a heavy stick with leathern thongs tied to it, the whole forming a pillory and whipping-post, rude, but satisfactory.

It was almost dark. The larger stars had come out, and the fireflies began to sparkle restlessly. The wind sighed in the pines, and a strong salt smell came from the sea. Overhead a whip-poor-will uttered its mournful cry.

The long day's work, from sunrise to sunset, was over, and the population of the quarter had drifted in from the fields of tobacco and maize, the boats, the carpenter's shop, the forge, the mill, the stables, and barns. Hard-earned rest was theirs, and they were prepared to enjoy it. It was supper-time. In the square a great fire of brush-wood had been kindled, and around it squatted a ring of negroes, busy with bowls of loblolly and great chunks of corn bread. They chattered like monkeys, and one who had finished his mess raised a chant in which one note was a yell of triumph, the next a long-drawn plaintive wail. The rich barbaric voice filled the night. A figure, rising, tossed aside an empty bowl, and began to dance in the red firelight.

The white men ate at their cabin doors, sitting upon logs of wood, or in groups of three or four messed at tables made by stretching planks from one tree-stump to another. It was meat-day; and they, too, made merry.

From the women's cabins also came shrill laughter. Snatches of song arose, altercations that suddenly began and as suddenly ceased, a babel of voices in many fashions of speech. Broad Yorkshire contended with the thin nasal tones of the cockney; the man from the banks of the Tweed thrust cautious sarcasms at the man from Galway. A mulatto, the color of pale amber, spoke sonorous Spanish to an olive-hued piece of drift-wood from Florida. An Indian indulged in a monologue in a tongue of a faraway tribe of the Blue Mountains.

The glare from the fire and from flaring pine-knots played fitfully over the motley throng, now bringing out in strong relief some one face or figure, then plunging it into profoundest shadow. It burnished the high forehead and scalp lock of the Indian, and made to gleam intensely the gold earring in the ear of the mulatto. The scarlet cloth wound about the head of a Turk seemed to turn to actual flame. Under the baleful light vacant faces of dully honest English rustics became malignant, while the negro, dancing with long, outstretched arms and uncouth swayings to and fro, appeared a mirthful fiend.

The three gentlefolk and their mad conductress gazed from out the shadow and at a safe distance. Sir Charles Carew, a man of taste, felt strong artistic pleasure in the Rembrandtesque scene before him—the leaping light, the weird shadows, resolving themselves into figures posed with savage freedom, the dancing satyr, the sombre pines above, and, beyond the pines, the stillness of the stars. Betty drew a little shuddering breath, and her hand went to clasp Patricia's. The latter was looking steadily upward at the slender crescent moon.

"Do not look, Betty," she said quietly. "I do not. It is a horror to me—a horror. I am going back," she said, turning.

But she had reckoned without Margery, who caught her by the arm. "Come," she said imperiously. "Come and see the breaking heart!" Patricia hesitated, then yielded to curiosity and the insistent pressure of the skeleton fingers.

The cabins nearest them were deserted, their occupants having joined themselves to the groups further down the lane where the firelight beat strongest and the torches were more numerous. With no more sound than a moth would make, flitting through the dusk, the mad woman led them to the outermost of these cabins. Within five paces of the door she stopped and pointed a long forefinger.

"The breaking heart!" she said in a triumphant whisper.

A man lay, face downwards, in the coarse and scanty grass. One arm was bent beneath his forehead, the other was outstretched, the hand clenched.

It was the attitude of one who has flung himself down in dumb, despairing misery. As they looked, he gave a long gasping sob that shook his whole frame, then lay quiet.

A burst of revelry came down the lane. The man raised his head impatiently, then let it drop again upon his arm.

Patricia turned and walked quickly back the way they had come. Betty and Sir Charles followed her; Margery, her whim gratified, had vanished into the darkness of the pines.

No one spoke until they were again amidst the wet and rustling corn. Then said Betty with tears in her voice, "O Patricia, darling! there is so much misery in the world, fair and peaceful as it looks to-night. That poor man!"

"That 'poor man,' Betty," answered Patricia in a hard voice, "is a criminal, a felon, guilty of some dreadful, sordid thing, a gaol-bird reclaimed from the gallows and sent here to pollute the air we breathe."

"It was the convict, Landless, was it not?" asked Sir Charles.

"Yes."

"But, Patricia," said the gentle Betty, "whatever he may have done, he is wretched now."

"He has sowed the wind; let him reap the whirlwind," said Patricia steadily.

They went on to the house and into the great room where the myrtle candles were burning softly, the dimity curtains shutting out the night. Mrs. Lettice was at the spinet, with Captain Laramore to turn the leaves of her song book, and the Governor, with the chess table out and the pieces in battle array, awaited (he said) the arrival of the Princess of the Castle in the Air.

CHAPTER V

IN THE THREE-MILE FIELD

In a far corner of the Three-mile Field Landless bent over tobacco plant after tobacco plant, patiently removing the little green shoots or "suckers" from the parent stem.

His back and limbs ached from the unaccustomed stooping, the fierce sunshine beat upon his head, the blood pounded behind his temples, his tongue clave to the roof of his mouth,—and the noontide rest was still two hours away. As, with a gasp of weariness, he straightened himself, the endless plain of green rose and fell to his dazzled eyes in misty billows. The most robust rustic required several months of seasoning before he and the Virginia climate became friends, and this man was still weak from privation and confinement in prison and in the noisome hold of the ship.

He turned his weary eyes from the vivid gold green of the fields to the shadows of the forest. It lay within a few yards of him, just on the other side of a little stream and a rail fence that zigzagged in gray lines hung with creepers. At the moment he defined happiness as a plunge into the cool, perfumed darkness, a luxurious flinging of a tired body upon the carpet of pine needles, a shutting out, forever, of the sunshine.

Suddenly he felt that eyes were upon him, and his glance traveled from the fringe of trees to meet that of an Indian seated upon a log in an angle of the fence.

He was a man of gigantic stature, dressed in coarse canvas breeches, and with a handkerchief of gaudy dye twisted about his head. His bold features wore the usual Indian expression of saturnine imperturbability, and he half sat, half reclined upon the log as motionless as a piece of carven bronze, staring at Landless with large, inscrutable eyes.

Landless, staring in return, saw something else. The rank growth of weeds in which the log was sunk moved ever so slightly. There was a flash as of a swiftly drawn rapier, and something long and mottled hung for an instant upon the shoulder of the Indian, and then dropped into its lair again.

With a sudden lithe twist of his body, the savage flung himself upon it, and holding it down with one hand, with the other beat the life out with a heavy stick. The creature was killed by the first stroke, but he continued to rain vindictive blows upon it until it was mashed to a pulp. Then, with a serenely impassive mien, he resumed his seat upon the log.

Landless sprang across the stream, and went up to him.

"You are bitten! Is there aught I can do?"

The Indian shook his head. With one hand he pulled the shoulder forward, trying, as Landless saw, to meet the wound with his lips; but finding that it could not be done, he desisted and sat silent, and to all appearance, unconcerned.

Landless cried out impatiently, "It will kill you, man! Do you know no remedy?"

The Indian grunted. "Snake root grow deep in the forest, a long way off. Besides, an Iroquois does not die for a little thing like a pale face or a dog of an Algonquin."

"Why did you try to reach the sting with your mouth?"

"To suck out the evil."

"Is that a cure?"

The Indian nodded. Landless knelt down and examined the shoulder. "Now," he said, "tell me if I set about it in the right way," and applied his lips to the swollen, blue-black spot.

The Indian gave a grunt of surprise, and his white teeth flashed in a smile; then he sat silent under the ministrations of the white man who sucked at the wound, spitting the venom upon the ground, until the dark skin was drawn and wrinkled like the hand of a washerwoman.

"Good!" then said the Indian, and pointed to the stream. Landless went to it, rinsed his mouth, and brought back water in his cap with which he laved the shoulder of his new acquaintance, ending by binding it up with the handkerchief from the man's head.

A guttural sound from the Indian made him look up. At the same instant the whip of the overseer, descending, cut him sharply across the shoulders. He sprang to his feet, the veins in his forehead swollen, his frame tense with impotent anger. The overseer, having gained his attention, thrust the whip back into his belt.

"If you don't want to get what will hurt as bad as a snake bite," he said grimly, "you had best tend to your tobacco and let vagrom Indians alone. That row is to be suckered before dinner-time or your pork and beans will go begging. As for you," turning to the Indian, "what are you doing on this plantation? Where's your pass?"

The Indian took from his waistband a slip of paper which he handed to the overseer, who looked at it and gave it back with a grudging—"It's all right this time, but you'd better be careful. It's my opinion that Major Carrington lets his servants run about a deal more than's good for them. Anyhow, you've no business in this field. Clear out!"

The Indian arose and went his way. But as he passed Landless, suckering a plant with angry energy, he touched him, as if by accident, with his sinewy hand.

"Monakatocka never forgives an enemy," came in a sibilant whisper too low to be heard by the watchful overseer. "Monakatocka never forgets a friend. Some day he will repay."

The red-brown body slipped away through the tall weeds and clumps of alder, like the larger edition of the thing that had hung upon its shoulder. The overseer strode off down the field, sending keen glances to right and left. He was a conscientious man, and earned every pound of his wages.

Landless, left alone, worked steadily on, for he had no mind to lose his midday meal, uninviting as he knew it would prove to be. Moreover, he was one who did with his might what his hand found to do. His body was weary, and his heart sick within him, but the green shoots fell thick and fast.

"Yon was a kindly thing you did. Pity 'twas in no better cause than the saving of a worthless natural."

The speaker, who was at work on the next row of plants, had caught up with Landless from behind, and now moved his nimble fingers more slowly, so as to keep pace with the less expert new hand.

Landless, raising his head, stared at a figure of positively terrifying aspect. Upon a skeleton body of extraordinary height was set a head bare of any hair. Scalp, forehead and cheeks were of one dull, ivory hue like an eastern carving. Upon the smooth, dead surface of the right cheek sprawled a great red R, branded into the flesh, and through each large protruding ear went a ragged hole. For the rest, the lips were of iron, and the small, deep-set eyes were so bright and burning that they gave the impression that they were red like the great letter. It might have been the face of a man of sixty years, though it would have been hard to tell wherein lay the semblance of age, so smooth was the skin and so brilliant the eyes.

"The Indian needed help. Why should I not have given it him?" said Landless.

"Because it is written, 'Cursed are the heathen who inhabit the land.'"

Landless smiled. "So you would not help an Indian in extremity. What if it had been a negro?"

"Cursed are the negroes! 'Ye Ethiopians also, ye shall be slain by the sword.'"

"A Quaker?"

"Cursed are the Quakers! 'Silly doves that have no heart.'"

Landless laughed. "You have cursed pretty well all the oppressed of the land. I suppose you reserve your blessings for the powers that be."

"The powers that be! May the plagues of Egypt light upon them, and the seven vials rain down their contents upon them! Cursed be they all, from the young man, Charles Stuart, to that prelatical, tyrannical, noxious Malignant, William Berkeley! May their names become a hissing and an abomination! Roaring lions are their princes, ravening wolves are their judges, their priests have polluted the sanctuary! May their flesh consume away while they stand upon their feet, and their eyes consume away in their holes, and their tongues consume away in their mouths, and may there be mourning among them, even as the mourning of Hadadrimmon in the valley of Megiddon!"

"You are a Muggletonian?"

"Yea, verily am I! a follower of the saintly Ludovick Muggleton, and of the saintlier John Reeve, of whom Ludovick is but the mouthpiece, even as Aaron was of Moses. They are the two witnesses of the Apocalypse. They are the two olive trees and the two candlesticks. To them and to their followers it is given to curse and to spare not, to prophesy against the peoples and kindred and nations and tongues whereon is set the seal of the beast. Wherefore I, Win-Grace Porringer, testify against the people of this land; against Prelatists and Papists, Presbyterians and Independents, Baptists, Quakers and heathen; against princes, governors, and men in high places; against them that call themselves planters and trample the vineyard of the Lord; against their sons and their daughters who are haughty, and walk with stretched-forth neck and wanton eyes, walking and mincing and making a tinkling with their feet. Cursed be they all! Surely they shall be as Sodom and Gomorrah, even the breeding of salt-pits and a perpetual desolation!"

"Your curses seem not to have availed, friend," said Landless. "Curses are apt to come home to roost. I should judge that yours have returned to you in the shape of branding-irons."

The man raised a skeleton hand and stroked the red letter.

"This," he said coolly, "was given me when I ran away the second time. The first time I was merely whipped. The third time I was shaven and this shackle put upon my leg." He raised his foot and pointed to an iron ring encircling the ankle. "The fourth time I was nailed by the ears to the pillory, whence come these pretty scars."

Landless burst into grim laughter. "And after your fifth attempt, what then?"

The man gave him a sidelong look. "I have not made my fifth attempt," he said quietly.

They worked in silence for a few minutes. Then said Master Win-Grace Porringer:—

"I was sent to the plantations, because, in defiance of the Act of Uniformity (cursed be it, and the authors thereof), I attended a meeting of the persecuted and broken remnant of the Lord's people. What was your offense, friend, for I reckon that you come not here of your free will, being neither a rustic nor a fool?"

"I came from Newgate," said Landless, after a pause. "I am a convict."

The man's hand stopped in the act of pulling off a shoot. He gave a slow upward look at the figure beside him, let his eyes rest upon the face, and looked slowly down again with a shake of the head.

"Humph!" he said. "The society in Newgate must be improved since my time."

They worked without speaking until they had nearly reached the end of the long double row, when said the Muggletonian:—

"You are too young, I take it, to have seen service in the wars?"

"I fought at Worcester."

"Upon which side?"

"The Commonwealth's."

"I thought as much. Humph! You were all, Parliament and Presbytery, Puritan and Independent, Hampden and Vane and Oliver, in the gall of bitterness and the bond of iniquity, very far from the pure light in which walk the followers of the blessed Ludovick. At the last the two witnesses will speak against you also. But in the mean time it were easier for the children of light to walk under the rule of the Puritan than under that of the lascivious house of Jeroboam which now afflicts England for her sins. But the Lord hath a controversy with them! An east wind shall come up, the wind of the Lord shall come up from the wilderness! They shall be moved from their places! They shall lick the dust like serpents, they shall move out of their holes like worms of the earth, and be utterly destroyed! Think you not as I do, friend?" he asked, turning suddenly upon Landless.

"I think," said Landless, "that you are talking that which, if overheard, might give you a deeper scar than any you bear."

"But who is to hear? the tobacco, the Lord in heaven, and you. The senseless plant will keep counsel, the Lord is not like to betray his servant, and as for you, friend,—" he looked long and searchingly at Landless. "Despite the place you come from, I do not think you one to bring a man into trouble for being bold enough to say what you dare only think."

Landless returned the look. "No," he said quietly. "You need have no fear of me."

"I fear no one," said the other proudly.

Presently he craned his long body across the plant between them until his lips almost touched the ear of the younger man.

"Shall you try to escape?" he whispered.

A smile curled Landless's lip. "Very probably I shall," he said dryly. He looked down the long lines of broad green leaves at the toiling figures, black and white, dull peasants at best, scoundrels at worst; and beyond to the huddled cabins of the quarter, and to the great house, rising fair and white from orchard and garden; seeing, as in a dream, a man, young in years but old in sorrow, disgraced, outcast, friendless, alone, creeping down a vista of weary years, day after day of soul-deadening toil, of association with the mean and the vile, of shameful submission to whip and finger. Escape! The word had beaten through brain and heart so long and so persistently, that at times he feared lest he should cry it aloud.

Win-Grace Porringer shook his head.

"It's not an easy thing to escape from a Virginia plantation. With dogs and with horses they hunt you down, yea, with torches and boats. They band themselves together against the fleeing sparrow. They call in the heathen to their aid. And it is a fearful land, for great rivers bar your way, and forests push you back, and deep quagmires clutch you and hold you until the men of blood come up. And when you are taken they cruelly maltreat you, and your term of service is doubled."

"And yet men have gotten away," said Landless.

"Yes, but not many. And those that get away are seldom heard of more. The forest swallows them up, and after a while their skulls roll about the hills, playthings for wolves, or the deep waters flow over their bones, or they lie in a little heap of ashes at the foot of some Indian torture stake."

"Why did you try to escape?" asked Landless.

The man gave him another sidelong look.

"I tried because I was a fool. I am no longer a fool. I know a better way."

"A better way!"

"Hush!" The man looked over his shoulder and then whispered, "Will you go with me to-night?"

"Go with you! Where?"

"To a man I know—a man who gives good advice."

"Many can do that, friend."

"Ay, but not show the way to profit by it as doth this man."

"Who is he?"

"A servant even as we are servants,—a learned and godly man, albeit not a follower of the blessed Ludovick. Listen! About the rising of the moon to-night, slip from your cabin and come to the blasted pine on the shore of the inlet. There will be a boat there and I will be in it. We will go to the cabin of the man of whom I speak. He is a cripple, and knowing that he cannot run away, the godless and roistering Malignant who calls himself our master hath given him a hut among the marshes, where he mendeth nets. Come! I may not say more than that it will be worth your while."

"If we are caught—"

"Our skins pay for us. But the Lord will shut the eyes of the overseers that they see not, and their ears that they hear not, and we will be safely back before the dawn. You will come?"

"Yes," said Landless. "I will come."

CHAPTER VI

THE HUT ON THE MARSH

It was shortly after midnight when the two servants slipped along the inlet, silently and warily, and keeping their boat well under the shore. It was a crazy affair, barely large enough for two, and requiring constant bailing. When they had made half a mile from the quarters, the Muggletonian, who rowed, turned the boat's head across the inlet, and ran into a very narrow creek that wound in mazy doubles through the marshes. They entered it, made the first turn, and the broad bosom of the inlet, lit by a low, crimson moon, was as if it had never been. On every side high marsh grass soughed in the night wind,—plains of blackness with the red moon rising from them. The tide was low. So close were the banks of wet, black earth, that they heard the crabs scuttling down them, and Porringer made a jab with his pole at a great sheepshead lying *perdu* alongside. The water broke before them into spangles, glittering phosphorescent ripples. A school of small fish, disturbed by the oars, rushed past them, leaping from the water with silver flashes. A turtle plunged sullenly. From the grass above came the sleepy cry of marsh hens, and once a great white heron rose like a ghost across their path. It flapped its wings and sailed away with a scream of wrath.

The boat had wound its tortuous way for many minutes before Porringer said in a low voice: "We can speak safely now. There is nothing human moving on these flats unless the witch, Margery, is abroad. Cursed may she be, and cursed those who give her shelter and food and raiment and lay offerings at her door, for surely it is written, 'Thou shalt not suffer a witch to live.'"

"Is there anything a Muggletonian will not curse?" asked Landless.

"Yea," answered the other complacently. "There are ourselves, the salt of the earth. There are a thousand or more of us."

"And the remainder of the inhabitants of the earth are reprobate and doomed?"

"Yea, verily, they shall be as the burning of lime, as thorns cut up will they be burned in the fire."

"Then why have you to do with me, and with the man to whom we are going?"

"Because it is written: 'Make ye friends of the mammon of unrighteousness;' and moreover there be degrees even in hell fire. I do not place you, who have some inkling of the truth, nor the Independents and Fifth Monarchy men (as for the Quakers they shall be utterly damned) in the furnace seven times heated which is reserved for the bigoted and bloody Prelatists who rule the land, swearing strange oaths, foining with the sword, and delighting in vain apparel; keeping their feast days and their new moons and their solemn festivals. They are the rejoicing city that dwells carelessly, that says in her heart, 'I am, and there is none beside me.' The day cometh when they shall be broken as the breaking of a potter's vessel, yea, they shall be violently tossed like a ball into a far country."

Here they struck a snag, well-nigh capsizing the boat. When she righted, and Landless had bailed her out with a gourd, they proceeded in silence. Landless was in no mood for speech. He did not know where they were going, nor for what purpose, nor did he greatly care. He meant to escape, and that as soon as his strength should be recovered and he could obtain some knowledge of the country, and he meant to take no one into his counsel, not the Muggletonian, whose own attempts had ended so disastrously, nor the 'man who gave good advice.' As to this midnight expedition he was largely indifferent. But it was something to escape from the stifling atmosphere of the cabin where he had tossed from side to side, listening to the heavy breathing of the convict Turk and peasant lad with whom he was quartered, to the silver peace of moon-flooded marsh and lapping water.

They made another turn, and in front of them shone out a light, gleaming dully like a will-of-the-wisp. It looked close at hand, but the creek turned upon itself, coiled and writhed through the marsh, and trebled the distance.

The Muggletonian rested on his oar, and turned to Landless.

"Yonder is our bourne," he said gravely. "But I have a word to say to you, friend, before we reach it. If, to curry favor with the uncircumcised Philistines who set themselves over us, thou speakest of aught thou mayest see or hear there to-night, may the Lord wither thy tongue within thy mouth, may he smite thee with blindness, may he bring thee quick into the pit! And if not the Lord, then will I, Win-Grace Porringer, rise and smite thee!"

"You may spare your invectives," said Landless coldly. "I am no traitor."

"Nay, friend," said the other in a milder tone. "I thought it not of thee, or I had not brought thee thither."

He shoved the nose of the boat into the shore, and caught at a stake, rising, water-soaked and rotten, from below the bank. Landless threw him the looped end of a rope, and together they made the boat fast, then scrambled up the three feet of fat, sliding earth to the level above where the ground was dry, none but the highest of tides ever reaching it. Fifty yards away rose a low hut. It stood close to another bend in the creek, and before it were several boats, tied to stakes, and softly rubbing their sides together. The hut had no window, but there were interstices between the logs through which the light gleamed redly.

When the two men had reached it, the Muggletonian knocked upon the heavy door, after a peculiar fashion, striking it four times in all. There was a shuffling sound within, and (Landless thought) two voices ceased speaking. Then some one said in a low voice and close to the door: "Who is it?"

"The sword of the Lord and of Gideon," answered the Muggletonian.

A bar fell from the door, and it swung slowly inwards.

"Enter, friends," said a quiet voice. Landless, stooping his head, crossed the threshold, and found himself in the presence of a man with a high, white forehead and a grave, sweet face, who, leaning on a stick, and dragging one foot behind him, limped back to the settle from which he had risen, and fell to work upon a broken net as calmly as if he were alone. Besides themselves he was the only inmate of the room.

A pine torch, stuck into a cleft in the table, cast a red and flickering light over a rude interior, furnished with the table, the settle, a chest and a straw pallet. From the walls and rafters hung nets, torn or mended. In one corner was a great heap of dingy sail, in another a sheaf of oars, and a third was wholly in darkness. Lying about the earthen floor were several small casks to which the man motioned as seats.

Leaving Landless near the door, Win-Grace Porringer dragged a keg to the side of the settle, and sitting down upon it, approached his death mask of a face close to the face of the mender of nets, and commenced a whispered conversation. To Landless, awaiting rather listlessly the outcome of this nocturnal adventure, came now and then a broken sentence. "He hath not the look of a criminal, but—" "Of Puritan breeding, sayest thou?" "We need young blood." Then after prolonged whispering, "No traitor, at least."

At length the Muggletonian arose and came towards Landless. "My friend would speak with you alone," he said, "I will stand guard outside." He went out, closing the door behind him.

The mender of nets beckoned Landless. "Will you come nearer?" he asked in a quiet refined voice that was not without a ring of power. "As you see, I am lame, and I cannot move without pain."

Landless came and sat down beside the table, resting his elbow upon the wood, and his chin upon his hand. The mender of nets put down his work, and the two measured each other in silence.

Landless saw a man of middle age who looked like a scholar, but who might have been a soldier; a man with a certain strong, bright sweetness of look in a spare, worn face, and underlying the sweetness a still and deadly determination. The mender of nets saw, in his turn, a figure lithe and straight as an Indian's, a well-poised head, and a handsome face set in one fixed expression of proud endurance. A determined face, too, with dark, resolute eyes and strong mouth, the face of a man who has done and suffered much, and who knows that he will both do and suffer more.

"I am told," said the mender of nets, "that you are newly come to the plantations."

"I was brought by the ship God-Speed a month ago."

"You did not come as an indented servant?"

Landless reddened. "No."

"Nor as a martyr to principle, a victim of that most iniquitous and tyrannical Act of Uniformity?"

"No."

"Nor as one of those whom they call Oliverians?"

"No."

The mender of nets tapped softly against the table with his thin, white fingers. Landless said coldly:—

"These are idle questions. The man who brought me here hath told you that I am a convict."

The other looked at him keenly. "I have heard convicts talk before this. Why do you not assert your innocence?"

"Who would believe me if I did?"

There was a silence. Landless, raising his eyes, met those of the mender of nets, large, luminous, gravely tender, and reading him like a book.

"I will believe you," said the mender of nets.

"Then, as God is above us," said the other solemnly, "I did not do the thing! And He knows that I thank you, sir, for your trust. I have not found another—"

"I know, lad, I know! How was it?"

"I was a Commonwealth's man. My father was dead, my kindred attainted, and I had a powerful enemy. I was caught in a net of circumstance. And Morton was my judge."

"Humph! the marvel is that you ever got nearer to the plantations than Tyburn. Your name is—"

"Godfrey Landless."

"Landless! Once I knew—and loved—a Warham Landless—a brave soldier, a gallant gentleman, a true Christian. He fell at Worcester."

"He was my father."

The mender of nets covered his eyes with his hand. "O Lord! how wonderful are thy ways!" he said beneath his breath, then aloud, "Lad, lad, I cannot wholly sorrow to see you here. Wise in counsel, bold in action, patient, farseeing, brave, was thy father, and I think thou hast his spirit. Thou hast his eyes, now that I look at thee more closely. I have prayed for such a man."

"I am glad you knew my father," said Landless simply.

After a long silence, in which the minds of both had gone back to other days, the mender of nets spoke gravely.

"You have no cause to love the present government?"

"No," said Landless grimly.

"You were heart and hand for the Commonwealth?"

"Yes."

"You mean to escape from this bondage?"

"Yes."

The mender of nets took from his bosom a little worn book. "Will you swear upon this that you will never reveal what I am about to say to you, save to such persons as I shall designate? For myself I would take your simple word, for we are both gentlemen, but other lives than mine hang in the balance."

Landless touched the book with his lips. "I swear," he said.

The man brought his serene, white face nearer.

"What would you have given," he asked solemnly, "for the cause for which your father died?"

"My life," said Landless.

"Would you give it still?"

"A worthless gift," said Landless bitterly. "Yea, I would give it, but the cause is dead."

The other shook his head. "The cause of the just man dieth not."

There was a pause broken by the mender of nets.

"Thou art no willing slave, I trow. The thought of escape is ever with thee."

"I shall escape," said Landless deliberately. "And if they track me they shall not take me alive."

The mender of nets gave a melancholy smile. "They would track you, never fear!" He leaned forward and touched Landless with his hand. "What if I show you a better way?" he asked in a whisper.

"What way?"

"A way to recover your liberty, and with it, the liberty of downtrodden brethren. A way to raise the banner of the Commonwealth and to put down the Stuart."

Landless stared. "A miserable hut," he said, "in the midst of a desolate Virginia marsh, and within it, a brace of slaves, the one a cripple, the other a convict,—and Charles Stuart on his throne in Whitehall! Friend, this dismal place hath turned your wits!"

The other smiled. "My wits are sound," he said, "as sound as they were upon that day when I gave my voice for the death (a sad necessity!) of this young man's father. And I do not think to shake England,—I speak of Virginia."

"Of Virginia!"

"Yea, of this goodly land, a garden spot, a new earth where should be planted the seeds of a mighty nation, strong in justice and simple right, wise, temperate, brave; an enlightened people, serving God in spirit and in truth, not with the slavish observance of prelatist and papist, nor with the indecent familiarity of the Independent; loyal to their governors, but exercising the God-given right of choosing those who are to rule over them; a people amongst whom liberty shall walk unveiled, and to whom Astræa shall come again; a people as free as the eagle I watched this morning, soaring higher and ever higher, strongly and proudly, rejoicing in its progress heavenward."

"In other words, a republic," said Landless dryly.

"Why not?" answered the other with shining, unseeing eyes. "It is a dream we dreamed ten years ago, I and Vane and Sidney and Marten and many others,—but Oliver rudely wakened us. Then it was by the banks of the Thames, and it was for England. Now, on the shores of Chesapeake I dream again, and it is for Virginia. You smile!"

"Have you considered, sir,—I do not know your name."

"Robert Godwyn is my name."

"Have you considered, Master Godwyn, that the Virginians do not want a republic, that they are more royalist and prelatical than are their brethren at home; that they out-Herod Herod in their fantastic loyalty?"

"That is true of the class with whom you have come into contact,—of the masters. But there is much disaffection among the people at large. And there are the Nonconformists, the Presbyterians, Independents, Baptists, even the Quakers, though they say they fight not. To them all, Charles Stuart is the Pharaoh whose heart the Lord hardened, and William Berkeley is his task-master."

"Any one else?"

"There are those of the gentry who were Commonwealth's men, and who chafe sorely under the loss of office and disfavor into which they have fallen."

"And these all desire a republic?"

"They desire the downfall of the royalists with William Berkeley at their head. The republic would follow."

"And when a handful of Puritan gentlemen, a few hundred Nonconformists, and the rabble of the colony shall have executed this project, have usurped the government, dethroning the king, or his governor, which is the same thing,—then will come in from the mouth of Thames a couple of royal frigates and blow your infant republic into space."

"I do not think so. The frigates would come undoubtedly, but I am of another opinion as to the result of their coming. They would not take us unprepared as those of the Commonwealth took William Berkeley in fifty-two. And with a plentiful lack of money and a Dutch war threatening, Charles Stuart could not send unlimited frigates. Moreover, if Virginia revolted, Puritan New England would follow her example, and she would find allies in the Dutch of New Amsterdam."

"You spin large fancies," said Landless, with some scorn. "I suppose you are plotting with these gentlemen you speak of?"

"No," said the man, with a scarcely perceptible hesitation. "No, they are few in number and scattered. Moreover, they might plot amongst themselves but never with—a servant."

"Then you are concerned with the Nonconformists?"

"The Nonconformists are timid, and dream not that the day of deliverance is at hand."

Landless began to laugh. "Do you mean to say," he demanded, "that you and I, for I suppose you count on my assistance, are to enact a kind of Pride's Purge of our own? That we are to drive from the land the King's Governor, Council, Burgesses and trainbands; sweep into the bay Sir William Berkeley and Colonel Verney, and all those gold-laced planters who dined with him the other day? That we are to take possession of the colony as picaroons do of a vessel, and hoisting our flag,—a crutch surmounted by a ball and chain on a ground sable,—proclaim a republic?"

"Not we alone."

"Oh, ay! I forgot the worthy Muggletonian."

"He is but one of many," said the mender of nets.

Landless leaned forward, a light growing in his eyes. "Speak out!" he said. "What is it that will break this chain?"

The mender of nets, too, bent forward from his settle until his breath mingled with the breath of the younger man.

"A slave insurrection," he said.

CHAPTER VII

A MENDER OF NETS

"A slave insurrection!"

Landless, recoiling, struck with his shoulder the torch, which fell to the floor. The flame went out, leaving only a red gleaming end. "I will get another," said the mender of nets, and limped to the corner where the shadow had been thickest. Landless, left in darkness, heard a faint muttering as though Master Robert Godwyn were talking to himself. It took some time to find the torch; but at length Godwyn returned with one in his hand, and kindled it at the expiring light.

Landless rose from his seat, and strode to and fro through the hut. His pulses beat to bursting; there was a tingling at his finger-tips; to his startled senses the hut seemed to expand, to become a cavern, interminable and unfathomable, wide as the vaulted earth, filled with awful, shadowy places and strange, lurid lights. The mender of nets became a far-off sphinx-like figure.

Godwyn watched him in silence. He had a large knowledge of human nature, and he saw into the mind and heart of the restless figure. He himself was a philosopher, and wore his chains lightly, but he guessed that the iron had entered deeply into the soul of the man before him. The sturdy peasants, indented servants with but a few short years to serve, better fed and better clad than their fellows at home, found life on a Virginia plantation no sweet or easy thing; the political and ecclesiastical offenders enjoyed it still less, while the small criminal class found their punishment quite sufficiently severe. To this man the life must be a slow *peine forte et dure*, breaking his body with toil, crushing his soul with a hopeless degradation. The thought of escape must be ever present with him. But escape in the conventional manner, through pathless forests and over broad streams, was a thing rarely attained to. Ninety-nine out of a hundred failed; and the last state of the man who failed was worse than his first.

Landless strode over to the table, and leaned his weight upon it.

"Listen!" he said. "God knows I am a desperate man! My attempt to escape failing, there is naught but His word between me and the deepest pool of these waters. I am no saint. I hate my enemies. Restore to me my sword, pit me against them one by one, and I will fight my way to freedom or die.... A fair fight, too, a rising of the people against oppression; a challenge to the oppressor to do his worst; a gallant leading of a forlorn hope.... But a slave insurrection! a midnight butchery! There was one who used to tell me tales of such risings in the Indies. Murder and rapine, fire rising through the night, planters cut down at their very thresholds, shrieking women tortured, children flung into the flames,—a carnival of blood and horror!"

"We are not in the Indies," said the other quietly. "There will be no such devil's work here. Sit down and listen while I put the thing before you as it is. There are, most iniquitously held as slaves in this Virginia, some four hundred Commonwealth's men, each one of whom, at home and in his own station, was a man of mark. Many were Ironsides. And each one is a force in himself,—cool, determined, intrepid,—and wholly desperate. With them are many victims of the Act of Uniformity, godly men, eaten up with zeal. For their freedom they would dare much; for their faith they would spill every drop of their blood."

"They are like our friend, the Muggletonian, fanatics all, I suppose," said Landless.

"Possibly. Your fanatic is the best fighting machine yet invented. Do you not see that these two classes form a regiment against which no trainbands, no force which these planters could raise, would stand?"

"But they are scattered, dispersed through the colony!"

"Ay, but they can be brought together! And to that end, seeing how few there are upon any one plantation, upon the day when they rise, they must raise with them servants and slaves. Then will they overpower masters and overseers, and gathering to one point, form there a force which will beat down all opposition. It is simple enough. We will but do that which it was proposed to do ten years ago. You know the instructions given by the Parliament to the four commissioners?"

"They were to summon the colony to surrender to the Commonwealth. If it did so, well and good; if not, war was to be declared, and the servants invited to rise against their masters and so purchase their freedom."

"Precisely. Berkeley submitted, and there was no rising. This time there will be no summons, but a rising, and a very great one. It will be, primarily, a rising of four hundred Oliverians, strong to avenge many and grievous wrongs; but with them will rise servants and slaves, and to the banner of the Commonwealth, beneath which they will march, will flock every Nonconformist in the land, and, when success is assured, then will come in and give us weight and respectability those (and they are not a few) of the better classes who long in their hearts for the good days of the Commonwealth, and yet dare not lift a finger to bring them back."

"And the royalists?"

"If they resist, their blood be upon them! But there shall be no carnage, no butchery. And if they submit they shall be unmolested, even as they were ten years ago. There is land enough for all."

"The servants and slaves?"

"They that join with us, of whatever class, shall be freed."

"This insurrection is actually in train?"

"Let us call it a revolution. Yes, it is in train as far as regards the Oliverians. We have but begun to sound servants and slaves."

"And you?"

"I am, for lack of a better, General to the Oliverians."

"And you believe yourself able to control these motley forces,—men wronged and revengeful, fanatics, peasants, brutal negroes, mulattoes (whom they say are devils), convicts,—to say to them, 'Thus far must you go, and no farther.' You invoke a fiend that may turn and rend you!"

Godwyn shaded his eyes with his hand. "Yes," he said at last, speaking with energy. "I do believe it! I know it is a desperate game; but the stake! I believe in myself. And I have four hundred able adjutants, men who are to me what his Ironsides were to Oliver, but none—" he stretched out his hand, thin, white, and delicate as a woman's, and laid it upon the brown one resting upon the table. "Lad," he said in a gravely tender voice, "I have none upon this plantation in whom I can put absolute trust. There are few Oliverians here, and they are like Win-Grace Porringer, in whom zeal hath eaten up discretion. Lad, I need a helper! I have spoken to you freely; I have laid my heart before you; and why? Because I, who was and am a gentleman, see in you a gentleman, because I would take your word before all the oaths of all the peasant servants in Virginia, because you have spirit and judgment; because,—in short, because I could love you as I loved your father before you. You have great wrongs. We will right them together. Be my lieutenant, my confidant, my helper! Come! put your hand in mine and say, 'I am with you, Robert Godwyn, heart and soul.'"

Landless sprang to his feet. "It were easy to say that," he said hoarsely, "for, in all the two years I lay rotting in prison, and in these weeks of sordid misery here in Virginia, yours is the only face that has looked kindly upon me, yours the only voice that has told me I was believed.... But it is a fearful thing you propose! If all go as you say it will,—why WELL! but if not, Hell will be in the land. I must have time to think, to judge for myself, to decide—"

The door swung stealthily inward, and in the opening appeared the dead white face, with the great letter sprawling over it, of Master Win-Grace Porringer.

"There are boats on the creek," he said. "Two coming up, one coming down."

Godwyn nodded. "I hold conference to-night with men from this and the two neighboring plantations. You will stay where you are and see and hear them. Only you must be silent; for they must not know that you are not entirely one with us, as I am well assured you will be."

"They are Oliverians?"

"All but two or three."

"I secured the mulatto," interrupted the Muggletonian.

"Ay," said Godwyn, "I thought it well to have one slave representative here to-night. These mulattoes are devils; but they can plot, and they can keep a still tongue. But I shall not trust him or his kind too far."

The peculiar knock—four strokes in all—sounded upon the door, and Porringer went to it. "Who is there?" passed on the one side, and "The sword of the Lord and of Gideon" on the other. The door swung open, and there entered two men of a grave and determined cast of countenance. Both had iron-gray hair, and one was branded upon the forehead with the letter that appeared upon the cheek of the Muggletonian. Again the knock sounded, the countersign was given, and the door opened to admit a pale, ascetic-looking youth, with glittering eyes and a crimson spot on each cheek, who stooped heavily and coughed often. He was followed by another stern-faced Commonwealth's man, and he in turn by a brace of broad-visaged rustics and a smug-faced man, who looked like a small shopkeeper. After an interval came two more Oliverians, grim of eye, and composed in manner.

Last of all came the mulatto of the pale amber color and the gold ear-rings; and with him came the long-nosed, twitching-lipped convict in whose company Landless had crossed the Atlantic. His name was Trail; and Landless, knowing him for a villainous rogue, started at finding him amongst the company.

His presence there was evidently unexpected. Godwyn frowned and turned sharply upon the mulatto. "Who gave you leave to bring this man?" he demanded sternly.

The mulatto was at no loss. "Worthy Señors all," he said smoothly, addressing himself to the company in general. "This Señor Trail is a good man, as I have reason to know. Once we were together in San Domingo, slave to a villainous cavalier from Seville. With the help of St. Jago and the Mother of God, we killed him and made our escape. Now, after many years, we meet here in a like situation. I answer for my friend as I answer for myself, myself, Luiz Sebastian, the humble and altogether-devoted servant of you all, worshipful Señors."

The man with the branded forehead muttered something in which the only distinguishable words were, "Scarlet woman," and "Papist half-breed," and the smug-faced man cried out, "Trail is a forger and thief! I remember his trial at the Bailey, a week before I signed as storekeeper to Major Carrington."

This speech of the smug-faced man created something of a commotion, and one or two started to their feet. The mulatto looked about him with an evil eye.

"My friend has been in trouble, it is true," he said, still very smoothly. "He will not make the worse conspirator for that. And why, worthy Señors, should you make a difference between him and one other I see in company? Mother of God! they are both in the same boat!" He fixed his large eyes on Landless as he spoke, and his thick lips curled into a tigerish smile.

Landless half rose, but Godwyn laid a detaining hand upon his arm. "Be still," he said in a low voice, "and let me manage this matter."

Landless obeyed, and the mender of nets turned to the assembly, who by this time were looking very black.

"Friends," he said with quiet impressiveness, "I think you know me, Robert Godwyn, well enough to know that I make no move in these great matters without good and sufficient reason. I have good and sufficient reason for wishing to associate with us this young man,—yea, even to make him a leader among us. He is one of us—he fought at Worcester. And that he is an innocent man, falsely accused, falsely imprisoned, wrongfully sent to the plantations, I well believe,—for I will believe no wrong of the son of Warham Landless."

There was a loud murmur of surprise through the room, and one of the Oliverians sprung to his feet, crying out, "Warham Landless was my colonel! I will follow his son were he ten times a convict!"

Godwyn waited for the buzz of voices to cease and then calmly proceeded, "As to this man whom Luiz Sebastian hath brought with him, I know nothing. But it matters little. Sooner or later we must engage his class,—as well commence with him as with another. He will be faithful for his own sake."

The dark faces of his audience cleared gradually. Only the youth with the hectic cheeks cried out, "I have hated the congregation of evil doers, and I will not sit with the wicked!" and rose as if to make for the door. Win-Grace Porringer pulled him down with a muttered, "Curse you for a fool! Shall not the Lord shave with a hired razor? When these men have done their work, then shall they be cut down and cast into outer darkness, until when, hold thy peace!"

The company now applied itself to the transaction of business. Trail was duly sworn in, not without a deal of oily glibness and unnecessary protestation on his part. The man who held the little, worn Bible now turned to Landless, but upon Godwyn's saying quietly, "I have already sworn him," the book was returned to the bosom of its owner.

Each conspirator had his report to make. Landless listened with grave attention and growing wonder to long lists of plantations and the servant and slave force thereon; to news from the up-river estates, and from the outlying settlements upon the Rappahannock and the Pamunkey, and from across the bay in Accomac; to accounts of secret arsenals slowly filling with rude weapons; to allusions to the well-affected sailors on board those ships that were likely to be in harbor during the next two months;—to the details of a formidable and far-reaching conspiracy.

The Oliverians spoke of the hour in which this mine should be sprung as the great and appointed day of the Lord, the day when the Lord was to stretch forth his hand and smite the malignants, the day when Israel should be delivered out of the hand of Pharaoh. The branded man apostrophized Godwyn as Moses. Their stern and rigid features relaxed, their eyes glistened, their breath came short and thick. Once the youth who had wished to avoid the company of the wicked broke into hysterical sobbing. The two rustics spoke little, but possibly thought the more. To them the day of the Lord translated itself the day of their obtaining a freehold. The smug-faced shopkeeper put in his oar now and again, but only to be swept aside by the torrent of Biblical quotation. The newly admitted Trail kept a discreet silence, but used his furtive greenish eyes to good purpose. Luiz Sebastian sat with the stillness of a great, yellow, crouching tiger cat.

Godwyn heard all in silence. Not till the last man had had his say did he begin to speak, approving, suggesting, directing, moulding in his facile hands the incongruous and disjointed mass of information and opinion into a rounded whole. The men, listening to him with breathless attention, gave grim nods of approval. At one point of his discourse the branded man cried out:—

"If the Puritan gentry you talk of would gird themselves like men, and come forth to the battle, how quickly would the Lord's work be done! They are the drones within the hive! They expect the honey, but do not the work."

"It is so," said Godwyn, "but they have lands and goods and fame to lose. We have naught to lose—can be no worse off than we are now."

"If the Laodicean, Carrington,"—began the branded man.

Godwyn interrupted him. "This is beside the matter. Major Carrington is a godly man who hath, though in secret, done many kindnesses to us poor prisoners of the Lord. Let us be content with that."

A moment later he said, "It waxeth late, friends, and loath would I be for one of you to be discovered. Come to me again a week from to-night. The word will be, 'The valley of Jehoshaphat.'"

The conspirators dropped away, in twos and threes, gliding silently off in their stolen boats between the walls of waving grass. When, last of all save Landless and the Muggletonian, Trail and Luiz Sebastian approached the door, Godwyn stopped them with a gesture.

"Stay a moment," he said. "I have a word to say to you. We may as well be frank with you. I distrust you, of course. It is natural that I should. And you distrust me as much. It is natural that you should. I would do without the aid of you and the class you represent if I could, but I cannot. You would do without my aid if you could, but you cannot. Betray me, and whatever blood money you get, it will not be that freedom which you want. We are obliged to work together, unequal yoke-fellows as we are. Do I make myself understood?"

"To a marvel, Señor," said Luiz Sebastian.

"Damn my soul, but you're a sharp one!" said Trail.

Godwyn smiled. "That is enough, we understand one another. Good-night."

The two glided off in their turn, and Godwyn said to the Muggletonian, "Friend Porringer, that mended sail must be bestowed in the large boat before the hut against Haines' coming for it in the morning. Will you take it to the boat for me? And if you will wait there this young man shall join you shortly."

The Muggletonian nodded, piled the heap of dingy sail upon his head and strode off. The mender of nets turned to Landless.

"Well," he said. "What do you think?"

"I think," said Landless, raising his voice, "that the gentleman in the dark corner must be tired of standing."

There was a dead silence. Then a piece of shadow detached itself from the other heavy shadows in the dark corner and came forward into the torch light, where it resolved itself into a handsome figure of a man, apparently in the prime of life, and wearing a riding cloak of green cloth and a black riding mask. Not content with the concealment afforded by the mask, he had pulled his beaver low over his eyes and with one hand held the folds of the cloak about the lower part of his face. He rested the other ungloved hand upon the table and stared fixedly at Landless. "You have good eyes," he said at last, in a voice as muffled as his countenance.

"It is a warm night," said Landless with a smile. "If Major Carrington would drop that heavy cloak, he would find it more comfortable."

The man recoiled. "You know me!" he cried incredulously.

"I know the Carrington arms and motto. *Tenax et Fidelis*, is it not? You should not wear your signet ring when you go a-plotting."

The Surveyor-General of the Colony dropped his cloak, and springing forward seized Landless by the shoulders.

"You dog!" he hissed between his teeth, "if you dare betray me, I'll have every drop of your blood lashed out of your body!"

Landless wrenched himself free. "I am no traitor," he said coldly.

Carrington recovered himself. "Well, well," he said, still breathing hastily, "I believe you. I heard all that passed to-night, and I believe you. You have been a gentleman."

"Had I my sword, I should be happy to give Major Carrington proof," said Landless sternly.

The other smiled. "There, there, I was hasty, but by Heaven! you gave me a start! I ask your pardon."

Landless bowed, and the mender of nets struck in. "I was sorry to keep you so long, Major Carrington, in such an uncomfortable position. But the arrival of the Muggletonian before he was due, together with your desire for secrecy, left me no alternative."

"I surmise, friend Godwyn, that you would not have been sorry had this young man proclaimed his discovery in full conclave," said Carrington with a keen glance.

Godwyn's thin cheek flushed, but he answered composedly, "It is certainly true that I would like to see Major Carrington committed beyond withdrawal to this undertaking. But he will do me the justice to believe that if, by raising my finger, I could so commit him, I would not do so without his permission."

"Faith, it is so!" said the other, then turned to Landless with a stern smile. "You will understand, young man, that Miles Carrington never attended, nor will attend, a meeting wherein the peace of the realm is conspired against by servants. If Miles Carrington ever visits Robert Godwyn, servant to Colonel Verney, 'tis simply to employ him (with his master's consent) in the mending of nets, or to pass an idle hour reading Plato, Robert Godwyn having been a scholar of note at home."

"Certainly," said Landless, answering the smile. "Major Carrington and Master Godwyn are at present much interested in the philosopher's pretty but idle conception of a Republic, wherein philosophers shall rule, and warriors be the bulwark of the state, and no Greek shall enslave a fellow Greek, but only outer barbarians—all of which is vastly pretty on paper—but they agree that it would turn the world upside down were it put into practice."

"Precisely," said Carrington with a smile.

"You had best be off, lad," put in Godwyn. "Woodson is an early riser, and he must not catch you gadding.... You will think on what you have heard to-night, and will come to me again as soon as you can make opportunity?"

"Yes," said Landless slowly. "I will come, but I make no promises."

He found Porringer seated in their boat, patiently awaiting him. They cast off and rowed back the way they had come through the stillness of the hour before dawn. The tide being full, the black banks had disappeared, and the grass, sighing and whispering, waved on a level with their boat. When they slid at last into the broader waters of the inlet, the stars were paling, and in the east there gleamed a faint rose tint, the ghost of a color. A silver mist lay upon land and water, and through it they stole undetected to their several cabins.

Meanwhile the two men, left alone in the hut on the marsh, looked one another in the face.

"Are you sure that he can be trusted?" demanded Carrington.

"I would answer for his father's son with my life."

"What of these scruples of his? Faith! an unusual conjunction—a convict and scruples! Will you manage to dispose of them?"

Godwyn smiled with wise, sad eyes. "Time will dispose of them," he said quietly. "He is new to the life. Let him taste its full bitterness. It will plead powerfully against his—scruples. He has as yet no special and private grievance. Wait until he gets into trouble with Woodson or his master. When he has done that and has taken the consequences, he will be ours. We can bide our time."

CHAPTER VIII

THE NEW SECRETARY

"Tell me not, sweet, I am unkind,

That from the nunnery

Of thy chaste breast and quiet mind,

To war and arms I flee....

"Yet this inconstancy is such

As you too shall adore.

I could not love thee, dear, so much,

Loved I not honor more."

The rich notes rang higher and higher, filling the languid air, and drowning the trill of the mockingbirds. Patricia, filling her apron with midsummer flowers, sang with a careless passion, her mind far away in the midst of a Whitehall pageant, described to her the night before by that silver-tongued courtier, Sir Charles Carew.

Still singing, she went up the steps of the porch and into the cool wide hall. In her face there was a languorous beauty born of the sunshine outside; a soft color glowed in her cheeks, her eyes were large and dreamy, little damp tendrils of gold strayed about her temples. She threw down her hat, and loosened the kerchief of delicate lawn from about her warm young throat; then, with the flowers still in her arms, she raised the latch of the door of a room held sacred to Colonel Verney, and entered, to find herself face to face with the convict, Godfrey Landless, who sat at a table covered with papers, busily writing.

She started violently, and the mass of flowers fell to the floor, shattering the petals from the roses and poppies. Landless came forward, knelt down, and, picking them up, restored them to her without a word.

"I thank you," she said coldly. "I thought my father was here."

"Colonel Verney is in the next room, madam."

She moved to the door leading into the great room with the gait of a princess, and Landless went back to his work.

Colonel Verney, on his knees before the richly carven chest containing his library, looked up from the two score volumes to behold a mass of brilliant blooms transferred from two white arms to the ground outside the open window.

"Well, sweetheart," he said. "What is it?"

"Papa," she said, coming to his side, and looking down upon him with a vexed face; "you promised me that you would employ no more convicts in the house."

"Why, so I did, my dear," answered her father, comfortably seating himself upon "Purchas: His Pilgrimmes." "And I meant to keep my word, but this is the way of it. The day after you went to Rosemead with Betty Carrington, down comes young Shaw with the fever, and has to be sent home to his mother. His illness came at a precious inconvenient season, for the gout was in my fingers again, and I was bent on disappointing William Berkeley, who hath wagered a thousand pounds of sweet scented that my 'Statement of the Evil Wrought by the Navigation Laws to His Majesty's Colony of Virginia' won't be finished in time for the sailing of the God-Speed. So I told Woodson to find me some one among the men who knew how to write. He brought me this fellow, and I vow he is an improvement on young Shaw. He doesn't ask questions, and he is a very pretty Latinist. The paper will be finished to-day. I was but searching for a neat quotation to close with. Then the fellow will go back to the tobacco, and you will be no longer annoyed by his presence in the house. Now kiss me, sweet chuck, and begone, for I am busied upon affairs of state."

Left alone, Colonel Verney pored over his books until he found what he wanted, when, after rearranging his library in the carved chest, he rose stiffly to his feet, and went into the next room and up to the writing-table. Landless rose from his seat, and, resigning it to his master, stood gravely by while the Colonel looked over the manuscript upon which he had been employed.

"Ha!" said the Colonel. "A very fair copy! You have numbered and headed the pages, I observe. Let me see, let me see, let me see," and he ran them over between his fingers. "Oppressive Nature of the Act.—Grave Dissatisfaction.—It advantageth No One save Small Traders at Home.—Increase of Revenue to His Majesty if 't were repealed.—Dutch Bottoms.—Trade with Russia.—His Majesty's Poor Planters Throw Themselves upon His Majesty's Mercy. Very good, very good!"

"It is nigh finished, sir," said Landless.

"Ay, ay! By the Lord Harry, William Berkeley will repent his wager! A pretty paper it is, and containeth many excellent points and much good Latin, and you have copied it fairly and cleanly. It is a pity, my man," he added not unkindly, "that you should have lived so evilly as to bring yourself to this pass, for you have in you the making of an excellent secretary."

"Is it your will, sir, that I finish the copy now?"

"Yes, but take it to the small table within the window there. I myself will sit here and jot down some ideas for my dedication which you can afterwards amplify."

The worthy colonel pulled the big Turkey worked chair closer to the table, turned back his ruffles and fell to work. Landless retired to the table within the window, and for a while naught was heard in the quiet room but the scratching of quills, as master and man drove them across the whitey-brown sheets.

At length the master pushed his chair back and stretched himself with a prodigious yawn. "The Lord be thanked!" he said, addressing the air. "That's done! And it is time to see to the dressing of that sore upon Prince Rupert's shoulder; and I remember Haines said that one of the hounds had been gored by Carrington's bull. Haines can't dress a wound. Haines is a bungler. But, by the Lord Harry! Richard Verney is as good a veterinary as he is a statesman."

He lifted his burly figure from the depths of the chair, and going over to Landless, dropped upon the table before him a page of hieroglyphics for him to decipher at his leisure. Then with another word of commendation for the beauty of the copy, he walked heavily from the room. A moment later Landless heard him whistle to his dogs, and then break into a stave of a cavalier drinking song, sung at the top of a full manly voice, and dying away in the direction of the stables.

Landless' hand moved to and fro across the paper with a tireless patience. He did not go back to the central table, for the light was better in the window, and a vagrant breath of air strayed in now and then. The window was a deep one, and heavy drugget curtains hung between it and the rest of the room.

The door opened and a man's voice said: "This room is darkened into delicious coolness. Shall we try it, cousin?"

Patricia entered like a sunbeam, and after her sauntered Sir Charles Carew, languid, debonair, and perfectly appareled.

Landless, seeing them plainly, did not realize that in the shadow of the heavy curtains he was himself unseen. He had grown so accustomed to the quiet insolence that overlooks the presence of an inferior as it does that of any other article of furniture, that he did not doubt that the fine lady and gentleman before him were perfectly aware of the presence in the room of the slave whom his master's caprice had raised for the moment to the post of secretary. It was some few minutes before he began to consider within himself that he might be mistaken.

CHAPTER IX

AN INTERRUPTED WOOING

Sir Charles pushed forward the big chair for Patricia, and himself dropped upon a stool at her feet. Taking her fan from her, he began to play with it, lightly commenting on the picture of the Rape of Europa with which it was adorned. Suddenly he closed it, tossed it aside, and leaning forward, possessed himself of her hand.

"Madam, sweet cousin, divinest Patricia," he exclaimed in a carefully impassioned tone; "do you not know that I am your slave, the captive of your bow and spear, that I adore you? I adore you! and you, flinty-hearted goddess, give no word of encouragement to your prostrate worshiper. You trample upon the offering of sighs and tears which he lays at your feet; you will not listen when he would pour into your ear his aspirations towards a sweeter and richer life than he has ever known. Will it be ever thus? Will not the goddess stoop from her throne to make him the happiest of mortals, to win his eternal gratitude, to become herself forever the object of the most respectful, the most ardent, the most devoted love?"

He flung himself upon his knee and pressed her hand to his heart with passion not all affected. He had come to consider it a piece of monstrous good luck, that, since he must make a wealthy match, Providence (or whatever as a Hobbist he put in place of Providence), had, in pointing him the fortune, pointed also to Patricia Verney. But the night before, in the privacy of his chamber, he had suddenly sat up between the Holland sheets with a startled and amused expression upon his handsome face, swathed around with a wonderful silken night-cap, and had exclaimed to the carven heads surmounting the bed-posts, "May the Lard sink me! but I'm in love!" and had lain down again with an astonished laugh. While sipping his morning draught he made up his mind to secure the prize that very day, in pursuance of which determination he made a careful toilet, assuming a suit that was eminently becoming to his blonde beauty. Also his valet slightly darkened the lower lids of his eyes, thereby giving him a larger, more languishing and melancholy aspect.

Patricia, from the depths of the Turkey worked chair, gazed with calm amusement upon her kneeling suitor.

"You talk beautifully, cousin," she said at length. "'Tis as good as a page from 'Artemène.'"

Sir Charles bit his lip. "It is a page from my heart, madam; nay, it is my heart itself that I show you."

"And would you forsake all those beautiful ladies who are so madly in love with you?—I vow, sir, you told me so yourself! Let me see, there was Lady Mary and Lady Betty, Mistress Winifred, the Countess of —— and Madame la Duchesse de ——. Will Corydon leave all the nymphs lamenting to run after a little salvage wench who does not want him?"

"'S death, madam! you mock me!" cried the baronet, starting to his feet.

"Sure, I meant no harm, cousin; I but put in a good word for the poor ladies at Whitehall. I fear that you are but a recreant wooer."

"Will you marry me, madam?" demanded Sir Charles, standing before her with folded arms.

She slowly shook her head. "I do not love you, cousin."

"I will teach you to do so."

"I do not think you can," she said demurely. "Though I am sure I do not know why I do not. You are a very fine gentleman, a soldier and a courtier, witty, brave and handsome—and this match"—a sigh—"is my father's dearest wish. But I do not love you, sir, and I shall not marry you until I do."

"Ah!" cried Sir Charles, and sunk again upon his knee. "You give me hope! I will teach you to love me! I will exhibit towards you such absolute fidelity, such patient devotion, such uncomplaining submission to your cruel probation, that you will perforce pity me, and pity will grow by soft degrees into blessed love. I do not despair, madam!" He pressed her hand to his lips and cast his fine eyes upward in a killing look.

Patricia gave a charming laugh. "As you please, Sir Charles. In the mean time let us be once more simply good friends and loving cousins. Tell me as much as you please of Lady Mary's charms, but leave Patricia Verney's alone."

Sir Charles rose from his knees, smarting under an amazed sense of failure, and very angry with the girl who had discarded him, Charles Carew, as smilingly as if he had been one of the very provincial youths whom he awed into awkward silence every time they came to Verney Manor. Without doubt she deserved the condign punishment which it was in his power to inflict by sailing away upon the next ship which should leave for England. But he was now obstinately bent upon winning her. If not to-day, to-morrow; and if not to-morrow, the next day; and if not that, the day after. He was of the school of Buckingham and Rochester. He could devote to the capture of a woman all the tireless energy, the strategic skill, the will, the patience, the daring, of a great general. He could mine and countermine, could plan an ambuscade here, and lead a forlorn hope there, could take one intrenchment by storm, and another by treachery. And victory seldom forsook her perch upon his banners.

Life in Virginia was pleasant enough, and he could afford to devote several months to this siege. As to how it would terminate he had not the slightest doubt. But just now it was the course of wisdom to retreat upon the position held yesterday, and that as quickly as possible. So he smoothed his face into a fine calm, modulated his voice into its usual tone of languor, and said with quiet melancholy:—

"You are pleased to be cruel, madam. I submit. I will bide my time until that thrice happy day when you will have learnt the lesson I would teach, when Love, tyrannous Love, shall compel your allegiance as he does mine."

"A far day!" said Patricia with soft laughter. "You had best return to Lady Mary. I do not think that I shall ever love."

She lifted her white arms, and clasping them behind her head, gazed at him with soft, bright, untroubled eyes and smiling lips. The sunlight, filtering through the darkened windows in long bright stripes, laid a shaft of gold athwart her shoulder and lit her hair into a glory. From out the distance came the colonel's voice:—

"In his train see sweet Peace, fairest Queen of the sky,

Ev'ry bliss in her look, ev'ry charm in her eye.

Whilst oppression, corruption, vile slav'ry and fear

At his wished for return never more shall appear.

Your glasses charge high, 'tis in great Charles' praise,

In praise, in praise, 'tis in great Charles' praise."

Some one outside the door coughed, and then rattled the latch vigorously. These precautions taken, the door was opened and there appeared Mistress Lettice, gorgeously attired, and with an extra row of ringlets sweeping her withered neck, and a deeper tinge of vermilion upon her cheeks,—for she had waked that morning with a presentiment that Mr. Frederick Jones would ride over in the course of the day. Sir Charles rose to hand her to a chair, but she waved him back with a thin, beringed hand.

"I thank you, Sir Charles; but I will not trouble you. I am going down to the summer-house by the road, as I think the air there will cure my migraine. Patricia, love, I am looking for my 'Clelie,'—the fourth volume. Have you seen it?"

"No, Aunt Lettice."

"It is very strange," said Mrs. Lettice plaintively. "I am sure that I left it in this room. 'Tis that careless slut of a Chloe who deserves a whipping. She hides things away like a magpie."

"Look in the window; you may have left it there," said Patricia.

Mrs. Lettice approached the window, laid a hand upon the curtain, and started back with a scream.

"What is it, madam?" cried the baronet.

"'Tis a man! a horrid, horrid man hiding there, waiting to cut all our throats in the dead of night as the Redemptioner did to the family at Martin-Brandon! Oh! Oh! Oh!" and Mrs. Lettice threw her apron over her head, and sank into the nearest chair.

Patricia started up. Sir Charles, striding hastily towards the window, his hand upon his sword, was met by the emerging figure of Landless.

The two gazed at each other, Sir Charles' first haughty surprise fast deepening into passion as he remembered that the man before him had assisted at the scene of a while before, had witnessed his discomfiture, had seen him upon his knees, baffled, repulsed, even laughed at!

He was the first to speak. "Well, sirrah," he said between his teeth, "what have you to say for yourself?"

"That I ask your pardon," said Landless steadily. "I should have made known my presence in the room. But at first I thought you aware of it; and when I discovered that you were not, I ... it seemed best to remain silent. I was wrong. I should have made some sign even then. Again, I beg your pardon." He turned to Patricia, who stood, tall, straight, and coldly indignant, beside the chair from which she had risen. "Madam," he said in a voice that faltered, despite himself, "I crave your forgiveness."

She bit her coral under lip, and looked at him from under veiled eyelids. It was a cruel look, very expressive of scorn, abhorrence, and perhaps of fear.

"My father hath many unmannerly servants," she said coldly and clearly, "who often provoke me. But I pardon them because they know no better. It seems that like allowance cannot be made for you. However," she smiled icily, "I shall not complain of you to my father, which assurance will doubtless content you."

Landless turned from burning red to deadly white. His eyes, fixed upon the floor, caught the rich shimmer of her skirts as she moved towards the door; a moment and she was gone, leaving the two men facing each other.

Between them there existed a subtle but strong antagonism. Sir Charles Carew, courtier in a coarse and shameless court masquerading under a glittering show of outward graces, had taken lazy delight in heaping quiet insults upon the man who could not resent them. This amusement had beguiled the tedium of the Virginia voyage; and when chance threw them together upon a Virginia plantation, where life flowed on in one long, placid lack of variety, the sport became doubly prized. It had to be pursued at longer intervals, but pursued it was. Heretofore the amusement had been all upon one side; now, Sir Charles felt a chagrined suspicion that it was he who had afforded the entertainment. Simultaneously with arriving at this conclusion he arrived at a point where he was coldly furious.

Landless returned his look coolly and boldly. He considered that he had made quite sufficient apology for an offense which was largely involuntary, and he was in no mood for further abasement.

"You are an insolent rascal," said the baronet smoothly.

Landless smiled. "Sir Charles Carew should be a good judge of insolence."

Sir Charles took a leisurely pinch of snuff, shook the fallen grains from his ruffles, snapped the lid of the box, looked languishingly at the miniature that adorned it, replaced the box in his pocket, and remarked, "Well, I am waiting!"

"And for what?"

"To hear your petition that I forbear to bring this matter to the notice of your master. The lady mercifully gave you her promise. I suppose I must follow so fair an example."

"Sir Charles Carew may wait till doomsday to hear that or any other request made by me to him or to the lady—who does not seem always mercifully inclined—" he broke off with a slight and expressive smile.

Sir Charles took another pinch of snuff. "May the Lard blast me," he drawled, "if they do not teach repartee at Newgate! But I forget that the tongue is the only weapon of women and slaves."

"Some day I hope to teach you otherwise."

The other laughed. "So the slave thinks he can use a sword? Where did he learn? In Newgate, from some broken captain, as payment for imparting the trick of stealing by the Book?"

Landless forced himself to stand quiet, his arms folded, his fingers tightly clenching the sleeves of his coarse shirt. "Shall I tell Sir Charles Carew where I first used my sword with good effect?" he said in an ominously quiet voice. "At Worcester I was but a stripling, but I fought by the side of my father. I remember that, young as I was, I disabled a very pretty perfumed and ringleted Cavalier. I think he was afterwards sold to the Barbadoes. And my father praised my sword play."

"Your father," said the other, bringing his strong white teeth together with a click. "Like father, like son. The latter a detected rogue, gaol-bird, and slave; the former a d—d canting, sniveling Roundhead hypocrite and traitor, with a text ever at hand to excuse parricide and sacrilege."

Landless sprang forward and struck him in the face.

He staggered beneath the weight of the blow; then, recovering himself, he whipped out his rapier, but presently slapped it home again. "I am a gentleman," he said, with an airy laugh. "I cannot fight you." And stood, slightly smiling, and pressing his laced handkerchief to his cheek whence had started a few drops of blood.

Mrs. Lettice, whom curiosity or the search for the fourth volume of "Clelie" had detained in the room, screamed loudly as the blow fell; and Colonel Verney, appearing at the door, stopped short, and stared from one to the other of the two men.

CHAPTER X

LANDLESS PAYS THE PIPER

The hut of the mender of nets stood upon a narrow isthmus connecting two large tracts of marsh. That to the eastward was partially submerged at high tide; that to the west, being higher ground, waved its long grass triumphantly above the reaching waters. Upon this side the marsh was separated from the mainland of forest and field by a creek so narrow that the great pines upon one margin cast their shadows across to the other, and one fallen giant quite spanned the sluggish waters.

The grass of this marsh was annually cut for hay; for though the great herds of cattle belonging to the different plantations roamed at large through all seasons of the year, seeking their sustenance from forest or marsh, the more provident of the planters were accustomed to make some slight provision against the winter, which might prove a severe one with snow and ice.

It was late afternoon, and the hay was cut. The half dozen mowers threw themselves down upon the stubble, stretching out tired limbs and pillowing heated foreheads upon their arms. They had been given until sunset to do the work. Having no task-master over them, and being hid from the tobacco-fields by a convenient coppice of pine and cedar, they had set to work in a fury of diligence, had cut and stacked the grass in a race with time, and now found themselves possessed of a precious hour in which to dawdle, and swap opinions and tobacco before the sunset horn should call them to quarters.

Three were indented servants, lumbering, honest-visaged youths whose aims in life were simple and well defined. Their creed had but four articles: "Do as little as you can consistently with keeping out of the overseer's black books; get your full share of loblolly and bacon, and some one else's if you are clever enough; embrace every opportunity for reasonable mischief that is offered you; honor Church and King, or say you do, and Colonel Verney will overlook most pranks." Of the others, one was the Muggletonian, one the mulatto, Luiz Sebastian, and one a convict, not Trail, but the red-haired, pock-marked, sullen wretch who had come to the plantation with Trail and Landless, and whose name was Roach.

One of the rustics, who seemed more intelligent than his fellows, and who had a good-humored deviltry in his young face and big blue eyes, began an excellent imitation of Dr. Nash's exhortation to submission and obedience delivered upon the last instruction day for servants, and soon had his audience of two guffawing with laughter. The mulatto and the convict edged by imperceptible degrees farther and farther away from the others, until, within the shadow of a stack of grass, they lay side by side and commenced a muttered conversation. The countenance of the white man, atrocious villainy written large in every lineament, became horribly intent as his amber-hued companion talked in fluent low tones, emphasizing what he had to say by a restless, peculiar, and sinister motion of his long, yellow fingers. At a little distance lay the Muggletonian, his elbows on the ground, his ghastly face in his hands, and his eyes riveted upon the Geneva Bible which he had drawn from his bosom.

When he had brought his entertainment to a finish, the blue-eyed youth rolled himself over and over the stubble to where the Muggletonian lay, intent upon a chapter of invective. The youth covered the page with one enormous paw and playfully attempted to insert the little finger of the other into the hole in Porringer's ear. "What now, old Runaway," he said, lazily, "hunting up fresh curses to pour on our unfort'net heads?"

"Cursed be he who makes a mock of age," said the Muggletonian, grimly. "May he be even as the wicked children who cried to the prophet, 'Go up, thou baldhead!'"

The boy laughed. "Tell me when you see brown bear a-coming," quoth he. "Losh! a bear steak would taste mighty good after eternal bacon!"

Porringer closed his book and restored it to his bosom. "Tell me," he said, abruptly, "have you seen aught of the young man called Landless?"

"'The young man called Landless,'" answered the other, petulantly, "has a d—d easy berth of it! Yesterday evening I carried water from the spring to the great house to water Mistress Patricia's posies, and every time I passes the window of the master's room I see that fellow a-sitting at his ease in a fine chair before a fine table, writing away as big as all out of doors. And every time I says to him, says I, 'I reckon you think yourself as fine as the Lord Mayor of London? A pretty sec'tary you make!'"

"Have you seen him to-day?"

"No, I haven't seen him to-day,—but I see someone else. Mates," he exclaimed, "Witch Margery's coming down t' other side of creek. I'll call her over."

Scrambling to his feet he gave a low halloo through his hands, "Margery! Margery! Come and find the road to Paradise!"

Margery waved her hand to signify that she heard and understood, and presently stepped upon the fallen tree that spanned the stream. It was a narrow and a slippery bridge, but she flitted across it with the secure grace of some woodland thing, and, staff in hand, advanced towards the men. Between them and the western sun she stood still, a dark figure against a halo of gold light, and threw an intent and searching glance over the unbroken green of the marsh and the blue of the waters beyond. Then with a wild laugh she came up to them and cast her staff wreathed with dark ivy upon the ground.

"The road is not here," she cried. "Here is all green grass, and beyond is the weary, weary, weary sea! There is no long, bright, shining road to Paradise." She sat down beside her staff, and taking her chin into her hand, stared fixedly at the ground.

The men gathered around her, with the exception of the Muggletonian, who, after audibly comparing her to the Witch of Endor, turned on his side and drew his cap over his eyes as if to shut out the hated sight. The convict took up the staff and began to pull from it the strings of ivy.

"Put it down!" she said quickly.

The man continued to strip it of its leafy mantle.

"Put it down, can't you?" said the youth. "She never lets any one touch it. She says an angel gave it to her to help her on her way."

With a snarling laugh the convict threw it from him with all his force. Whirling through the air it struck the water midway from shore to shore. Margery sprang to her feet with a loud cry. The boy rose also.

"D—n you!" he said, wrathfully. "I'd like to break it over your misshapen back! Here, Margery, don't fret. I'll get it for you."

He ran to the bank, dived into the water, and in three minutes was back with the dripping mass in his arms. He gave it into Margery's hands, saying kindly while he shook himself like a large spaniel; "There! it isn't hurt a mite!"

With a cry of delight Margery seized the "angel's gift" and kissed the hand that restored it. Then she turned upon the convict.

"When I go back to my cabin in the woods," she said, solemnly, and with her finger up, "I shall whistle all the fairy folk into a ring, all the elves and the pixies, and the little brown gnomes who burrow in the leaves and look for all the world like pine cones, and I shall tell them what you did, and to-night they will come to your cabin, and will pinch you black and blue, and stick thorns into you, and rub you with the poison leaf until you are blotched and swelled like the great bull frog that croaks, croaks, in these marshes."

There was an uneasy ring in the convict's laugh, full of bravado as he meant it to be. Margery continued with an ominously extended forefinger. "And then they will fly to the great house where the master lies sleeping, and they will whisper to him that you took away the angel's gift from poor, lost Margery, and he will be angry, for he is good to Margery, and to-morrow he will make Woodson do to you what he did to-day to the Breaking Heart."

"To the Breaking Heart!" exclaimed her auditors.

Margery nodded. "Yes, the Breaking Heart. You call him Landless."

The Muggletonian sat up. "What dost thou mean, wretched woman! fit descendant of the mother of all evil?"

Margery, offended by his tone, only pursed up her lips and looked wise.

"What did the master have done to Landless, Margery?" asked the youth.

Margery threw her worn figure into a singular posture. Standing perfectly straight, she raised her arms from her sides and spread them stiffly out, the hands turned inward in a peculiar fashion. Then, still with extended arms, she swayed slightly forward until she appeared to lean against, or to be fastened to, some support. Next she threw her head back and to one side, so that her face might be seen in three quarter over her shoulder. Her mobile features wreathed themselves in an expression of pain and rage. Her brows drew downward, her thin lips curled themselves away from the gleaming teeth, and, at intervals of half a minute or more, her eyelids quivered, she shuddered, and her whole frame appeared to shrink together.

The pantomime was too expressive to be misunderstood by men each of whom had probably his own reasons for recognizing some one or all of its features. The convict broke into a yelling laugh, in which he was joined, though in a subdued and sinister fashion, by Luiz Sebastian. The rustics looked at each other with slow grins of comprehension, and the blue-eyed youth uttered a long shrill whistle. The great letter upon the cheek of the Muggletonian turned a deeper red, and his eyes burned. The youth was curious.

"Tell us all about it, Margery," he said, coaxingly, "and when the millons are ripe, I'll steal you one every night."

Margery was nothing loth. She had attained the reputation of an accomplished *raconteuse*, and she was proud of it. Her crazed imagination peopled the forest with weird uncanny things, and fearful tales she told of fays and bugaboos, of spectres and awful voices speaking from out the dank stillness of twilight hollows. Often she sent quaking to their pallets men who would have heard the war-whoop with scarcely quickened pulses.

And she could tell of every-day domestic happenings as well as of the doings of the powers of darkness.

Her audience listened greedily to the instance of plantation economy which she proceeded to relate.

"When was this, woman?" demanded the Muggletonian, when she had finished.

Margery pointed to the declining sun and then upwards to a spot a little past the zenith.

"Just after the nooning," said the Muggletonian, and began to curse.

Margery stood up, her staff in her hand, and said airily, "Margery must be going. The sun is growing large and red, and when he has slipped away behind the woods, the voices will begin to call to Margery from the hollow where the brook falls into the black pool. She must be there to answer them." She moved away with a rapid and gliding step, flitted across the fallen tree, and was lost to sight in the shadow of the pines beyond.

As the last flutter of her light robe vanished, a figure appeared, walking rapidly along the opposite margin of the creek. The youth's sight was keen. He sent a piercing glance across the intervening distance and broke into an astonished laugh. "Lord in Heaven! it's the man himself!" he cried in an awed tone. "Ecod! he must be made of iron!"

Landless crossed the bridge and came towards the staring group. His face was white and set, and there were dark circles beneath his eyes, which had the wide unseeing stare of a sleep-walker. He walked lightly and quickly, with a free, lithe swing of his body. The men looked at one another in rough wonder, knowing what was hidden by the coarse shirt. He passed them without a word, apparently without knowing that they were there, and went on towards the hut of the mender of nets. Presently they saw him enter and shut the door.

The rustics and the convict, after one long stare of amazement at the distant hut, began to comment freely and with much recondite blasphemy upon the transaction recorded by Margery. Luiz Sebastian only smiled amiably, like a lazy and well-disposed catamount, and the boy whistled long and thoughtfully. But the countenance of Master Win-Grace Porringer wore an expression of secret satisfaction.

CHAPTER XI

LANDLESS BECOMES A CONSPIRATOR

As Landless entered the hut Godwyn looked up with a pleased smile from the net he was mending. The two men had not seen each other since the night upon which Landless had been brought to the hut by the Muggletonian. Twice had Landless laid his plans for a second visit, only to be circumvented each time by the watchfulness of the overseer.

The smile died from Godwyn's face as he observed his visitor more closely.

"What is it?" he asked quickly.

Landless came up to him and held out his hand. "I am with you, Robert Godwyn, heart and soul," he said steadily.

The mender of nets grasped the hand. "I knew you would come," he said, drawing a long breath. "I have needed you sorely, lad."

"I could not come before."

"I know: Porringer told me you were prevented. I—" He still held Landless' hand in both his own, and as he spoke his slender fingers encircled the young man's wrist.

"What is the matter with your pulse?" he demanded. "And your eyes! They are glazing! Sit down!"

"It is nothing," said Landless, speaking with effort.

"I have been a physician, young man," retorted the other. "Sit down, or you will fall."

He forced him down upon a settle from which he had himself risen, and stood looking at him, his hand upon his shoulder. Presently his glance fell to the shoulder, and he saw upon the white cloth where his hand pressed it against the flesh, a faint red stain grow and spread.

The face of the mender of nets grew very dark. "So!" he said beneath his breath.

He limped across the hut and drew from some secret receptacle above the fireplace a flask, from which he poured a crimson liquid into an earthen cup; then hobbled back to Landless, sitting with closed eyes and head bowed upon the table.

"Drink, lad," he said with grave tenderness. "'Tis a cordial of mine own invention, and in the strength it gave me I fled from Cropredy Bridge though woefully hacked and spent. Drink!"

He held the cup to the young man's lips. Landless drained it and felt the blood gush back to his heart and the ringing in his ears to cease. Presently he raised his head. "Thank you," he said. "I am a man again."

"How is it that you are here?"

Landless smiled grimly. "I imagine it's because Woodson thinks me effectually laid by the heels. When he goes the rounds at supper time he will be surprised to find my pallet empty."

"You must be in quarters before then. You must not get into further trouble."

"Very well," was the indifferent reply.

They were silent for a few moments, and then Landless spoke.

"I am come to tell you, Master Godwyn, that I will join in any plan, however desperate, that may bring me release from an intolerable and degrading slavery. You may use me as you please. I will work for you with hands and head, ay, and with my heart also, for you have been kind to me, and I am grateful."

The mender of nets touched him softly upon the hand. "Lad," he said, "I once had a son who was my pride and my hope. In his young manhood he fell at the storming of Tredah. But the other night when I talked with you, I seemed to see him again, and my heart yearned over him."

Landless held out his hand. "I have no father," he said simply.

"Now," at length said Godwyn, "to business! I must not keep you now, but come to me to-morrow night if you can manage it. You may speak to Win-Grace Porringer, and he will help you. I will then tell you all my arrangements, give you figures and names, possess you, in short, with all that I, and I alone, know of this matter. And my heart is glad within me, for though my broken body is tied to my bench here, I shall now have a lieutenant indeed. I have conceived; you shall execute. The son of Warham Landless, if he have a tithe of his father's powers, will do much, very much. For more than a year I have longed for such an one."

"Tell me but one thing," said Landless, "and I am content. You have so planned this business that there shall be no wanton bloodshed? You intend no harm, for instance, to the family yonder?" with a motion of his head towards the great house.

"God forbid!" said the other quickly. "I tell you that not one woman or innocent soul shall suffer. Nor do I wish harm to the master of this plantation, who is, after the lights of a Malignant, a true and kindly man, and a gentleman. This is what will happen. Upon an appointed day the servants, Oliverian, indented and convict, upon all the plantations seated upon the bay, the creeks, the three rivers, and over in Accomac, will rise. They will overpower their overseers and those of their fellows who may remain faithful to the masters, will call upon the slaves to follow them, and will march (the force of each plantation under a captain or captains appointed by me), to an appointed place in this county. All going well, there should be mustered at that place within the space of a day and a night a force of some two thousand men—such an army as this colony hath never seen, an army composed in large measure of honest folk, and officered by four hundred men who, bold and experienced, and strong in righteous wrath, should in themselves be sufficient to utterly deject the adversary. We will make of that force, motley as it is, a second New Model, as well disciplined and as irresistible as the first; and who should be its general but the son of that Warham Landless whom Cromwell loved, and whose old regiment is well represented here? Then will we fight in honest daylight with those who come against us—and conquer. And we will not stain our victory. Your nightmare vision of midnight butchery is naught. There will be no such thing."

Through the quiet of the evening came to them the clear, sweet, and distant winding of a horn.

"'Tis the call to quarters," said Godwyn. "You must go, lad."

Landless rose. "I will come to-morrow night if I can. Till then, farewell,—father." He ended with a smile on his dark, stern face that turned it into a boy's again.

"May the Lord bless thee, my son," said the other in his gravely tender voice. "May he cause His face to shine upon thee, and bring thee out of all thy troubles."

As Landless turned to leave the hut the mender of nets had a sudden thought. "Come hither," he said, "and let me show you my treasure house. Should aught happen to me, it were well that you should know of it."

He took up the precious flask from the table, and followed by Landless, limped across the hut to the fireplace. The logs above it appeared as solid, gnarled and stained by time as any of the others constituting the walls of the hut, but upon the pressure of Godwyn's finger upon some secret spring, a section of the wood fell outwards like the lid of a box, disclosing a hollow within.

From this hollow came the dull gleam of gold, and by the side of the little heap of coin lay several folded papers and a pair of handsomely mounted pistols.

Godwyn touched the papers. "The names or the signs of the Oliverians are here," he said, "together with those of the leaders of the indented servants concerned with us. It is our solemn League and Covenant—and our death warrant if discovered. The gold I had with me, hidden upon my person, when I was brought to Virginia. The pistols were the gift of a friend. Both may be useful some day."

"Hide them! Quick!" said Landless in a low voice, and wheeled to face a man who stood in the doorway, blinking into the semi-darkness of the room.

The lid of the hollow swung to with a click, the log assumed its wonted appearance, and the mender of nets, too, turned upon the intruder.

It was the convict Roach who had pushed the door open and now stood with his swollen body and bestial face darkening the glory of the sunset without. There was no added expression of greed or of awakened curiosity upon his sullenly ferocious countenance. He might have seen or he might not. They could not tell.

"What do you want?" asked Landless sternly.

"Thought as you might not have heard the horn, comrade, and so might get into more trouble. So I thought I'd come over and warn you." All this in a low, hoarse and dogged voice.

"Don't call me comrade. Yes: I heard the horn. You had best hasten or you may get into trouble yourself."

The man received this intimation with a malevolent grin. "Talking big eases the smart, don't it?" and he broke into his yelling laugh.

"Get out of this," said Landless, a dangerous light in his eyes.

The man stopped laughing and began to curse. But he went his way, and Landless, too, after waiting to give him a start, left the hut and turned his steps towards the quarters.

Upon the other side of the creek, sitting beneath a big sweet gum, and whittling away at a piece of stick weed, he found the boy who, the day before, had accused him of feeling as fine as the Lord Mayor of London. He sprang to his feet as Landless approached, and cheerfully remarking that their paths were the same, strode on side by side with him.

"I say," he said presently with ingenuous frankness, "I asks your pardon for what I said to you yesterday. I dessay you make a very good Sec'tary, and Losh! the Lord Mayor himself mightn't have dared to strike that d—d fine Court spark. They say he has fought twenty duels."

"You have my full forgiveness," said Landless, smiling.

"That's right!" cried the other, relieved. "I hates for a man to bear malice."

"I have seen you before yesterday. I forget how they call you."

"Dick Whittington."

"Dick Whittington!"

"Ay. Leastways the parish over yonder," a jerk of his thumb towards England, "called me Dick, and I names myself Whittington. And why? Because like that other Dick I runs away to make my fortune. Because like him I've little besides empty pockets and a hopeful heart. And because I means to go back some fine day, jingling money, and wearing gold lace, and become the mayor of Banbury. Or maybe I'll stop in Virginia, and become a trader and Burgess. I could send for Joyce Whitbread, and marry her here as well as in Banbury."

Landless laughed. "So you ran away?"

"Yes; some four years ago, just after I came to man's estate." (He was about nineteen.) "Stowed myself away on board the Mary Hart at Plymouth. Made the Virginny voyage for my health, and on landing was sold by the captain for my passage money. Time's out in three years, but I may begin to make my fortune before then, for—" He stopped speaking to give Landless a sidelong glance from out his blue eyes, and then went on.

"A voice speaks through the land, from the Potomac to the James, and from the falls of the Far West to the great bay. What says the voice?"

Landless answered, "The voice saith, 'Comfort ye, my people, for the hour of deliverance is at hand.'"

"It's all right!" cried the boy gleefully. "I thought you was one of us. We are all in the fun together!"

"We are in for a desperate enterprise that may hang every man of us," said Landless sternly. "I do not see the 'fun,' and I think you talk something loudly for a conspirator."

The boy was nothing abashed. "There's none to hear us," he said. "I can be as mum as t' other Dick's cat when there are ears around. As for fun, Losh! what better fun than fighting!"

"You seem to have a pretty good time as it is."

"Lord, yes! Life's jolly enough, but you see there's mighty little variety in it."

"I have found variety enough," said Landless.

"Oh, you've been here only a few weeks. Wait until you've spent years, and have gone through your experience of to-day half a dozen times, and you will find it tame enough."

"I shall not wait to see."

"Then a man gets tired of working for another man, and hankers for the time when he can set up for himself, especially if there's a pretty girl waiting for him." A tremendous sigh. "And then there's the fun of the rising. Losh! a man must break loose now and then!"

"For all of which good reasons you have become a conspirator?"

"Ay, it doesn't pay to run away. You are hunted to death in the first place, and well nigh whipped to death if you are caught, as you always are. And then they double your time. This promises better."

"If it succeeds."

"Oh, it will succeed! Why shouldn't it with old Godwyn, who is more cunning than a red fox or a Nansemond medicine-man, at its head? Besides, if it fails, hanging is the worst that can happen, and we will have had the fun of the rising."

"You are a philosopher."

"What's that?"

"A wise man. Tell me: If this plot remains undiscovered, and the rising actually takes place, there will be upon each plantation before we can get away an interval of confusion and perhaps violence. 'Tis then that the greatest danger will threaten the planters and their families. You yourself have no ill feeling towards your master or his family? You would do them no unprovoked mischief?"

The boy opened his big blue eyes, and shook his head in a vehement negative.

"Lord bless your soul, no!" he cried. "I wouldn't hurt a hair of Mistress Patricia's pretty head, nor of Mistress Lettice's wig, neither. As for the master, if he lets us go peaceably, we'll go with three cheers for him! Bless you! they're safe enough!"

The sanguine youth next announced that he smelt bacon frying, and that his stomach cried "Trencher!" and started off in a lope for the quarters, now only a few yards distant. Landless followed more sedately, and reached his cabin without being observed by the overseer.

CHAPTER XII

A DARK DEED

Three weeks passed, weeks in which Landless saw the mender of nets some eight times in all, making each visit at night, stealthily and under constant danger of detection. Thrice he had assisted at conferences of the Oliverians from the neighboring plantations, who now, by virtue of his descent, his intimacy with Godwyn, and his very apparent powers, accepted him as a leader. Upon the first of these occasions he had set his case before them in a few plain, straightforward words, and they believed him as Godwyn had done, and he became in their eyes, not a convict, but, as he in truth was, an Oliverian like themselves, and a sufferer for the same cause. The remaining interviews had been between him and Godwyn alone. In the lonely hut on the marsh, beneath starlight or moonlight, the two had held much converse, and had grown to love each other. The mender of nets, though possessed of a calm and high serenity of nature that defied trials beneath which a weaker soul had sunk, was a man of many sorrows; he had the wisdom, too, of years and experience, and he sympathized with, soothed, and counseled his younger yoke-fellow with a parental tenderness that was very grateful to the other's more ardent, undisciplined, and deeply wounded spirit.

Upon the night of their eighth meeting they held a long and serious consultation. Affairs were in such train that little remained to be done, but to set the day for the rising, and to send notice by many devious and underground ways to the Oliverian captains scattered throughout the Colony. Landless counseled immediate action, the firing of the fuse at once by starting the secret intelligence which would spread like wildfire from plantation to plantation. Then would the mine be sprung within the week. There was nothing so dangerous as delay, when any hour, any moment might bring discovery and ruin.

Godwyn was of a different opinion. It was then August, the busiest and most unhealthy season of the year, when the servants and slaves, weakened by unremitting toil, were succumbing by scores to the fever. It was the time when the masters looked for disaffection, when the overseers were most alert, when a general watchfulness pervaded the Colony. The planters stayed at home and attended to their business, the trainbands were vigilant, the servant and slave laws were construed with a harshness unknown at other seasons of the year. There were few ships in harbor compared with the number which would assemble for their fall lading a month later, and

Godwyn counted largely upon the seizure of the ships. In a month's time the tobacco would be largely in,—a weighty consideration, for tobacco was money, and the infant republic must have funds. The ships would be in harbor, and their sailors ready for anything that would rid them of their captains; the heat and sickness of the summer would be abated; the work slackened, and discipline relaxed. The danger of discovery was no greater now than it had been all along, and the good to be won by biding their time might be inestimable. The danger was there, but they would face it, and wait,—say until the second week in September.

Landless acquiesced, scarcely convinced, but willing to believe that the other knew whereof he spoke, and conscious, too, that his own impatience of the yoke which galled his spirit almost past endurance might incline him to a reckless and disastrous haste.

It was past midnight when he rose to leave the hut on the marsh. Godwyn took up his stick. "I will walk with you to the banks of the creek," he said. "'Tis a feverish night, and I have an aching head. The air will do me good, and I will then sleep."

The young man gave him his arm with a quiet, protecting tenderness that was very dear to the mender of nets, and leaning upon it, he limped through the fifty feet of long grass to the border of the creek.

"Shall I not wait to help you back?" asked Landless.

"No," said the other, with his peculiarly sweet and touching smile. "I will sit here awhile beneath the stars and say my hymn of praise to the Creator of Night. You need not fear for me; my trusty stick will carry me safely back. Go, lad, thou lookest weary enough thyself, and should be sleeping after thy long day of toil."

"I am loth to leave you to-night," said Landless.

Godwyn smiled. "And I am always loth to see you go, but it were selfish to keep you listening to a garrulous, wakeful old man, when your young frame is in sore need of rest. Good-night, dear lad."

Landless gave him his hands. "Good-night," he said.

He stood below the other at the foot of the low bank to which was moored his stolen boat. Godwyn stooped and kissed him upon the forehead. "My heart is tender to-night, lad," he said. "I see in thee my Robert. Last night I dreamed of him and of his mother, my dearly loved and long-lost Eunice, and ah! I sorrowed to awake!"

Landless pressed his hand in silence, and in a moment the water widened between them as Landless bent to his oars and the crazy little bark shot out into the middle of the stream. At the entrance of the first labyrinthine winding he turned and looked back to see Godwyn standing upon the bank, the moonlight silvering his thin hair and high serene brow. In the mystic white light, against the expanse of solemn heaven, he looked a vision, a seer or prophet risen from beneath the sighing grass. He waved his hand to Landless, saying in his quiet voice, "Until to-morrow!" The boat made the turn, and the lonely figure and the hut beyond it vanished, leaving only the moonlight, the wash and lap of water, and the desolate sighing of the marsh grass.

There were many little channels and threadlike streams debouching from the main creek, and separated from it by clumps and lines of partially submerged grass, growing in places to the height of reeds. While passing one of these clumps it occurred to Landless that the grass quivered and rustled in an unusual fashion. He rested upon his oars and gazed at it curiously, then stood up, and parting the reeds, looked through into the tiny channel upon the other side. There was nothing to be seen, and the rustling had ceased. "A heron has its nest there, or a turtle plunged, shaking the reeds," said Landless to himself, and went his way.

Some three hours later he was roused from the heavy sleep of utter fatigue by the voice of the overseer. Bewildered, he raised himself upon his elbow to stare at Woodson's grim face, framed in the doorway and lit by the torch held by Win-Grace Porringer, who stood behind him. "You there, you Landless!" cried the overseer, impatiently. "You sleep like the dead. Tumble out! You and Porringer are to go to Godwyn's after that new sail for the Nancy. Sir Charles Carew has taken it into his head to run over to Accomac, and he's got to have a spick and span white rag to sail under. Hurry up, now! He wants to start by sun up, and I clean forgot to send for it last night. You're to be back within the hour, d' ye hear? Take the four-oared shallop. There's the key," and the overseer strode away, muttering something about patched sails being good enough for Accomac folk.

Landless and the Muggletonian stumbled through the darkness to the wharf behind the quarters, where they loosed the shallop, and in it shot across the inlet towards the mouth of the creek.

"I will row," said the Muggletonian with grim kindness; "you look worn out. I suppose you were out last night?"

Landless nodded, and the other bent to the oars with a will that sent them rapidly across the sheet of water. A cold and uncertain light began to stream from the ashen east, and the air was dank and heavy with the thick mist that wrapped earth and water like a shroud. It swallowed up the land behind them, and through it the nearer marshes gloomed indistinctly, dark patches upon the gray surface of the water. The narrow creek was hard to find amidst the universal dimness. The Muggletonian rowed slowly, peering about him with small, keen eyes. At length with a grunt of satisfaction he pointed to a pale streak dividing two masses of gray, and had turned the boat's head towards it, when through the stillness they caught the sound of oars. The next moment a boat glided from the creek and began to skirt the shores of the inlet, hugging the banks and moving slowly and stealthily. It was still so dark that they could tell nothing more than that it held one man.

"Now, who is that?" said the Muggletonian. "And what has he been doing up that creek?"

"Hail him," Landless replied.

Porringer sent a low halloo across the water, but if the man heard he made no sign. The boat, one of the crazy dugouts of which every plantation had store, held on its stealthy way, but being over close to the bank presently ran upon a sand bar. Its occupant was forced to rise to his feet in order to shove it off. He stood upright but a moment, but in that moment, and despite the partial darkness, Landless recognized the misshapen figure.

"It is the convict, Roach!" he exclaimed.

"Ay," said the Muggletonian, "and an ill-omened night bird he is! May he be cursed from the sole of his foot to the crown of his head! May there be no soundness in him! May—What are you about, friend?" he cried, interrupting himself. "There's no need of two pair of oars. We have plenty of time."

Landless bent to the second pair of oars. "He came down the creek," he said in a voice that sounded strained and unnatural.

The other stared at him. "What do you mean?" he demanded.

"Nothing: but let us hasten."

Porringer stared, but fell in with the humor of his companion, and the shallop, impelled by strong arms, shot into the creek and along its mazy windings with the swiftness of a bird.

Landless rowed with compressed lips and stony face, a great fear tugging at his heart. Porringer too was silent. The vapor hung so heavily upon the plains of marsh level with their heads that they seemed to be piercing a dense, low cloud. The light was growing stronger, but the earth still lay like a corpse, livid, dumb, cold and still. There was a chill stagnant smell in the air.

Arriving at the stake in the bank below the hut, they fastened the boat to it, and stepping out, moved through the dense mist to where the hut loomed indistinctly before them, looking in the blank and awful stillness like a forlorn wreck drifting upon an infinite sea of soundless foam.

"The door is open," said Landless.

"Ay, I see," answered Porringer. "Does he wish to die before his time of the fever, that he lets this graveyard mist and stench creep in upon him in his sleep?"

They spoke in low tones as though they feared to waken the sleeper whom they had come to waken. When they reached the hut, they knocked upon the lintel of the door and called Godwyn by name, once, twice, thrice. There was no answer.

"Come on!" said Landless hoarsely, and entered the hut, followed by the other. The cold twilight, filtering through the low and narrow doorway, was powerless to dispel the darkness within. Landless groped his way to the pallet and stooped down.

"He is not here," he said.

The Muggletonian stumbled over a sheaf of oars, sending them to the floor with a noise that in the utter stillness, and to their strained ears, sounded appalling.

"It's the darkness of Tophet," muttered Porringer. "If I could find his flint and steel; there are pine knots, I know, in the corner—God in Heaven!"

"What is it? What is the matter?" cried Landless, as he staggered against him.

"It's his face!" gasped the other. "There upon the table! I put my hand upon it. It's cold!"

Landless rushed to the fireplace where he knew the tinder-box to be kept, and then groped for and found the heap of pine knots. A moment more and the fat wood was burning brightly, casting its red light throughout the hut, and choking back the pale daylight.

The familiar room with its familiar furnishing of chest and settle and pallet, of hanging nets and piles of dingy sail, sprung into sight, but with it sprung into sight something unfamiliar, strange, and dreadful.

It was the body of the mender of nets, flung face upwards across the rude table, the head hanging over the edge, and the face, which but a few short hours before had looked upon Landless with such a bright and patient serenity, blackened and distorted. Upon the throat were dark marks, the print of ten murderous fingers.

With a bitter cry Landless fell upon his knees beside the table, and pressed his face against the cold hand flung backwards over the head of the murdered man. Porringer began to curse. With white lips and burning eyes he hurled anathemas at the murderer. He cursed him by the powers of light and darkness, by the earth, the sea, and the air; by all the plagues of the two Testaments. Landless broke the torrent of his maledictions.

"Silence!" he said sternly. "*He* would have forgiven." Presently he rose from the ground, and taking the body in his arms, placed it upon the pallet, and reverently composed the limbs. Then he turned to the fireplace. It was easy to see that the hiding place had been visited. The spring was broken, and the lid had been struck and jammed into place by a powerful and hasty hand. Landless wrenched it off. Before him lay the pistols; but the gold and papers were gone. He turned to the Muggletonian, standing beside him with staring eyes.

"Listen!" he said. "There was gold here. The wretch whom we passed but now knew of it—never mind how—and for it he has murdered the only friend I had on earth. There will come a day when I will avenge him. There were papers here, lists with the signatures of Oliverians, Redemptioners, sailors,—of all classes concerned in this undertaking, save only the slaves and the convicts. There were letters from Maryland and New England, and a correspondence which would provide whipping-post and pillory for other Nonconformists than the Quakers. All these, the actual proofs of this conspiracy, are in his—that murderer's—hands,—where they must not stay."

"What wilt thou do, friend?" said the Muggletonian eagerly. "Wilt thou take the murderer aside in the gate to speak with him quietly, and smite him under the fifth rib, as did Joab to Abner the son of Ner, who slew his brother Asahel?"

"God forbid," said Landless. "But I will take them from him before he knows their contents. One moment, and we will go."

He crossed to the pallet and stood beside it, looking down on the shell that lay upon it with a stern and quiet grief. One of the cold white hands was clenched upon something. He stooped, and with difficulty unclasped the rigid fingers. The something was a ragged lock of coarse red hair.

"You see," he said.

"Ay," said the Muggletonian grimly. "It's evidence enough. There's but one man in this county with hair like that. Leave that lock where it is, and that dead man holds the rope that will hang his murderer."

"It shall be left where it is," said Landless, and reclosed the fingers upon it.

He took a piece of sail-cloth from the floor, and with it covered the dead man from sight. Next he turned to the hollow above the fireplace, and took from it the pistols, concealing them in his bosom. "I may need them," he said. "Come."

They left the hut and its dead guardian, and rowed back through the summer dawn. The sky was barred with crimson and gold, the fiery rim of the sun just lifting above the eastern waters, the mist, a bridal veil of silver and pearl drawn across the face of a virgin earth.

They rowed in silence until they neared the wharf, when Porringer said, "You are leader now."

The other raised his haggard eyes. "It is a trust. I will go through with it, God helping me. But I would I were lying dead beside him in yonder hut."

They left the boat at the wharf, and went towards the quarters. Meeting one of the blowzed and slatternly female servants, Landless asked where they might find the overseer. He had gone to the three-mile field half an hour ago, after bestowing upon the two dilatory servants a hearty cursing, and promising to reckon with them at dinner-time. "Where was the master?" He had gone to the mouth of the inlet with Sir Charles Carew, who had grown impatient, and had sailed away under the Nancy's patched sail. The under overseer was in the far corn-field, two miles off.

"Are all the men in the fields, Barb?" asked Landless.

Barb informed him that they were, "as he might very well know, seeing that the sun was half an hour high."

"Have you seen the man called Roach?"

No: Barb had not seen him; but she had heard the overseer tell Luiz Sebastian to take two men and go to the strip of Orenoko between the inlet and the third tobacco house, and Luiz Sebastian had been calling for Roach and Trail.

Landless thanked her, and moved away without offering to bestow upon her that which Barb probably thought her information merited.

"Do you find Woodson," he said to the Muggletonian, "and report this murder, saying nothing, however, of what we know. I myself will go to the tobacco house."

"Had I not best come with thee to hold up thy hands?" said Porringer. "I would take up my text from the thirty-fifth of Numbers, and from Revelation, twenty-second, thirteen, and deal mightily with the murderer."

"No," answered Landless. "Woodson must be seen at once, or we ourselves will fall under suspicion. And, friend, ask that thou and I may be the ones to bury *him*."

CHAPTER XIII

IN THE TOBACCO HOUSE

The third tobacco house was built upon a point of land jutting into the larger inlet, and screened off from the wide expanse of fields by a belt of cedars. It was a lonely, retired spot, and the high, dark, windowless structure with its heavy, low-browed door had a menacing aspect. Landless expected to find the men within the building, instead of outside attending to their work, and he was not disappointed. As he walked through the doorway into the pungent gloom, the three started up from the debris of casks, sticks, and pegs, amidst which they had been squatting, with their heads ominously close together.

Landless strode up to Roach. "You murderer!" he said.

The convict recoiled; then with a bestial sound, half snarl, half bellow of rage, he gathered himself for a rush. Landless awaited him with bent body and sinewy, outstretched arms; but the mulatto interposed. Laying his long, beautifully shaped, yellow hands upon Roach, he forced him back against a cask, and, pinning him there, whispered in his ear. The face of the wretch gradually resumed its usual expression of low brutality, though an ugly sweat broke out upon it, and the mouth opened and shut as though he had been running. He turned upon Landless with a half threatening, half cringing air.

"So you've found out what I was about last night, eh, pardner? But you'll keep a still tongue. You're not one to peach on your comrade as was in hell or Newgate with you, and as crossed the ocean with you to this d—d Virginia, and as has always liked you, and has the same spite as you have against the man what bought us. You say naught, comrade, and you'll not stand to lose by it."

"I go from here to give you up to Colonel Verney," said Landless.

The wretch gave a snarl of rage and fear. Luiz Sebastian laid a soothing hand upon his shoulder.

"If I thought that," snarled the convict, "you'd never live to reach that door."

"I shall live to see you hanged," said the other coolly.

Here the mulatto slipped something into Roach's hand. "So you'll give me up?" said the latter in a peculiar voice.

"I have said so."

"Then, by the Lord! I'll be even with you!" Roach cried with savage triumph. "Do you see this, and this, and this?" fluttering a mass of folded papers before the other's eyes. "Ah! I was wise, I was, when I couldn't hide everything about me, to take the papers, and leave the weapons. I've got you now. Here's the lists that the old fool who is dead and gone to hell had hidden behind the gold! Here's enough to hang you and your d—d Cromwellians higher than Haman. There will be more than one giving up, I'm thinking! I've got you under my thumb, and I'll squeeze you!"

"You cannot read; you do not know what those papers contain," said Landless steadily.

"But I can," put in Trail smoothly. "I was but just running them over to our friend whose education has been so sadly neglected, when you came in."

Landless drew a pistol from his bosom, cocked it, and leveled it at the murderer. "You see," he said with an ominously quiet eye and voice, "you were not altogether wise to leave the weapons. Now, give me those lists."

"Damnation!" cried the convict, and Luiz Sebastian glided towards the door.

Landless, quick of eye and active of body, saw the movement, and sprang backwards to the opening before the other could reach it. He covered the three with his pistol.

"I will shoot the first of you that stirs," he said sternly. "You, Roach, lay those papers upon that bit of board, and push them towards me with your foot."

"I'll go to hell first," was the sullen reply.

"As you please. I will give you until I count twenty. If those papers are not in my hands, then I will shoot you like the dog you are."

The murderer uttered a dreadful curse. Landless began to count. Roach made an irresolute motion of the hand that held the lists. Landless counted on, "fifteen, sixteen, seventeen, eighteen—" With another oath and a grin of rage Roach dropped the papers upon the board at his feet. "Now push it towards me," said Landless.

With a brow like midnight the other did as he was bid. Still covering his men, Landless stooped quickly, and took up the precious papers, assured himself that they were all there, and placed them in his bosom.

"Now," he said, leaning his back against the doorpost, and regarding the three baffled rogues with a grim eye, "I have a few words to say to you. I speak first to you, Trail, and to you, Luiz Sebastian. These papers have told you little that you did not know before. It was not the information that you gained from them that made them so valuable; it was the possession of them, the possession of actual proofs of this conspiracy which you might hold over our heads, or, if the notion took you, might sell to Colonel Verney?"

"Señor Landless sees the thing as it is," said Luiz Sebastian.

"Well, you no longer possess these proofs, and are therefore just where you were yesterday."

"Listen, Señor Landless," said Luiz Sebastian gloomily. "This plot does not please us. It is too much in the hands of those who call themselves soldiers and martyrs, whom our master calls fanatic Oliverians, and whom I, Luiz Sebastian, call accursed heretics. The servants have no say in the matter; they are to follow like sheep where these others lead. The slaves are not even to know of it until the last moment. A handful of us who have white blood in our veins are let into the secret, that we may incite the blacks when the time is come; but are we consulted? Are our opinions asked, our wishes deferred to? I, Luiz Sebastian, who have been through three insurrections in the Indies, and who know how such things should be managed; has my advice been craved as to this or that? You make us promises. Mother of God! how do we know that those promises will be kept? By St. Jago! the insurrection may arrive, and the planters be put down, and next year may find us slaves still, with but a change of masters!"

"It is too late now for such questions," said Landless steadily. "You must accept the conspiracy as it is. In liberating themselves, these men will of necessity free you even as they will free me, who am not, as you know, of their class. I shall take my chance, as I think you will take yours."

The mulatto played with a tobacco peg, striking it against his great, white teeth. At length he said slowly and with a sinister upward glance at the figure by the door, "Certainly, Señor Landless, it seems our best, our only chance, for freedom."

And with this Landless had perforce to be content. He turned to the murderer, saying sternly, "Now for my word with you. I hold your life in my hands, for I heard you last night in the marsh, and Porringer and I saw you stealing from the creek this morning, and I can swear that you knew of the gold hidden in the hut. You have it on you at this moment. I could hold you here with this pistol until the overseer should come and search you. But I let you go, choosing rather your safety than the endangerment of that which was dearer than life to the man you murdered. The unsupported assertion of a murderer as to the contents of papers which he had not got to show, might not go for much, but I prefer that you should not make it. I have warned you;—you had best make your escape at once."

"If you hold your tongue, there's no reason why I should run."

"Oh, yes, there is! There is a reason in the hut on the marsh."

"What do you mean?"

"I mean that clasped in the hand of the man you murdered is the missing half of that torn lock upon your forehead."

With a yell Roach sprang to the door only to be confronted by the muzzle of Landless' pistol.

"Wait a moment," he said composedly. "Oh, you need not be afraid! I intend to let you go. But you don't leave this tobacco house until after I have left it myself."

"Curse you!" cried the other, foaming at the lips.

"You are ungrateful. I not only promise not to witness against you, but I aid you to escape."

"For reasons of your own," suggested Trail.

"Precisely; for reasons of my own. If you are taken, I will hold my tongue just so long as you hold yours. If you escape now, I will pray that my day of reckoning will yet come. And it will be a heavy reckoning."

"Ay, that it will!" cried the murderer with brutal fury. "You've got the upper hand now; but wait! Every dog has his day, and I'll have mine! and when it comes, I'll do for you! I'll smash your beauty! I'll draw more blood from you than ever the whip of the overseer did! I'll use you worse than I used that old man last night, who writhed and struggled, and tried to pray! I'll—"

With white lips and blazing eyes Landless sprang forward, and clapped the mouth of the pistol to the ruffian's temple. Roach recoiled, then sunk upon his knees with an abject whine for mercy.

Landless let his hand drop, and moved slowly back to the door. "You had need to cry for mercy," he said in a low, distinct voice, "for you were never so near to death before. I let you go now, but one day I shall kill you. Until which day—take care of yourself!" Still with his face upon them he passed out of the door, then turned and walked away with a steady step, but with a heart bleeding for the loss of his friend, and heavy with forebodings for the future.

In the tobacco house the murderer, the forger, and the mulatto sat stricken into silence until the last crisp footfall had died away. Then amidst a torrent of curses Roach made for the door. Trail plucked him back. "Where are you going?" he cried.

"I don't know! To the devil!"

"The bloodhounds will be upon your trail before noon."

The wretch cried out and struck his hand against the wall with a force that laid the knuckles bare and bleeding.

"There is a way," said Luiz Sebastian slowly, "a way that only I know. You must take to the inlet here, and swim up it until you come to the mouth of the brook yonder in the forest. You must wade up that brook until you come to a second, and up that until you come to a third. When you have gone a mile up that one, leave it, and strike through the woods, going towards the north. Another mile will bring you to a village of the Chickahominies upon the Pamunkey.[1] They are at odds with Governor and Council, and they will hide you. Moreover, I once did their sachem a service, and they are my friends."

"I'm off," said Roach, breaking from the detaining grasp.

"Wait," said Luiz Sebastian. "There is time enough. Woodson will not come for a long while. When he does, he shall find Señor Trail and myself busily at work there outside, and we will say that you left us, and went down the inlet a long time before. But now we want to talk to you."

"Be quick then," growled the other, "I've no mind to swing for this job."

Luiz Sebastian brought his handsomely malevolent face close to the other's hideous countenance.

"Would you not like to ruin that devil who but now robbed you of your hard-earned property?"

"Would I not?" cried the murderer with a tremendous oath. "I'd give everything but life and gold to do it, as that cunning devil well knew. I'd give my soul!"

"Would you like to be shown how to get more gold than old Godwyn's store, twenty times told? To get your freedom? To have some black, sweet hours in which to work your will on them at the house yonder? To plunge your arms to the elbow in the master's money chest; to become drunken with his wine; to strike him down, and that smiling imp his cousin, and that other devil, Woodson; to hear the women cry for mercy—and cry in vain? You would like all this?"

"Show me the way!" cried the brute with a ferocious light in his bloodshot eyes. "Show me the way to do it safely, and I'll—" He broke off and threatened the air with malignant fists.

"Go to the village on the Pamunkey," said Luiz Sebastian with his most feline expression. "I will come to you there the first night I can slip away, I and our friend, the Señor Trail. There we will have our little conference. Mother of God! Señor Landless may find that others can plot as well as he and his accursed heretics."

[1] The modern York.

CHAPTER XIV

A MIDNIGHT EXPEDITION

Four nights later, the hour before midnight found Landless walking steadily through the forest, bound upon a mission which he had had in his mind since the night after the murder of Godwyn. This was the first night since that event upon which he had deemed it advisable to leave the quarters, having no mind to be captured as a runaway by one of the many search parties which were scouring the peninsula between the two great rivers for the murderer of Robert Godwyn. But the search was now trending northward towards Maryland, to which colony runaways usually turned their steps, and he felt that he might venture.

There was little undergrowth in the primeval forest, and the rows of vast and stately trees were as easy to thread as the pillared aisles of a cathedral. When he came to one of the innumerable streamlets that caught the land in a net of silver, he removed his coarse shoes and stockings, and waded it. The great branches overhead shut in a night that was breathlessly hot and still. He could see the stars only when he crossed the streams or emerged into one of the many little open glades. He walked warily, making no sound, and now and then stopping to listen for the distant halloo, or bark of a dog, which might denote that he was followed, or that there was a search party abroad, but he heard nothing save the usual forest sounds,—the dropping of acorns, the sighing leaves, the cry of some night bird,—sounds that seemed to make the night more still than silence.

He was nearing his destination when from out a shadowy clump of alders, standing upon the bank of the stream which he had just crossed, there shot a long arm, and the next moment he was wrestling with a dark and powerful figure whose naked body slipped from his hold as though it had been greased. But Landless, too, was strong and determined, and the two swayed and strained backwards and forwards through the darkness, wary and resolute, neither giving his antagonist advantage. The hand of the unknown writhed itself from the other's clasp and stole downwards towards his waist. Landless felt the motion and intercepted it. Then the figure, with an angry guttural sound, began to put forth its full strength. The arms encircled Landless with a slowly tightening iron band; the great dark shoulder came forward with the force of a battering-ram; the limbs twined like boa-constrictors around the limbs of the other. Locked together, the two reeled into a little fairy glade, where the short grass, pearled with dew, lay open to the moon. Here, borne backwards by the overwhelming force of his assailant, Landless fell heavily to the ground. The figure falling with him, pinned him to the earth with its knee upon his breast. In the moonlight he saw the gleam of the lifted knife.

He had had but time for a half-uttered, half-thought prayer when the pressure upon his breast relaxed; the knife fell, indeed, but harmlessly upon the grass, and the figure rose to its height with an astonished "Ugh!"

Landless, rising also, began to think that he recognized the gigantic form towering through the pale moonlight.

"Ugh!" said the figure again. "The great Spirit threw us into the light in time. Monakatocka had been forever shamed had his knife drunk the life of his friend."

"Why did you set upon me?" demanded Landless, still breathless from the struggle, while the Indian was as calmly composed as upon the day of their first meeting.

"Monakatocka took you for the man for whom they hunt with dogs through the forest, scaring the deer from the licks and the partridge from the fern. Two nights ago Major Carrington said to Monakatocka, 'Find me that man and kill him, and to the twenty arms' length of roanoke which the county will pay to Monakatocka, I will add a gun with store of powder, and with a bullet for every stag between Werowocomico and Machot.' When he heard you a long way off, moving over the leaves, trying to make no sound, Monakatocka thought he held the gun of the paleface Major in his hand. But now—" he waved his hand with a gesture eloquent of resignation.

"I am sorry to disappoint you," said Landless, amused at his air of calm regret.

"I am glad to have proved the strength of my brother," was the sententious reply. "Where goes my brother through the woods, which are full of danger to him to-night? Or has he a pass?"

"I have business at Rosemead," answered Landless. "I am close to the house, I think?"

The Indian pointed through the trees. "It lies twelve bowshots before you. The overseer with the dogs has gone to the great swamp to look for the man with the red hair."

"Thanks for the information, friend," said Landless. "I ask you, moreover, to say nothing of this encounter. I have no pass."

"I have but one friend," answered the Indian. "His secret is my secret."

"Are you, too, then, so lonely?" asked Landless, touched by his tone.

"Listen," said the Indian, leaning his back against a great oak. "I will tell my brother who I am.... Many years ago the Conestogas, they whom the palefaces call the Susquehannocks, came down the great bay and fought with the palefaces. Monakatocka was then but a lad on his first warpath. Agreskoi was angry: he hid his face behind a cloud. With their guns the palefaces beat the Conestogas like fleeing women back to their village on the banks of a great river, and themselves returned in triumph to their board wigwams, bearing with them many captives. Monakatocka, son to a great chief, was one. The palefaces made him to work like a squaw in their fields of tobacco and maize. When he ran away they put forth a long arm and plucked him back and beat him. Agreskoi was angry, for Monakatocka had not any offering to make him. One by one his fellow captives have dropped away like the leaves that fall in the moon of Taquetock, until, behold! he is left alone. The palefaces are his enemies. He thinks of the village beside the pleasant stream, and he hates them. A warrior of the long house takes no friend from the wigwam of an Algonquin. Monakatocka is alone."

He spoke with a wild pathos, his high, stern features working in the moonlight, and his bold glance softened into an exquisite melancholy.

"I too am friendless," said Landless, "and bound to a far more degrading captivity than that you suffer. Our fate is the same."

The Indian took his hand in his, and raising it, pressed the forefinger against a certain spot upon his shoulder. "You have a friend," he said.

"You make too much of a very slight service," said Landless. "But I embrace your offer of friendship—there's my hand upon it. And now I must be going upon my way. Good-night!"

The Indian gave a guttural "Good-night," and Landless strode on through the thinning woods. Shortly he emerged from the forest and saw before him tobacco fields and a house, and beyond the house the vast sheet of the Chesapeake slumbering beneath the moon. There was a beaten path leading to the house. Landless struck into it and followed it until it led him beneath a window which (having been once sent with a message to the Surveyor-General), he knew to belong to the sleeping-chamber of Major Carrington. Stopping beneath this window he listened for any sound that might warn him of aught stirring within or without the mansion,—all was silent, the house and its inmates locked in slumber.

He took a handful of pebbles from the path and threw them, one by one, against the wooden shutter, the thud of the last pebble being answered by a slight noise from within the room. Presently the shutter was opened and an authoritative voice demanded:—

"Who is it? What do you want?"

Landless came closer beneath the window. "Major Carrington," he said in a low voice, "It is I, Godfrey Landless. I must have speech with you."

There was a moment's silence, and then the other said coldly, "'Must' is a word that becomes neither your lips nor my ears. I know no reason why Miles Carrington *must* speak with the servant of Colonel Verney."

"As you please: Godfrey Landless craves the honor of a word with Major Carrington."

"And what if Major Carrington refuses?" said the other sharply.

"I do not think he will do so."

The Surveyor-General hesitated a moment, then said:—

"Go to the great door. I will open to you in a moment. But make no noise."

Landless nodded, and proceeded to follow his directions. Presently the door swung noiselessly inward, and Carrington, appearing in the opening, beckoned Landless within, and led the way, still in profound silence, across the hall to the great room. Here, after softly closing the door, he lighted candles, saw to it that the heavy wooden shutters were securely drawn across the windows, and turned to face his visitor in a somewhat different guise than the riding suit and jack boots, the mask and broad flapping beaver, in which he had appeared in their encounter in the hut on the marsh. His stately figure was now wrapped in a night-gown of dark velvet, his bare feet were thrust into velvet slippers, and a silken night-cap, half on and half off, imparted a rakish air to his gravely handsome countenance. He threw himself into a great armchair and tapped impatiently upon the table.

"Well!" he said dryly.

Landless standing before him began to speak with dignity and to the point. Godwyn, the head of a great conspiracy, was dead, leaving him, Landless, in some sort his successor. In a conference of the leading conspirators held but a few nights before the murder, Godwyn had announced that not only had he given to the son of Warham Landless his complete confidence, but that in case aught should happen to himself before the time for action, he would wish the young man to succeed him in the leadership of the revolt. There had been some demur, but Godwyn's influence was boundless, and on his advancing reason after reason for his preference, the Oliverians had acquiesced in his judgment and had given their solemn promise to respect his wishes. Three nights later, Godwyn was murdered. Since that dreadful blow, Landless had seen only such of the conspirators as were in his immediate neighborhood. Confounded at the turn affairs had taken, and utterly at a loss, they had turned eagerly to him as to one having authority. For his own freedom, for the sake of his promise to the dead man, he would do his utmost. He had come to-night to discover, if possible, Major Carrington's intentions—

Carrington, who had listened thus far with grave attention, frowned heavily.

"If my memory serves me, sirrah, I told you once before that Miles Carrington stirs not hand or foot in this matter. I may wish you well, but that is all."

"'Tis a poor friend that cries 'Godspeed!' to one who struggles in a bog, and gives not his hand to help him out."

"Your figure does not hold," said the other, dryly. "I have not cried 'Godspeed!' I have said nothing at all, either good or bad. I have nothing to do with this conspiracy. You are the only man now living that knows that I am aware that such a thing exists. And I hope, sir, that you will remember how you gained that knowledge."

"I am in no danger of forgetting."

"Very well. Your journey here to-night was a useless as well as a dangerous one. I have nothing to say to you."

"Will you tell me one thing?" said Landless, patiently. "What will Major Carrington have to say to me upon the day when I speak to him as a free man with free men behind me?"

"Upon that day," said the other, composedly, "Miles Carrington will submit to the inevitable with a good grace, having been, as is well known, a friend to the Commonwealth, and having always, even when there was danger in so doing, spoken against the cruel and iniquitous enslavement of men whose only offense was non-conformity, or the having served under the banners of Cromwell."

"If he should be offered Cromwell's position in the new Commonwealth, what then?"

"Pshaw! no such offer will be made."

"We must have weight and respectability, must identify ourselves with that Virginia in which we are strangers, if we are to endure," said Landless, with a smile. "A fact that we perfectly recognize—as does Major Carrington. He probably knows who is of, and yet head and shoulders above, that party in the state upon whose support we must ultimately rely, who alone could lead that party; who alone might reconcile Royalist and Puritan;—and to whom alone the offer I speak of will be made."

Carrington smiled despite himself. "Well, then, if the offer is made, I will accept it. In short, when your man is out of the bog I will lend my aid to cleanse him of the stains incurred in the transit. But he must pull himself out of the mire. I am safe upon the bank, I will not be drawn with him into a bottomless ruin. Do I make myself plain?"

"Perfectly," said Landless, dryly.

The other flushed beneath the tone. "You think perhaps that I play but a craven part in this game. I do not. God knows I run a tremendous risk as it is, without madly pledging life and honor to this desperate enterprise!"

"I fail to see the risk," said Landless, coldly.

The other struck his hand against the table. "I risk a slave insurrection!" he said.

A noise outside the door made them start like guilty things. The door opened softly and a charming vision appeared, to wit, Mistress Betty Carrington, rosy from sleep and hastily clad in a dressing-gown of sombre silk. Her little white feet were bare, and her dark hair had escaped from its prim, white night coif. She started when she saw a visitor, and her feet drew demurely back under the hem of her gown, while her hands went up to her disheveled hair; but a second glance showing her his quality, she recovered her composure and spoke to her father in her soft, serious voice.

"I heard a noise, my father, and looking into your room, found it empty, so I came down to see what made you wakeful to-night."

"'Tis but a message from Verney Manor, child," said her father. "Get back to bed."

"From Verney Manor!" exclaimed Betty. "Then I can send back to-night the song book and book of plays lent me by Sir Charles Carew, and which, after reading the first page, I e'en restored to their wrappings and laid aside with a good book a-top to put me in better thoughts if ever I was tempted to touch them again. I will get them, good fellow, and you shall carry them back to their owner with my thanks, if it so be that I can find words that are both courteous and truthful."

"Stop, child!" said her father as she turned to leave the room. "The volumes, which you were very right not to read, may rest awhile beneath the good book. This is a secret mission upon which this young man has come. It is about a—a matter of state upon which his master and I have been engaged. No one here or at Verney Manor must know that he has been at Rosemead."

"Very well, my father," said Betty, meekly, "the books can wait some other opportunity."

"And," with some sternness, "you will be careful to hold your tongue as to this man's presence here to-night."

"Very well, father."

"You are not to speak of it to Mistress Patricia or to any one."

"I will be silent, my father."

"Very well," said the Major. "You are not like the majority of women. I know that your word is as good as an oath. Now run away to bed, sweetheart, and forget that you have seen this messenger."

"I am going now, father," said Betty, obediently. "Is Mistress Patricia well, good fellow?"

"Quite well, I believe, madam."

"She spake of crossing to Accomac with Mistress Lettice and Sir Charles Carew, when the latter should go to visit Colonel Scarborough. Know you if she went?"

"I think not, madam. I think that Sir Charles Carew went alone."

"Ah! They have fallen out then," said Betty, half to herself, and with a demure satisfaction in her wild flower face. "I am glad of it, for I like him not. Thanks, good fellow, for your answering my idle questions."

Landless bowed gravely. Betty bent her pretty head, and with a hasty, "I am going, father!" in answer to an impatient movement on the part of the Major, vanished from the room.

Carrington waited until the last light footfall had died away, and then said, "Our interview is over. Are you satisfied?"

"At least, I understand your position."

"Yes," said Carrington, thoughtfully, "it is as well that you should understand it. It is simple. I wish you well. I am in heart a Commonwealth's man. I love not the Stuarts. I would fain see this fair land freed from their rule and returned to the good days of the Commonwealth. And I may as well acknowledge, since you have found it out for yourself,"—a haughty smile,—"that I have my ambitions. What man has not?" He rose and began to pace the room, his hands clasped behind him, his handsome head bent, his rich robe trailing upon the ground behind him.

"I could rule this land more acceptably to the people than can William Berkeley with his parrot phrases, 'divine right,' and 'passive obedience.' I know the people and am popular with them, with Royalist and Churchman as well as with Nonconformist and Oliverian. I know the needs of the colony—home rule, self taxation, free trade, a more liberal encouragement to emigrants, religious tolerance, a rod of iron for the Indians, the establishment of a direct slave trade with Africa and the Indies. I could so rule this colony that in a twelvemonth's time, Richard Verney or Stephen Ludlow, hot Royalists though they be, would be forced to acknowledge that never, since the day Smith sailed up the James, had Virginia enjoyed a tithe of her present prosperity."

"'Tis a consummation devoutly to be desired,'" said Landless, dryly. "In the mean time, like the cat i' the adage—"

"You are insolent, sirrah!"

"When a stripling I served under one who took the bitter with the sweet, the danger as well as the reward, who led the soldiers from whom he took his throne."

"Cromwell, sirrah," said Carrington sternly, "led soldiers. You would require Miles Carrington to lead servants, to place himself, a gentleman and a master, at the head of a rebellion which, if it failed, would plunge him into a depth of ignominy and ruin proportionate to the height from which he fell. He declines the position. When you have won your freedom he will treat with you. Not before."

"Then," said Landless slowly, "upon the day on which the flag of the Commonwealth floats over the Assembly hall at Jamestown, then—"

"Then I will join myself to you as I have said, and I will bring with me those without whom your revolution would be but short-lived—the Puritan and Nonconformist element in the colony, gentle and simple."

"That is sufficiently explicit," said Landless, "and I thank you."

"I have trusted you fully, young man," said the other, stopping before him, "not only because you cannot betray me if you would, seeing that not one scrap of writing exists to inculpate me in this matter, and that your word would scarce be taken before mine, but because I believe you to be trustworthy. I believe also"—graciously—"that Robert Godwyn (whose death I sincerely mourn) showed his usual wisdom and knowledge of mankind when he chose you as his confidant and co-worker. I wish you well through with a dangerous and delicate piece of work and in enjoyment of your reward, namely, your freedom, and the esteem of the Commonwealth of Virginia. I will myself see to it that any past offenses which you are supposed to have committed (for myself, I believe you to have been harshly used), shall not stand in your light."

"Major Carrington is very good," said Landless, calmly. "I shall study to deserve his commendation."

The other took a restless turn or two through the room, stopping at length before the younger man.

"You may tell me one thing," he said in a voice scarcely above a whisper, and with his eyes bent watchfully upon the other's composed face. "Had Godwyn set the day?"

"Yes."

"And you will adhere to it?"

"Yes."

"What day?"

"The thirteenth of September."

"Humph! Two weeks off! Well, my tobacco will be largely in, and I shall send my daughter upon a visit to her Huguenot kindred upon the Potomac. Good night."

"Good night," answered Landless.

CHAPTER XV

THE WATERS OF CHESAPEAKE

Patricia was ennuyée to the last degree. That morning Sir Charles had ridden to Green Spring with her father; Mistress Lettice was in the still room decocting a face wash from rose leaves, dew and honey; young Shaw on his knees in the master's room, disconsolately poring over piles of musty papers in search of a misplaced deed which the colonel had ordered him to find against his return. It was a hot and listless afternoon. Patricia read a page of "The Rival Ladies," tried her spinet, had a languid romp with her spaniels, and finally sauntered into the porch, and leaning her white arms upon the railing, looked towards the dazzling blue waters of the Chesapeake. Presently an idea came to her. She went swiftly into the hall, and called for Darkeih. When that handmaiden appeared:—

"Darkeih, go down to the quarters, and tell the first man you meet to find Woodson, and send him to me."

Darkeih departed, and in half an hour's time the overseer appeared at the foot of the porch steps, red and heated from his rapid walk from the Three-Mile field.

"What's wrong, Mistress Patricia?" he asked quickly.

Patricia opened her lovely eyes. "Nothing is wrong, Woodson. What should be? I sent for you, because I want to go to Rosemead."

"To Rosemead!" exclaimed the overseer.

"Yes, to Rosemead, and I want a couple of men to take me."

The overseer gave a short, vexed laugh. "I can't spare the men, Mistress Patricia. You ought to have known that every man jack on the plantation is busy cutting. If I had a known this was all that was wanted! Fegs! I thought something dreadful was the matter."

"Something dreadful is the matter," said the young lady calmly. "I am bored to death."

"Sorry for ye, missy, but I can't spare the men."

"Oh, yes, you can!" said Patricia with unruffled composure.

The overseer, knowing his lady, began to weaken.

"Anyhow, you wouldn't want two men. You might go on a pillion behind old Abraham. I could spare *him*."

"I shall not go a-horseback. 'Tis too hot and dusty. I shall go in one of the sail-boats—the Bluebird, I think."

"Now, in the name of all that's contrary, what do you want to do that for, Mistress Patricia?" cried the harassed overseer. "It's twice as far by water."

"I'll reach Rosemead before dark. The men can bring the boat back to-night, and Major Carrington will send me home on a pillion to-morrow."

"Have you forgotten that to-morrow is Sunday?" said the overseer severely, and with a new-born anxiety for the proper observance of the holy day. "Will you have the Colonel pay a fine for you?"

"I will go to service with the Carringtons then, and come home on Monday," said the lady serenely.

"There's a squall coming up this afternoon."

"There isn't a cloud in the sky," said his mistress with calm conviction, looking straight before her at a low, tumbled line of creamy peaks along the horizon.

"If the Colonel were here—"

"He would say, 'Woodson, do exactly as Mistress Patricia tells you.'" This with great sweetness.

The overseer gave it up. "I reckon he would, missy," he said with a grin. "You wind him and all of us around your finger."

"'Tis all for your good, Woodson," with a soft, bright laugh. Then, coaxingly, "Am I to have the Bluebird?"

"I reckon so, Mistress Patricia, seeing that you have set your heart upon it," said the still reluctant overseer.

"That's a good Woodson. I want Regulus to be one of the boatmen. You can send any other you choose. I shall take Darkeih with me."

"You can't have Regulus, Mistress Patricia," answered the overseer positively. "He's worth any two men in the field. I can't let him go."

"Let him be at the wharf in half an hour. I will be ready by then."

"You can't have him, Missy."

Patricia stamped her pretty foot. "Am I mistress of this plantation, or am I not, Woodson?"

"Lord knows you are!" groaned the overseer.

"Then when I say I want Regulus, I will have Regulus and no other."

The overseer sighed resignedly. "Very well, Mistress Patricia, I'll send for him."

Patricia danced away, and the overseer strode down the path, viciously crunching the pebbles and bits of shell beneath his feet. At the wharf he found a detachment of the infant population of the quarters busily crabbing; all of whom, save two little Indians who fished stoically on, scrambled to their feet, and pulled a forelock. The overseer touched one urchin upon the shoulder with the butt end of his whip.

"You, Piccaninny, run as fast as your legs will carry you to the field by the swamp, and tell Regulus to leave his work, and come to the big wharf. Mistress Patricia wants to go a pleasuring."

Piccaninny's black shanks and pink heels flew up and out, and he was away like a flash. The overseer kept on to the end of the wharf, where were clustered the boats, some tied to the piles, some anchored a little way out. "Haines was to send a man to caulk a seam in the Nancy," he muttered. "Whoever he is, he'll have to go in the Bluebird. I'm not going to take another man from the tobacco. What fools women are! But they get their way,—the pretty ones at least." He leaned over the railing, and called,—

"You there, in the Nancy!"

Godfrey Landless looked up from his work. "What is it?"

The overseer chuckled grimly. "It's that fellow Landless who angered her once before," he said to himself with a malicious grin. "Well, 't isn't my business to know which of all the servants on this plantation she most dislikes to come near her. She'll have to put up with him to-day. There isn't a better boatman on the place anyhow."

To Landless he said, "Bring the Bluebird up to the wharf, and see that she is sweet and clean inside. Mistress Patricia starts for Rosemead in half an hour, and you and Regulus are to take her. You'll bring the boat back to-night. Step lively now!"

Landless brought the Bluebird, a sixteen-foot open boat, up to the wharf, made the inside, and especially the seat in the stern, spotlessly clean, put up the sail, and sat down to wait. Presently Regulus appeared above him, and swung himself down into the boat with a grin of delight, for he much preferred sailing with "'lil missy" to cutting tobacco. He had a great burly form and a broad, ebony face, and he was the devoted slave of Patricia, and of Patricia's maid, Darkeih. Moreover, he enjoyed the distinction of being the first negro born in the Colony, his parents having been landed from the Dutch privateer which in 1619 introduced the slave into Virginia. Viewed through a vista of nigh three hundred years, he appears a portent, a tremendous omen, a sign from the Eumenides. Upon that tranquil summer afternoon in the Virginia of long ago he was simply a good-humored, docile, happy-go-lucky, harmless animal.

"'Lil Missy's comin'," he remarked, with bonhommie, to his fellow boatman.

Darkeih, laden with cushions, appeared at the edge of the wharf. Landless, standing in the bow below her, relieved her of her burdens, and taking her by the hands, swung her down into the boat. She thanked him with a smile that showed every tooth in her comely brown countenance, and tripped aft, where, with the assistance of Regulus, she proceeded to arrange a cushioned seat for her mistress.

Landless waited for the lady of the manor to come forward. In the act of extending her hands to the boatman, she glanced at him, crimsoned, and drew back. Landless, interpreting color and action aright, buckled his armor of studied quiet more closely over a hurt and angry heart.

"I was ordered to attend you, madam," he said proudly. "But if you so desire, I will find the overseer and tell him that you wish for some one else in my place."

"There is not time," was the cold reply. "And as well you as any other. Let us be going."

Landless held out his arms again. She measured with her eyes the distance between her and the boat. "I do not need any help," she said. "If you will stand aside, I can spring from here to the prow."

"And strike the water instead, madam," said Landless, grimly, "when I would have to touch more than your hand in order to pull you out."

She colored angrily, but held out her hands. Landless lifted her down and steadied her to her seat in the stern. She thanked him coldly, and began at once to talk to Regulus with the playful familiarity of a child. Regulus grinned delight; he had been "'lil Missy's" slave from her childhood. Landless untied the boat from the piles and pushed her off; Regulus, who was to steer, pulled the tiller towards him, and the little Bluebird glided from the wharf, made a wide and graceful sweep, and proceeded leisurely down the inlet towards the waters of the great bay.

Landless seated himself in the bow, and turned his face away from the group in the stern. Patricia leaned back amidst her cushions, and opened a book; Darkeih, upon the other side of the rudder, held a whispered flirtation with Regulus, squatting at her feet, the tiller in his hand. There was but little wind, but what there was came from the land, and the Bluebird moved steadily though listlessly down the inlet, between the velvet marshes. The water broke against the sides of the boat with a languid murmur. It was very hot, and the sky above was of a steely, unclouded blue that hurt the eyes. Only in the southwest the line of cloud hills was erecting itself into an Alpine range. The glare of the sun upon the white pages of her book dazzled Patricia's eyes; the heat and the lazy swaying motion made her drowsy. With a sigh of oppression she closed her book, and taking her fan from Darkeih, laid it across her face, and curled herself among her cushions.

"I will sleep awhile," she said to her handmaiden, and serenely glided into slumberland.

She was in a balcony with Sir Charles Carew, looking down upon a fantastic procession that wound endlessly on, with flaunting banners, and to the sound of kettle-drums and trumpets, when she was aroused by Landless' voice. She opened her eyes and looked up from her nest of cushions to see him standing above her.

"What is it?" she asked frigidly.

"I grieve to waken you, madam, but there is a heavy squall coming up."

She sat up and looked about her. The Bluebird had left the inlet and was rising and falling with the long oily swell of the vast sheet of water that stretched before them to a horizon of vivid blue. North and east the water met the sky; a mile to the westward was the low wooded shore which they were skirting.

"The sun is shining," said Patricia, bewildered. "The sky is blue."

"Look behind you."

She turned and uttered an exclamation. The Alpine range had vanished, and a monstrous pall of gray-black cloud was being slowly drawn upward and across the smiling heaven. Even as she looked, it blotted out the sun.

"We had better make for the shore at once," said Landless. "We can reach it before the storm breaks and can find shelter for you until it is over."

Patricia exclaimed: "Why, we cannot be more than three miles from Rosemead! Surely we can reach it before that cloud overtakes us!"

"I think not, madam."

"Regulus!" cried his mistress imperiously. "We can reach Rosemead before that storm breaks, can we not?"

Among other amiable qualities, Regulus numbered a happy willingness to please, even at the expense of truth.

"Sho-ly, 'lil Missy," he said with emphasis.

"And it will not be much of a squall, besides, will it, Regulus?"

"No, 'lil Missy, not much ob squall," answered the obliging Regulus.

"There is much wind in it," said Landless. "Look at those white clouds scudding across the black; and these squalls strike with suddenness and fury. I may put the boat about, madam?"

"Certainly not. Regulus, who must know the Chesapeake and its squalls much better than you possibly can, says there is no danger. I have no mind to be set ashore in these woods with night coming on and Indians or wolves prowling around."

"I beg that you will be advised by me, madam."

She looked at him as she had done that day in the master's room. "Is it that you are *afraid* of a Virginia squall? If so, you will have to conquer your tremor. Regulus, keep the boat as it is."

Landless went back to his seat in the bow, with tightened lips. The wind freshened, coming in hot little puffs, and the Bluebird slid more swiftly over the low hills. The water turned to a livid green and the air slowly darkened. Across the black pall, looming higher and higher, shot a jagged streak of fierce gold, followed by a low rumble of thunder. A mass of gray-white, fantastically piled clouds whirled up from the eastern horizon to meet the vast blank sullen sheet overhead. There came a more vivid flash and a louder roll of thunder.

Landless walked aft and took the tiller from Regulus' hand, motioning him forward to the place he had himself occupied. The negro stared, but went with his accustomed docility. Patricia sat upright in indignant surprise.

"What are you doing?"

"I am about to head the boat for the shore," suiting the action to the word.

Her eyes blazed. "Did you not hear me say that I wished to proceed to Rosemead?"

"Yes, madam, I did."

"I order you, sir—"

"And I choose to disobey."

"I shall report you to Colonel Verney."

"As you please, madam."

From the prow, where he had been taking observations, Regulus cried in a startled voice: "De win 's comin'! De win 's comin' mighty quick!"

Landless thrust the tiller into Patricia's hands. "Keep it there, just where it is, for your life!" he cried authoritatively, and bounded forward to where Regulus was already struggling with the sail. They got it in and lashed to the mast just in time, for, with the shriek of a thousand demons, the squall whirled itself upon them. In an instant they were enveloped in a blinding horror of furious wind and rain, glare of lightning and incessant, ear-splitting thunder. A leaden darkness, illuminated only by the lightning, settled around them, and the air grew suddenly cold. Beneath the whip of the wind the Chesapeake woke from slumber, stirred, and rose in fury. The Bluebird danced dizzily upon white crests or swooped into black and yawning chasms. Steadying himself by the thwarts, Landless went back to Patricia, sitting pale and with clasped hands, but making no sound. Darkeih, with a moan of fear, had thrown herself down at her mistress' feet, and was hiding her face in her skirts. Landless took a scarf from among the pile of cushions, and wrapped it around Patricia. "'Tis a poor protection against wet and cold," he said, "but it is better than nothing."

"Thank you," she said then, with an effort. "Do you think this squall will last long?"

"I cannot tell, madam. It is rather a hurricane than a squall. But we must do the best we can."

As he spoke there came a fresh access of wind with a glare of intolerable light. The mast bent like a reed, snapped off clear to the foot and fell inward, the loosened beam striking Regulus upon the head, and bearing him down with it. The boat careened violently, and half filled with water. Darkeih screamed, and Patricia sprang to her feet, but sat down again at Landless' stern command, "Sit still! She will right in a moment."

He lifted and flung overboard the mass of splintered wood and flapping cloth, then fell to bailing with all his might, for the danger of swamping was imminent. Presently Patricia touched him upon the arm. "I will bail if you will see to Regulus," she said, in a low, strained voice. "I think he is dead."

Landless resigned the pail into her hands and lifted the negro's head and shoulders from the water in which he was lying, pillowing them upon the stern seat. He was unconscious, and bleeding from a cut on the forehead.

"He is not dead nor like to die," Landless said. "He will revive before long."

The girl gave a long, quivering sigh of relief. Landless finished the bailing and sat down at her feet.

Some time later she asked faintly: "Do you not think the worst is over now?"

"I am afraid not," he answered gently. "There is a lull now, but I am afraid the storm is but gathering its forces. But we will hope for the best—"

Another flash and crash cut him short. It was followed by rain that fell, not in drops, but in sheets. The wind, which had been blowing a heavy gale, rose suddenly into a tornado. With it rose the sea. The masses of water, hissing and smoking under the furious pelting of the rain, flung themselves upon the hapless Bluebird, laboring heavily in the trough of the waves, or staggering over their summits. A constant glare lit the heaving, tossing world of waters, and the air became one roar of wind, rain, and thunder.

Darkeih crouched moaning at her mistress' feet. Regulus lay unconscious, breathing heavily. Suddenly, with a quick intake of his breath, Landless seized Patricia, pulled her down into the bottom of the boat, and held her there.

"I see," she said in a low, awed voice. "It is Death!"

Through the glare a long green wall bore down upon them. The Bluebird leaped to meet it. It lifted her up, up to meet the lightning, then hurled her into black depths, and passed on, leaving her staggering in the trough, water-logged and helpless.

CHAPTER XVI

THE FACE IN THE DARK

Patricia lifted her white face from her hands. "We rode that dreadful wave?" she cried incredulously.

"By God's mercy, yes," said Landless gravely.

"Is there any hope for us?"

Landless hesitated. "Tell me the truth," she said imperiously.

"We are in desperate case, madam. The boat is half filled with water. Another such sea will sink us."

"Why do you not bail the boat?"

"The bucket is gone; the tiller also."

She shivered, and Darkeih began to wail aloud. Landless laid a heavy hand upon the latter's shoulder. "Silence!" he said sternly. "Here! I shall lay Regulus' head in your lap, and you are to watch over him and not to think of yourself. There's a brave wench!"

Darkeih's lamentations subsided into a low sobbing, and Landless turned to her mistress.

"Try to keep up your courage, madam," he said. "Our peril is great; but while there is life there is hope."

"I am not afraid," she said. "I—" The pitching of the boat threw her against Landless, and he put his arm about her. "You must let me hold you, madam," he said quietly. She shrank away from his touch, saying breathlessly, "No, oh no! See! I can hold quite well by the gunwale." He acquiesced in silence, only lifting her into a more secure position. "I thank you," she said humbly.

The storm continued to rage with unabated fury. Flash and detonation succeeded flash and detonation; the rain poured in torrents; and the wind whooped on the angry sea like a demon of destruction. The Bluebird pitched and tossed at the mercy of the great waves that combed above her. Time passed, and to the darkness of the storm was added the darkness of the night. The occupants of the boat, drenched by the rain and the seas she had shipped, shivered with cold. Regulus began to stir and mutter. "He is coming to himself," Landless cried to Darkeih. "When you see that he is conscious, make him lie still. He must not move about."

"Do you know where we are?" asked Patricia.

"No, madam; but I fear that the wind is driving us out into the bay."

"Ah!"

She said it with a sob, for a sudden vision of home flashed across the cold and darkness; and presently Landless could hear that she was weeping.

The sound went to his heart. "I would God I could help you, madam," he said gently. "Take comfort! You are in the hands of One who holds the sea in the hollow of His hand."

In a little while she was quiet. There passed another long interval of silent endurance, broken by Patricia's saying piteously, "My hands are so numbed with cold that I cannot hold to the side of the boat. And my arms are bruised with striking against it."

Without a word Landless put his arm around her, and held her steady amidst the tossings of the boat. "You are shivering with cold!" he said. "If I had but something to wrap you in!"

She drooped against him, and the lightning showed him her face, still and white, with parted lips, and long lashes sweeping her marble cheek.

"Madam, madam!" he cried roughly. "You must not swoon! You must not!"

With a strong effort she rallied. "I will try to be brave," she said plaintively. "I am not frightened,—not very much. But oh! I am cold and tired!"

He drew her head down upon his knee. "Let it lie there," he said, speaking as to a tired child. "I will hold you quite steady. Now shut your eyes and try to sleep. The storm is no worse than it was; and since the boat has lived this long in this sea, she may live through the night. And with morning may come many chances of safety. Try to rest in that hope."

Faint and exhausted from cold and terror, she submitted like a child, and lay with closed eyes in a sort of stupor within his arms.

There was less lightning now, and the thunder sounded in long booming peals, instead of short, sharp cannon cracks. The rain, too, had ceased; but the wind blew furiously, and the sea ran in tremendous waves. Regulus stirred, groaned, and struggled into a sitting posture. "Lie down again!" ordered Darkeih. "We 's all on de way to Heaben, but if nigger shake de boat, we'll get dere befo' de Lawd ready for us. Lie down!" Regulus, muttering to himself, looked stupidly about him, then dropped his head back into her lap. In three minutes he was snoring. Darkeih's whimpering died away, and her turbaned head sank lower and lower, until it rested upon that of Regulus, and she, too, slept.

Landless sat very still, holding his burden lightly and tenderly, and staring into the darkness. Against the steep slope of the sea, a picture framed itself, melted away, and was followed by others in long procession. He saw a ruinous, ivy-grown hall, and an old, grave, formal garden, where, between long box hedges broken by fantastic yews, there walked a boy, book in hand. A man with a stately figure and a stern, careworn face met the boy, and they leaned upon a broken dial, and the father reasoned with the son of Right and Truth and Liberty, and something touched upon the Tyrannicides of old. The yew trees drooped their sombre boughs about the figures, and they were gone, and in their place roared and swelled the Chesapeake.... The sound of the storm became the sound of a battle-cry. He saw a clanging fight where sword clashed upon armor, and artillery belched fire and thunder, and horse and man went down in the melée, and were trampled under foot amidst shrieks and oaths and stern prayers. The boy who had leaned upon the dial fought coolly, desperately, drunk with the joy of battle, stung to fierce effort by his father's eyes. The great banner, blazoned with the Cross of Saint George, streamed in crimson and azure between the battle and the lonely watcher in the storm-tossed boat, and the vision was gone.... The spires of a great city, where men walked with long faces and church bells made the only music, rose through the gloom, and he saw a dingy chamber in a dingy stack of buildings, and within it, bending over great tomes of law, a man, impoverished and orphaned, but young, strong, and full of hope,—a man well spoken of and allowed to be on the road to high preferment. The chamber wavered into darkness; but the city spires flashed light, and the slow ringing changed to mad peals from joy bells. Some one had been restored—to drop balm upon the bleeding heart of a nation, to bring light to them that sit in darkness,—so said the joy bells.... He saw a loathsome prison, and the man who had sat in the dingy chamber lying therein under accusation of a crime which he had not committed. He saw him pining there, week after week, month after month, untried, forgotten, at the mercy of an enemy to his house whose day had come with the Restored One.... The prison vanished, and the waves that tossed around him were the waves of the Atlantic. A ship ploughed her way through them. He saw into her hold,—a horrible place of stench and filth and darkness,—a place where hounds would not have kenneled. Men and women were there who cursed and fought for the scanty, worm-eaten food that was thrown them. Some wore gyves: they were heavy upon the wrists and ankles of the man of his vision. He saw a face looking down upon this man, a handsome supercilious face, with insolent amusement in the languid eyes and in the curves of the lips. The hatches were battened down upon the cargo of misery, and the ship with its brutal captain and its handful of gold-laced, dicing, swearing passengers vanished.... He saw a sandy, grass-grown street, and a row of mean houses, and a low, brick building with barred windows. There was a crowd before this building, and a man standing upon the platform of a pillory was selling human flesh and blood. He saw the boy who had stood beneath the yews of the old Hall, who had fought at Worcester beneath his father's eye; the man who had lain in prison and in the noisome hold of the ship, put up and sold to the highest bidder. He saw him carried away with other merchandise to the home of his purchaser. He saw a Virginia plantation lying fair and serene beneath a Virginia heaven; and a wide porch, and standing therein an angelic vision, all grace and beauty, vivid youth and splendor.

The picture vanished into the night that raved about him, and with a long shaken sigh he let his eyes fall from the watery steeps to the face of the woman who lay within his arms. He had not looked at her before, conceiving that she might be awake and feel his glance upon her. Now he could tell from her breathing that she slept. He gazed upon the pure pale face with the golden hair falling about it, in a passion of pity and tenderness. She moaned now and then in her sleep, or turned uneasily in his arms. Once she spoke a few words, and he bent eagerly to catch them, thinking that she had awakened and was speaking to him. They were:—

"Ah, your Excellency! where I reign there shall be only good Churchmen and loyal Cavaliers—no Roundheads, no rebel or convict servants!" and she laughed in her sleep.

Landless shrank as from a mortal blow, then broke into a bitter laugh, and said to himself, "Thou art a fool, Godfrey Landless. It were but too easy to forget to-night what thou art and what thou must seem to her. Thou art answered according to thy folly." He sighed impatiently, and withdrawing his gaze from the sleeping face, fell into a sombre reverie.

He was roused to active consciousness by a sudden and death-like pause in the gale. The lightning showed the pall of cloud hanging low, black, and unbroken; but the wind had sunk into an ominous calm. He looked anxiously around him, then softly disengaging himself from Patricia, leaned across her, and shook Regulus awake. The negro started up, stupid from sleep and from his wound.

"What is it, massa?" he queried. "Wake mighty early at Rosemead.... Lawd hab mercy! we 's still on de Chesapeake!"

"We will be in the Chesapeake in a moment," said Landless sternly, "if you stagger about in that way. Sit down and pull your wits together. You are like to need them all directly." He touched Darkeih and said, as her eyes, wide with alarm, opened upon him, "Listen, my wench! Whatever happens, you are to trust yourself to Regulus. He is a strong swimmer and he will take care of you. You hear, Regulus!"

"What is it?" exclaimed Patricia, as he bent over her. "Why have you waked Regulus? And oh! has not that dreadful wind died away?"

"It has stopped, madam, stopped suddenly and utterly," he said gravely. "But it will come upon us from another quarter, and it will bring the sea with it." He raised her, and held her with his arm. "Trust yourself to me when it comes," he said gently. "If I can save you, I will."

There was no time for more. Above them broke a new and more terrible storm. A ball of fire shot from the cloud into the sea; it was followed by a crash that seemed to shake the earth. A cataract of rain descended. From the northeast there swooped upon them a wind to which the gale of an hour before seemed a zephyr. It drove the boat before it as if she had been the bird from which she took her name. It piled wave on wave until the sea ran in mountains. Athwart the storm came a dull booming roar, and above the great hills of water appeared a long ridge crested with white.

"It is coming," said Landless.

Patricia looked up at him with great, despairing, courageous eyes. "I have caused your death," she said. "Forgive me."

There came a vivid flash, and a loud scream from Darkeih. "De lan'! de bressed, bressed, lan'!"

Landless wheeled. Silhouetted against the lit sky he saw a fringe of pines, and below it a low, shelving shore where the waves were breaking in foam and thunder. The Bluebird, driven by the wind, was hurrying towards it in mad bounds. The great wave overtook her, bore her onward with it, and sunk her within fifty feet of the shore.

Ten minutes later Landless, breathless and exhausted, staggered from out the hell of pounding waves and blinding, stinging spray on to the shore. Unlocking Patricia's arms from about his neck, he laid her gently down upon the sand and turned to look for the other occupants of the hapless Bluebird. They were close behind him. In a few minutes the two men, battling against wind and rain, had borne the women out of reach of the waves, and had placed them in the shelter of a low bank of sand. As Landless set his burden down he said reverently, "I thank God, madam."

"And I thank God," she answered, in the same tone.

He tried to shield her from the wind with his body. "It is frightful," he said, "that you should be exposed to such a night. I pray God that you take no harm."

"Would it not be more sheltered higher up the shore, under those trees?"

"Perhaps, but I fear to risk you there with the lightning so near. Later, when the storm subsides, we will try it."

He seated himself so as to screen her as much as possible from wind and rain, and a silence fell upon the party so suddenly snatched from death. Regulus stretched himself upon the sand and pulled Darkeih down beside him. Within a few minutes they were both asleep. The white man and woman sat side by side without speaking, watching the storm.

By degrees it raved itself out. The rain fell in less and less volume, the lightning became infrequent, the thunder pealed less loudly, and the wind died from a hurricane into a breeze. In two hours' time from the swamping of the boat the booming of the sea, and a ragged mass of cloud, lit by an occasional flash and slowly falling away from a pale and watery moon, were the only evidences of the tornado which had raged so lately.

"The storm is over," said Patricia, breaking a long silence.

"Yes," said Landless. "You have nothing to fear now. Would you not like to walk a little? You must be sadly chilled and weary with long sitting."

"Yes, I would," she answered, with a sigh of relief. "Let us walk towards those trees, and see if forest or water be beyond them."

He helped her to her feet, and they left the slaves sleeping upon the ground, and moved slowly, for she was numbed with cold, towards the fringe of pines.

Landless walked beside her without speaking. A while ago she had been simply a woman in danger of death—something for him to protect and to save. He had well nigh forgotten: he knew that she had quite forgotten. She was safe now, and was become once more the lady of the manor to whose soil he was fettered. He had remembered, and she was beginning to remember, for presently she said timidly and sweetly, but with condescension in her voice;—

"I am not ungrateful for all that you have done for me to-night, for saving my life. And, trust me, you will not find your mas—my father, ungrateful either. We will find some way to reward—"

"I neither merit nor desire reward, madam," said Landless, proudly and sadly, "for doing but my duty as a man and as your servant."

"But—" she began kindly, when he interrupted her with sudden passion.

"Unless you wish to cut me to the heart, to bitterly humiliate me, you will not speak of payment for any service I may have done you. I have been a gentleman, madam. For this one night treat me as such."

"I beg your pardon," she said at once.

They reached the belt of trees and entered it. Outside, the broken clouds had permitted an occasional gleam of watery moonshine; within the shadow of the trees it was gross darkness. Above them the wet branches, moved by the wind which still blew strongly, clashed together with a harsh and mournful sound, showering them with heavy raindrops. Their feet sank deeply in cushions of soaked moss and rotting leaves.

"There is nothing to be done here," said Landless. "It is better beneath the open sky."

There came a last, vivid flash of lightning that for a moment lit the wood, showing long colonnades of glistening tree trunks, with here and there a blasted and fallen monster. It showed something more, for within ten feet of them, from out a tangle of dripping, rain-beaten vines looked the face of the murderer of Robert Godwyn.

CHAPTER XVII

LANDLESS AND PATRICIA

For one moment the parties to this midnight encounter stared at each other with starting eyeballs; the next, down came the curtain of darkness between them.

With a cry of terror Patricia seized and clung to Landless's arm, trembling violently, and with her breath coming in long, gasping sobs. Exhausted by the previous terrors of the night, this last experience completely unnerved her—she seemed upon the point of swooning. Divining what would soonest calm her, Landless hurried her out of the wood and down the shore to the bank, beneath which lay the sleeping slaves. Here she sank upon the sand, her frame quivering like an aspen. "That dreadful face!" she said in a low, shaken voice. "It is burned upon my eyeballs. How came it there? Was it—dead?"

"No, no, madam," Landless said soothingly. "'Tis simple enough. The murderer is in hiding within these woods, and we stumbled upon his lair."

She gazed fearfully around her. "I see it everywhere. And may he not follow us down here? Oh, horrible!"

"He is not likely to do that," said Landless, with a smile. "You may rest assured that he is far from this by now."

She drew a long breath of relief. "Oh! I hope he is!" she cried fervently. "It was dreadful! No storm could frighten me as did that face!" and she shuddered again.

"Try not to think of it," he said. "It is gone now; try to forget it."

"I will try," she said doubtfully.

Landless did not answer, and the two sat in silence, watching out the dreary night. But not for long, for presently Patricia said humbly:—

"Will you talk to me? I am frightened. It is so still, and I cannot see you, nor the slaves, only that horrid, horrid face. I see it everywhere."

Landless came nearer to her, and laid one hand upon the skirt of her wet robe. "I am here, close to you, madam," he said; "there can nothing harm you."

He began to speak quietly and naturally of this and that, of what they should do when the day broke, of Regulus's wound, of the storm, of the great sea and its perils. He told her something of these latter, for he knew the sea; piteous tales of forlorn wrecks, brave tales of dangers faced and overcome, of heroic endurance and heroic rescue. He told her tales of a wild, rockbound Devonshire coast with its scattered fisher villages; of a hidden cave, the resort of a band of desperadoes, half smugglers, half pirates, wholly villains; of how this cave had been long and vainly searched for by the authorities; of how, one night, a boy climbed down a great precipice, scaring the seafowl from their nests, and lighted upon this cavern with the smugglers in it, and in their midst a defenseless prisoner whom they were about to murder. How he had shouted and made wailing, outlandish noises, and had sent rocks hurtling down the cliffs, until the wretches thought that all the goblins of land and sea were upon them, and rushed from the cavern, leaving their work undone. Whereupon, the boy reclimbed the cliff, and hastening to the nearest village, roused the inhabitants, who hurried to their boats, and descending upon the long-sought-for cave, surprised the smugglers, cut them down to a man, and rescued the prisoner.

The man who told these things told them well. The wild tales ran like a strain of sombre music through the night. His audience of one forgot her terror and weariness, and listened with eager interest.

"Well—" she said, as he paused.

"That is all. The ruffians were all killed and the prisoner rescued."

"And the boy?"

"Oh, the boy! He went back to his books."

"Did you know him?"

"Yes, I knew him. See, madam, it has quite cleared. How the moon whitens those leaping waves!"

"Yes, it is beautiful. I am glad the prisoner escaped. Was he a fisherman?"

"No; an officer of the Excise—a gallant man, with a wife and many children. Yes, I suppose he prized life."

"And I am glad that the smugglers were all killed."

Landless smiled. "Life to them was sweet, too, perhaps."

"I do not care. They were wicked men who deserved to die. They had murdered and robbed. They were criminals—"

She stopped short, and her face turned from white to red and then to white again, and her eyes sought the ground.

"I had forgotten," she muttered.

The hot color rose to Landless's cheek, but he said quietly:—

"You had forgotten what, madam?"

She flashed a look upon him. "You know," she said icily.

"Yes, I know," he answered. "I know that the perils of this night had driven from your mind several things. For a little while you have thought of, and treated me, as an equal, have you not? You could not have been more gracious to,—let us say, to Sir Charles Carew. But now you have remembered what I am, a man degraded and enslaved, a felon,—in short, the criminal who, as you very justly say, should not be let to live."

She made no answer, and he rose to his feet.

"It is almost day, and the moon is shining brightly. You no longer fear the face in the dark? I will first waken the slaves, and then will push along the shore, and strive to discover where we are."

She looked at him with tears in her eyes. "Wait," she said, putting out a trembling hand. "I have hurt you. I am sorry. Who am I to judge you? And whatever you may have done, however wicked you may have been, to-night you have borne yourself towards a defenseless maiden as truly and as courteously as could have done the best gentleman in the land. And she begs you to forget her thoughtless words."

Landless fell upon his knee before her. "Madam!" he cried, "I have thought you the fairest piece of work in God's creation, but harder than marble towards suffering such as may you never understand! But now you are a pitying angel! If I swear to you by the honor of a gentleman, by the God above us, that I am no criminal, that I did not do the thing for which I suffer, will you believe me?"

"You mean that you are an innocent man?" she said breathlessly.

"As God lives, yes, madam."

"Then why are you here?"

"I am here, madam," he said bitterly, "because Justice is not blind. She is only painted so. Led by the gleam of gold she can see well enough—in one direction. I could not prove my innocence. I shall never be able to do so. And any one—Sir William Berkeley, your father, your kinsman—would tell you that you are now listening to one who differs from the rest of the Newgate contingent, from the coiners and cheats, the cut-throats and highway robbers in whose company he is numbered, only in being hypocrite as well as knave. And yet I ask you to believe me. I am innocent of that wrong."

The moonlight struck full upon his face as he knelt before her. She looked at him long and intently, with large, calm eyes, then said softly and sweetly:—

"I believe you, and pity you, sir. You have suffered much."

He bowed his head, and pressed the hem of her skirt to his lips.

"I thank you," he said brokenly.

"Is there nothing?" she said after a pause, "nothing that I can do?"

He shook his head. "Nothing, madam. You have given me your belief and your divine compassion. It is all that I ask, more than I dared dream of asking an hour ago. You cannot help me. I must dree my weird. I would even ask of your goodness that you say nothing of what I have told you to Colonel Verney or to any one."

"Yes," she said thoughtfully. "If I cannot help you, it were wiser not to speak. I might but make your hard lot harder."

"Again I thank you." He kissed the hem of her robe once more, and rose to his feet with a heart that sat lightly on its throne.

The day began to break. With the first faint flush Landless woke the slaves, who at length yawned and shivered themselves into consciousness of their surroundings. "What are we to do now?" demanded Patricia.

"We had best strike through that belt of woods until we come to some house, whence we may get conveyance for you to Verney Manor."

"Very well. But oh! do not let us enter the forest here where we saw that fearful face. Let us walk along the shore until the light grows stronger. It is still night within the woods."

Landless acquiesced with a smile, and the four—he and Patricia in front, the negroes straying in the rear—set out along the shore. The air was chill and heavy, but there was no wind, and the unclouded sky gave promise of a hot day. In the east the rosy flush spread and deepened, and a pink path stretched itself across the fast subsiding waters. The wet sand dragged at their feet, and made walking difficult; moreover Patricia was chilled and weary, so their progress was slow. There were dark circles beneath her eyes, and her lips had a weary, downward curve; her golden hair, broken from its fastenings, hung in damp, rich masses against her white throat and blue-veined temples, and amidst the enshrouding glory her perfect face looked very small and white and childlike. The magnificent eyes carried in their clear, brown depths an expression new to Landless. Heretofore he had seen in them scorn and dislike; now they looked at him with a grave and wondering pity.

As the sun rose, the shipwrecked party left the shore, and entered the forest. A purple light filled its vast aisles. Far overhead bits of azure gleamed through the rifts in the foliage, but around them was the constant patter and splash of rain drops, falling slow and heavy from every leaf and twig. There was a dank, rich smell of wet mould and rotting leaves, and rain-bruised fern. The denizens of the woodland were all astir. Birds sang, squirrels chattered, the insect world whirred around the yellow autumn blooms and the purpling clusters of the wild grape; from out the distance came the barking of a fox. The sunlight began to fall in shafts of pale gold through openings in the green and leafy world, and to warm the chilled bodies of the wayfarers.

"It is like a bad dream," said Patricia gayly, as Landless held back a great, wet branch of cedar from her path. "All the storm and darkness, and the great hungry waves and the danger of death! Ah! how happy we are to have waked!"

Her glance fell upon Landless's face, and there came to her a sudden realization that there were those in the world, to whom life was not one sweet, bright gala day. She gazed at him with troubled eyes.

"I hope you care to live," she said. "Death is very dreadful."

"I do not think so," he answered. "At least it would be forgetfulness."

She shuddered. "Ah! but to leave the world, the warm, bright, beautiful world! To die on your bed, when you are old—that is different. But to go young! to go in storm and terror, or in horror and struggling as did that man who was murdered! Oh, horrible!"

The thought of the murdered man brought another thought into her mind.

"Do you think," she said, "that we had better tell that we saw the murderer at the first house to which we come, or had we best wait until we reach Verney Manor?"

Landless gave a great start. "You will tell Colonel Verney that?"

She opened her eyes widely. "Why, of course! What else should we do? Is not the country being scoured for him? My father is most anxious that he should be captured. Justice and the weal of the State demand that such a wretch should be punished." She paused and looked at him gravely as he walked beside her with a clouded face. "You say nothing! This man is guilty, guilty of a dreadful crime. Surely you do not wish to shield him, to let him escape?"

"Not so, madam," said Landless in desperation. "But—but—"

"But what?" she asked as he stopped in confusion.

He recovered himself. "Nothing, madam. You are right, of course. But I would not speak before reaching Verney Manor."

"Very well."

Landless walked on, bitterly perplexed and chagrined. The strife and danger of the night, the intoxicating sweetness of the morning hours when he knew himself believed in and pitied by the woman beside him, had driven certain things into oblivion. He had been dreaming, and now he had been plucked from a fool's paradise, and dashed rudely to the ground. Yesterday and the life and thoughts of yesterday, which had but now seemed so far away, pressed upon him remorselessly. And to-morrow! He did not want Roach to be taken. Always there would have been danger to himself and his associates in the capture of the murderer, but now when the vindictive wretch would assuredly attribute his disaster to the man to whom the lightning flash had revealed his presence on the shores of the bay, the danger was trebled. And it was imminent. He had little doubt that another night would see Roach in custody, and he had no doubt at all that the scoundrel would make a desperate effort to save his neck by betraying what he knew of the conspiracy—and thanks to Godwyn's lists he knew a great deal—to Governor and Council.

Patricia began to speak again. "It imports much that men should see that there is no weakness in the arm the law stretches out to seize and punish offenders. My father and the Governor and Colonel Ludlow believe that there is afoot an Oliverian plot—- What is the matter?"

"Nothing, madam."

"You stood still and caught your breath. Are you ill, faint?"

"It is nothing, madam, believe me? You were saying?"

"Oh! the Oliverians! Nothing definite has been discovered as yet, but there is thunder in the air, my father says, and I know that he and the Governor and the rest of the council are very watchful just now. But yesterday my father said that those few hundred men form a greater menace to the Colony than do all the Indians between this and the South Sea."

They walked on in silence for a few moments, and then she broke out. "They are horrible, those grim, frowning men! They are rebels and traitors, one and all, and yet they stand by and shake curses on the heads of true men. They slew the best man, the most gracious sovereign; they trampled the Church under foot, they made the blood of the noble and the good to flow like water, and now when they receive a portion of their deserts, they call themselves martyrs! They, martyrs! Roundhead traitors!"

"Madam," interrupted Landless with a curious smile upon his lips, "did you not know that I was, that I am, what you call a Roundhead?"

"No," she said, "I did not know," and stood perfectly still, looking straight before her down the long vista of trees. He saw her face change and harden into the old expression of aversion. The slaves came up to them, and Regulus asked if 'lil Missy wanted anything. "No, nothing at all," she answered, and walked quietly onward.

Landless, an angry pain tugging at his heart, kept beside her, for they were passing through a deep hollow in the wood where the gnarled and protruding roots of cypress and juniper made walking difficult, and where a strong hand was needed to push aside the wet and pendent masses of vine. Regulus, fifty yards behind them, began to sing a familiar broadside ballad, torturing the words out of all resemblance to English. The rich notes rang sweetly through the forest. Down from the far summit of a pine flashed a cardinal bird, piercing the gloom of the hollow like a fire ball thrown into a cavern. Landless held aside a curtain of glistening leaves that, mingled with purple clusters of fruit, hung across their path. Patricia passed him, then turned impulsively. "You think me hard!" she said. "Many people think me so, but I am not so, indeed.... And there are good Puritans. Major Carrington, they say, is Puritan at heart, and he is a good man and a gentleman.... And you saved my life.... At least you are not like those men of whom I spoke. You would not plot against the good peace which we enjoy! You would not try to array servant against master?"

It was a direct question asked with large, straightforward eyes fixed upon his. He tried to evade it, but she asked again with insistence, and with a faint doubt lurking in her eyes, "If these men are plotting, which God forbid! you know nothing of it? You have great wrongs, but you would take no such dastard way to right them?"

Landless's soul writhed within him, but he told the inevitable lie that was none the less a lie that it was also the truth. He said in a low voice, "I trust, madam, that I will do naught that may misbecome a gentleman."

She was quite satisfied. He saw that he had regained the ground lost by his avowal of a few minutes before, and he cursed himself and cursed his fate.

Soon afterwards they emerged from the forest upon a tobacco patch, from the midst of which rose a rude cabin, in whose doorway stood a woman serving out bowls of loblolly to half a dozen tow-headed children.

Half an hour later, Patricia, rested and refreshed, took her seat behind the oxen, which the owner of the cabin had harnessed up, with much protestation of his eagerness to serve the daughter of Colonel Verney, emptied her purse in the midst of the open-mouthed children, and bade kindly adieu to the good wife. Darkeih curled herself up in the bottom of the cart, and Landless and Regulus walked beside it.

In two hours' time they were at Verney Manor, where they found none but women to greet them, Rendered uneasy by the storm, Woodson had despatched a messenger to Rosemead, who had returned with the tidings that no boat from Verney Manor had reached that plantation. The overseer had ill news with which to greet the Colonel and Sir Charles when at midnight they arrived unexpectedly from Green Spring. Since then every able-bodied man had deserted the plantation. There were no boats at the wharf, no horses in the stables. The master and Sir Charles were gone in the Nancy, the two overseers on horseback. A Sabbath stillness brooded over the plantation, until a negro woman recognized the occupants of the ox-cart lumbering up the road. Then there was noise enough of an exclamatory, feminine kind. The shrill sounds penetrated to the great room, where, behind drawn curtains, surrounded by essences, and an odor of burnt feathers, with Chloe to fan her, and Mr. Frederick Jones to murmur consolation, reclined Mistress Lettice. As Patricia stepped upon the porch, Betty Carrington flew down the stairs and through the hall, and the two met with a little inarticulate burst of cries and kisses. Mistress Lettice in the great room went into hysterics for the fifth time that morning.

CHAPTER XVIII

A CAPTURE

At noon the next day returned the search party, dispatched by the Colonel on receipt of his daughter's information, and headed by Woodson and Sir Charles Carew. In their midst, bound with ropes, and seated behind one of the mounted men, was Roach. His clothing hung from him in tatters, and witnessed, moreover, to the quagmires and mantled pools through which he had struggled; his arm had been injured, and was tied with a bloody rag; blood was caked upon his villainous face, scratched and torn in his breathless bursting through thickets; his red hair fell over his eyes in matted elf-locks; his lips were drawn back in a snarl over discolored fangs; he panted like a dog, his thick red tongue hanging out. He looked hardly human. The man behind whom he rode was Luiz Sebastian.

The party dismounted in the small square, in the midst of the quarters. It being the noon rest, the entire servant population was on hand, and leaving its cabins and smoking messes of bacon and succotash, it hastened to a man to the square, where, beneath the dead tree and its sinister appendage, stood the master, listening to Woodson's account of the capture, and to Sir Charles's airy interpolations. Roach, dragged from the horse by a dozen officious hands, staggered with exhaustion. Luiz Sebastian caught him by the arm and so held him during the ensuing interview.

When the unusual bustle, the neighing of the horses, and the excited voices of the crowd brought the news of the capture to Landless, sitting, sunk in anxious thought, within his cabin, he rose and began to pace to and fro in the narrow room. Past his door hurried men, women, and children on their way to the square. One or two beckoned him to follow, but he shook his head. "If he betray me," he thought, "my fate will come to me soon enough. I will not go to meet it."

In his restless pacing to and fro, he stopped before a shelf where, beside some coarse eating utensils and the heap of tobacco pegs, the cutting of which occupied his spare moments, lay a little worn book. It had been Godwyn's. He opened it at random, and read a few verses. With a heavy sigh he laid his arm along the shelf and rested his burning forehead upon it. "'Let not your heart be troubled,'" he said beneath his breath; and again, "'Let not your heart be troubled.'" He recommenced his pacing up and down the room. "'Peace I leave with you, My peace I give unto you.'" Going to the doorway, he leaned against it and looked out into a world of sunshine, and up to where the topmost branches of a pine slept against the blue. "There may be peace beyond," he said. "I have not found it here."

Down the lane came a murmur of voices; then the overseer's harsh tones; then a light and mocking laugh. Seized by an uncontrollable impulse he left the cabin and directed his steps towards the square. As he passed a cabin some doors from his own, a gaunt figure arose from the doorstep and joined itself to him.

"The murderer is here," said the sepulchral voice of Master Win-Grace Porringer. "Verily the blood hath been taken out of his mouth, and his abominations from between his teeth. Cursed be the shedder of innocent blood!"

"Amen," said Landless; then, "This capture is like to be our ruin. This wretch will not keep silence."

"But he has no proofs. Since you destroyed those lists there exists not a scrap of writing about this affair. And we have covered our tracks as carefully as if we were the cursed heathen of the land upon the warpath. Let him say what he will. The Malignants, besotted fools! will think he lies to save his neck."

"A week ago they might have thought so," said Landless. "But not now. Something has gotten abroad. Already Governor and Council think they smell a plot."

The Muggletonian caught his breath. "How do you know this?"

"No matter how: I know it."

Porringer raised his scarred face to heaven. "God," he said, "we are thy people! Save us! Let destruction come upon them unawares; let them go down a dark and slippery way to death; make them to be as blind and deaf adders that see not the foot of the destroyer! Yea, shake thy hand upon these Malignants and make them a spoil to their servants!" He turned his ghastly face and burning eyes upon Landless. "Curse them with me!" he cried.

Landless shook his head. "Thou, and I look not alike at things, friend," he said.

"Thou art a Laodicean!" cried the other wildly. "Thou hast not an eye single to the Lord's work as had thy father before thee. Thou wouldst not smite the Amalekites hip and thigh, root and branch! One damsel would thou save alive, and for her sake thy heart is soft towards the whole accursed brood! Look to it lest the Lord spew thee out of His mouth! Woe, woe, to him that putteth his hand to the plough and looketh back!" He laughed wildly and tossed out his arms.

"I think thou hast eaten of the Jamestown weed!" said Landless fiercely. "Collect thy senses, man! And speak something less loudly, or Roach's betrayal will be superfluous. As to myself, if I curse not, I act; and as for my motives for what you call luke-warmness, and I call common humanity, you will please to let them alone!"

The excitement faded from the fanatic's face, and he said more quietly, "You are right, friend. I was mad for a moment, mad to see that freedom which is so near us so imperiled. I meant not to quarrel with you who have shown in the conduct of this work the discernment of a young Daniel, yea, who have so borne yourself, that I have grown to care for you as I never thought to care again for human being. I have prayed much that you should be brought from the twilight of Calvinism into the pure light wherein walk the disciples of the blessed Ludovick."

They reached the square and mingled with the motly crowd that lined its sides, leaving the centre occupied only by the murderer, his captors, and the master. Followed by the Muggletonian, Landless made his way to where the yellow locks of young Dick Whittington towered above the crowd. The boy saw him coming, and edging past a knot of blacks, met him in a little open space, whose only occupants were two or three women, and an Indian squatting upon the ground. Leaning against a pine, and fixing his gaze and, to all appearance, his attention upon the central group where the overseer was just finishing a circumstantial account of the chase, Landless said quietly:—

"You were of the party that took him?"

"That I was!" answered the boy gleefully. "Losh! but it was fun!" His blue eyes danced with impish delight; a noiseless laugh showed all his strong white teeth. "We went straight to the spot where you and Mistress Patricia saw him by the lightning. There the dogs struck his trail and the fun commenced. Over streams and fallen trees, and chinquepin ridges; through bogs and myrtle thickets and miles of grape vines—swounds! but it was hot work! Just look at the scratches on my face and hands! Joyce Whitbread wouldn't know me! The Court spark, he wore a mask and saved his beauty. He's a well-plucked one, though, took the lead and kept it, and when it was over, treated us to usquebaugh at Luckey Doughty's store. Well, we run the fox to earth in a Chickahominy village. Lord! I'm sorry for the half king of the Chickahominies! He'll have to answer to Governor and Council for letting red fox burrow in his village. Found him squatted in a sassafras patch. Snarled and fought and tried to bite like the beast he is. Woodson and the Court spark took him."

"Do you know what will be done with him now?"

"He'll be taken on to the gaol at the court-house."

"That is five miles from here," said Landless.

"Yes, near to the village where we took him. He'll be kept there until they can try him. And they'll make short work of him. He'll be food for crows directly."

The throng pressed upon them, forcing them nearer to the group beneath the dead tree. The overseer had finished his account, and the master was clearing his throat to speak. Landless found himself upon the inner verge of the mass of spectators, directly opposite the murderer, and confronted by him with a look so dark, wild and malignant, that he could not doubt the intention that lay behind those scowling eyes. Luiz Sebastian, still with the murderer's arm in his grasp, gave him a peculiar look which he could not translate. In the background he saw Trail's sinister face peering over the shoulder of an Indian.

"You dog!" said the planter, addressing himself directly to Roach. "What have you to say for yourself?"

The murderer made an uncertain sound with his dry lips, and his bloodshot eyes roamed around the circle from one staring face to another, until they returned to rest upon the watchful, amber-hued countenance beside him.

"Speak!" said his master sternly.

"I'll say nothing," was the dogged reply, "until I stands my trial. I demands a fair trial."

"Remember that this is your last chance to speak to me, to speak to any one in authority before you are tried. Of course you will hang for this. Have you anything to say? Do you wish to speak to me in private?"

The murderer raised his head, and shaking the tangled hair from about his face, cast at Landless, standing ten paces beyond the planter, such a look of deadly and blasting hatred, that for a moment the blood ran cold in the young man's veins. He set his teeth and braced himself to meet the blow at plans and hopes and life that should follow such a look.

To his astonishment the blow did not fall. Roach changed the basilisk gaze with which he had regarded him to a vacant stare.

"I've naught to say," he whined, "except that I hopes your honor will see that I has a fair trial—no d—d Tyburn or Newgate hocus-pocussing."

The master beckoned to the overseer. "Take him away," he said. "Take two or three men and carry him on to the gaol."

He turned on his heel and walked to where Sir Charles Carew leaned against a tree, idly flicking the mud from his boots with his riding cane. Landless standing near and listening with strained ears heard the master say in answer to the other's lifted brows:—

"Nothing to be learnt in that quarter. If there's rebellion brewing, he knows nothing of it."

Fresh horses were brought from the stables. "You, Luiz Sebastian, Taylor, and Mathew," said the overseer, swinging himself into the saddle. The men designated mounted, and Roach, bound and scowling, was hoisted to his former seat behind Luiz Sebastian. The cavalcade started. As the horse that bore the double load passed Landless, the murderer twisted himself about in his seat, and, with a venomous look, spat at him. Luiz Sebastian smiled evilly.

The shaven head and fleshless face of Win-Grace Porringer protruded themselves over Landless's shoulder.

"What does it mean?" he muttered.

"God knows," answered the other. "Come to the trysting place to-night. We must act, and act quickly."

That night ten men met in the deserted hut on the marsh, having stolen with the caution of Indians from their respective plantations. Five were men who had fought at Edgehill and Naseby and Worcester, or had followed Cromwell through the breach at Drogheda. Four were victims of the Act of Uniformity; darker, sterner, more determined if possible, than the veterans of the New Model. The tenth man was Landless. When, late at night, he and Porringer crept stealthily back to the quarters, it was with the conviction that this was the last time they should so steal through the darkness. The date of the rising had been fixed for the thirteenth of September; this night, by Landless's advice, it was brought forward to the tenth—and it was now the sixth.

Groping his way past the slumbering forms of the three other occupants of his cabin, Landless threw himself down upon his pallet with a heavy sigh.

"Liberty!" he said beneath his breath. "Goddess, whom I and mine have sought through long years, whom once we thought we held, and waked to find thee gone,—once I thought thee fairer than aught beside; thought no price too great to pay for thee. But now!"

He hid his face in his hands with a stifled groan. When at length he fell into a troubled sleep, it was to see again a storm-tossed boat, and a woman's face, set like a star against the blackness of the night.

CHAPTER XIX

THE LIBRARY OF THE SURVEYOR-GENERAL

At a long, low table stood Mistress Betty Carrington, her slender figure enveloped in an apron of blue dowlas, her sleeves of fine holland rolled above her elbows, and her white and rounded arms plunged deep into a great bowl filled with the purple globes of the wild grape. A row of children knelt on the brick floor at her feet, busily stripping the fruit from the stems, and negresses, hard by, strained with sinewy hands the crimson juice from the pulpy mass into jars of earthenware. To this group suddenly entered a breathless urchin.

"Ohé, mistis! de Gov'nor an' Massa Peyton comin' up de road!"

Betty suspended her operations with a little cry. "The Governor!" she exclaimed in dismay. "And my father is gone a-processioning;—and my gown is not seemly;—and he cannot be kept waiting!" She threw off her apron, dipped her hands into the water the slaves poured for her, and was at the hall door in time to courtesy to the Governor, as, followed by a groom, and attended by Mr. Peyton, he rode up to the house.

With the agility of youth his Excellency sprung from his horse, threw the reins to the groom, and advanced to greet the lady. A richly laced riding-suit became his still slight and elegant figure to a marvel; his gilt-spurred, Spanish leather boots were of the newest, most approved cut; his periwig was fresh curled, and framed with distinction a handsome, if somewhat withered, countenance. He doffed his Spanish hat with a bow and flourish: Betty courtesied profoundly.

"Welcome to Rosemead, your Excellency."

"I greet you well, pretty Mistress Betty," said the Governor, and took a governor's privilege. Mr. Peyton looked as though he would have liked to follow his Excellency's example, but was fain to content himself with the lady's hand, resigned to the respectful pressure of his lips with a charming blush and a dropping of long-fringed eyelids.

"Where is your father, sweetheart?" demanded the Governor.

"Ah! your Excellency, he is unfortunate. The vestry hath appointed this day for the examination of boundaries in this parish, and as his Majesty's Surveyor-General he leads the procession. But will not your Excellency await his return? He will be here anon, and with him Colonel Verney."

"Then will I wait, pretty one; for I have weighty matters to discuss both with him and with Dick Verney."

Betty ushered them into the great room, cool, dark, and fragrant of roses.

"If your Excellency will permit me to withdraw, I will order some refreshment for you after your long ride."

The Governor sank into an armchair, and smiled graciously.

"Faith! a bit of pasty comes not amiss after a morning canter. And prithee see to the sack thyself, Mistress Betty. And a dish of pippins and cheese," continued the Governor, meditatively, "and a rasher of bacon."

"There was a fine comb taken from the hive this morning. Will your Excellency choose a bit? And there are dates, sent my father by the captain of the Barbary vessel, and a quince tart—"

"We will taste of it all," said his Excellency, graciously, "and afterwards a pipe and a saucer of sweet scented, and your company, my love. Mr. Peyton, the lady may find the honeycomb too heavy for her lifting. We will excuse you to her assistance."

"I am your Excellency's most obedient servant," quoth Mr. Peyton with due submission, and hastened after his blushing mistress.

The Governor, left alone, strolled to the window and looked out upon the Chesapeake, lying blue and unruffled beneath the dazzling sunshine; to the mantel-piece, and smelt of the roses in the blue china bowl; to the spinet, and picked out "Here's to Royal Charles" with one finger;—and finally brought up before a corner cupboard, found the key in the door, turned it, and came upon the Surveyor-General's library.

"H'm, what has he here?" soliloquized his Excellency. "'Purchas; His Pilgrimes,' of course; 'General History of Virginia, New England and the Summer Isles,' well and good; 'Good News from Virginia,' humph! that must have been before my time; 'Public Good without Private Interest,' humph! What's this? 'Areopagitica,' John Milton! John Hypocrite and Parricide! A pretty author, and a pretty cause he advocates,—I thank God there are no schools and no printing presses in this colony, nor are like to be,—and a courageous Surveyor-General to keep by him such pestilent stuff in the present year of grace. 'Abuses Stript and Whipt,' 'Anglia Rediva,' 'Diary of Nehemiah Wallington,' 'Bastwick's Litany!' Miles Carrington, Miles Carrington! I have my eye on thee! Thou hadst need to walk warily! 'Zion's Plea against Prelacy,' damnation! 'Speech of Mr. Hampden,' death and hell! 'Eikonoklastes,' may the foul fiend fly away with my soul!"

And the Governor closed the cupboard door with a bang, and, with a very red and frowning face, went back to his seat, and there sank into a reverie, which lasted until the entrance of Mistress Betty and Mr. Peyton, followed by two slaves bearing an ample repast.

An hour later came home the Surveyor-General, bringing with him Colonel Verney, Sir Charles Carew, and Captain Laramore.

The Surveyor-General made stately apologies to his Excellency for his unavoidable absence: his Excellency, holding himself very erect, heard him out, and then said coldly, "Major Carrington may rest at ease. I was sufficiently amused."

"Truly the county knows Mr. Peyton's powers of entertainment," said the Surveyor-General with a bow and smile for that young gentleman.

"Mr. Peyton had other occupation," said the Governor dryly. "And I fear that his is too cavalier a wit, and that his sonnets and madrigals savor too much of loyalty to the Anointed of the Lord and to His Church to have proved acceptable to the worshipful company with whom I have been engaged. I have to congratulate his Majesty's Surveyor-General on the possession of such a library as, I dare swear, is to be found in no other house in this, his Majesty's *loyal* dominion of Virginia."

Carrington glanced towards the cupboard, and bit his lip.

"I am pleased," he said stiffly, "that your Excellency hath found wherewithal to pass an idle hour."

"It is, indeed, a choice collection," said the Governor, with a smooth tongue, but with an angry light in his eyes. "May I ask by whom it was chosen; who it was that so carefully culled nightshade and poison oak?"

"*I* choose my own reading," said Carrington haughtily. "And I see not why Sir William Berkeley should concern himself—"

"This passes!" exclaimed the Governor, giving rein to his fury and striking his hand against the table. "It doth concern me much, Major Carrington, both as a true man, and as the Governor of this Colony, the representative of his blessed Majesty, King Charles the Second, may all whose enemies, private and open, be confounded! that a gentleman who holds a high office in this Colony should have in his possession—ay! and read, too, for 'tis a well-thumbed copy—that foul emanation from a fouler mind, that malicious, outrageous, damnable, proscribed book, called 'Eikonoklastes!'"

"If Sir William Berkeley doubts my loyalty—" began Carrington fiercely.

"Major Carrington, you are too popular a man!" broke in the Governor as fiercely. "When, upon that black day, ten years ago, the usurper's frigates entered the Chesapeake, and taking us unprepared, compelled (God forgive me!) my submission, who but Miles Carrington welcomed and entertained the four commissioners (commissioners from a Roundhead Parliament to a King's Governor!)? Who but Miles Carrington was hand in glove with the shopkeeper Bennett and the renegade Matthews? Oh! they used their power mildly, I deny it not! They were gracious and long-suffering; they left to the loyal gentlemen, their sometime friends, life and lands; they contented themselves with banishing a loyal Governor to his own manor-house, and not, as they might have done, to the wilderness, to perish amongst the savages. O, they were exemplary despots! What, when a turn of Fortune's wheel brought them up, could grateful, loyal gentlemen, could a grateful King's Governor do, but follow the example set them and be civil to the officers of the late Commonwealth, and something more than civil to the gentleman who so gracefully avowed that he had but bowed to the times, and that the restored sovereign had no more faithful subject than he? When his Majesty was graciously pleased to continue that gentleman (at the solicitation of his loyal kindred at home) in the office of Surveyor-General to this colony, sure, we all rejoiced. It is not with the past of Major Carrington that I quarrel; it is with the present. In his case, that which should speak loudest for his recovered loyalty is wanting. Others there are who have that witness. Let Mr. Digges ride abroad, and from his cabin-door some prick-eared cur cried out, 'Renegade!' (Pardon me, the word is not mine.) The Oliverian and schismatic servants spit at him. Is it so with Major Carrington? By G—d, no! These people uncover to him as though he were the arch rebel himself. Speak of his Majesty's Surveyor-General before an Oliverian, and the fellow pricks up his ears like a charger that scents the battle. Nay, I am told that in their conventicles the schismatics pray for him, that he may be brought back into the fold, and may become a second Moses, and lead them out of Egypt! Even the Quakers have a good word for him. Major Carrington asks me if I question his loyalty. I answer that I know not, but I do know that the discontented and mutinous of the land do look upon him with too favorable a regard. And his loyalty is of that tender age that it may well be susceptible to the influence of the evil eye." The Governor, who was now in a white heat of passion, stopped for breath.

"Sir William Berkeley, you shall answer to me for this!" said the Surveyor-General, with white lips.

"With all the pleasure in life," said the Governor, clapping his hand to his rapier.

Carrington folded his arms. "Not now," he said, with stern courtesy. "I believe your Excellency sleeps at Verney Manor? I, too, am invited thither.

There, and it please you, we will adjust our little difference. For the present, you are my guest."

The Governor choked down his passion, though with difficulty. "Till to-night then—" he began, when Colonel Verney interposed.

"Neither to-night, nor at any other time," he said sturdily. "Gadzooks! have not his Majesty's servants enough on hand without employing their time in pinking one another? Here are the Chickahominies restive, and those plaguy Ricahecrians amongst us, and the Nansemond Independents prophesying the end of the world, and the witches' trial coming on, and the Quakers to be routed out, and on top of it all this story that Ludlow brings of a redemptioner's assertion that there is afoot an Oliverian plot. And his Majesty's Governor, and his Majesty's Surveyor-General with drawn rapiers! For shame, gentlemen! Major Carrington, my good friend and neighbor, for whose loyalty to our present gracious sovereign I would answer for as I would for my own, forget the hasty words which I am sure Sir William Berkeley already regrets. Come, Sir William, acknowledge that you were over-choleric."

"I'll be d—d if I do!" cried the Governor.

"We meet to-night," said the Surveyor-General.

The Colonel turned to Sir Charles Carew, who had been a highly amused spectator of this little scene.

"Charles," he said impressively, "report hath it that you have figured in more affairs of honor than any man of your age at court. You should be a nice judge of such gear. Join me in assuring these gentlemen that they may be reconciled, and their honor receive not the least taint; and so avert a duel which would be a scandal to the community, and a menace to the state."

Sir Charles glanced from the pacific Colonel to the sternly collected Surveyor-General, and thence to the fiery Governor, whose white, jeweled fingers twitched with impatience.

"Certainly, sir," he said lazily, "you are welcome to my poor opinion, which is that, considering the nature of the provocation, and the standing of the parties, there is one way out of the affair with honor."

"Exactly!" said the Colonel eagerly.

Sir Charles locked his hands behind his head. "There's a very pretty piece of ground behind your orchard, sir," he said, dreamily regarding the ceiling. "I noticed it the other day, and sink me! if I did not wish for Harry Bellasses with whom I have fought three times. 'Tis ever a word and a blow with Harry! The light just at sunset is excellent, though your twilight cometh over soon. May I venture to suggest to your Excellency that your *riposte* is more brilliant than safe? Major Carrington, your parade is somewhat out of fashion. I could teach you the newest French mode in five minutes."

"I am obliged for your offer, sir," said the Surveyor-General dryly. "The other has served my turn, and must do so again."

"Sir Charles Carew will do me the honor to be my second?" asked the Governor of that gentleman, who answered with a low bow, and a "The honor is mine."

"Captain Laramore?" said the Surveyor-General.

"At your service, Major," cried the Captain, a dashing, black-a-vised personage, with large gold rings in his ears, a plume a yard long in his castor, and a general Drawcansir air.

"Will Captain Laramore fight?" inquired Sir Charles. "I have had the honor of changing the date for sailing for several gentlemen of his profession."

"Even so accomplished a swordsman as Sir Charles Carew is allowed to be, hath yet a lesson to learn," said the doughty captain.

"And that is—"

"Pride shall have a fall—to-night."

Sir Charles smiled politely. "The ship that is anchored off yonder point is yours, is it not? Would you not like to take a last look at her? Or to leave instructions for your lieutenant and successor? There is time for you to gallop to the point and back."

"Am I to have the honor of crossing swords with you, Colonel Verney?" asked Mr. Peyton.

"No, sir!" exclaimed the vexed Colonel. "You are not! I wash my hands of this foolish fray. William Berkeley, I have never scrupled to tell thee when I thought thee in the wrong. I think so now. Charles, thou art an impudent fellow! I have it in my mind to wish that the Captain may give thee the lesson he talks of."

"Thank you, sir," drawled the gentleman addressed. "Mr. Peyton looks quite disconsolate. Sink me! if it's not a shame to leave him out in the cold. If he will wait his turn I will be happy to oblige him when I have disposed of the Captain."

"You will do no such thing!" retorted his kinsman. "Mr. Peyton, take your hand off your sword! At least there shall be two sane men at this meeting. I suppose, gentlemen, you agree with me that this affair cannot be kept too private? To that end you had best ride with me to Verney Manor, and there have it out on this plot of ground Charles talks of. It is at least retired."

"'Tis a most sweet spot," said Sir Charles.

"Good!" quoth the Governor. "And now that this little matter is settled, I am once more, and for the present, sir, simply your obliged guest and servant," and he bowed to the Surveyor-General.

Carrington returned the bow. "We will drink to our better acquaintance to-night. Pompey! the sack and the aqua vitæ. And, Pompey! a handful of mint."

The company fell to drinking, and then to tobacco. The Governor, whose fits of passion were as short as they were violent, arrived by rapid degrees at a pitch of high good humor. The company listened gravely for the fiftieth time to stories of the court of the first James; of Buckingham's amours, of the beauty of Henrietta Maria, of a visit to Paris, an interview with Richelieu, a duel with a captain of Mousquetaires, a kiss imprinted upon the fair hand of Anne of Austria. The charmed stream of the old courtier's reminiscences flowed on—he stopped for breath, and Sir Charles took the word and proceeded to unfold before their dazzled eyes a gorgeous phantasmagoria. The King, the Duke, Sedley and Buckingham, Mesdames Castlemaine, Stuart and Gwynne, Dryden and Waller and Lely, the King's house, the Queen's chapel, the Queen's duennas, the Tityre Tus, Paul's Walk, the Russian Ambassador, astrologers, orange girls, balls, masques, pageants, duels, the court of Louis le Grand, the King's hunting parties, Madame d'Orleans, Olympe di Mancini.

The Governor listened with dilating nostrils and sparkling eyes; Colonel Yerney's vexed countenance smoothed itself; Captain Laramore, sitting with outstretched legs, and head hidden in clouds of tobacco smoke, rumbled from out that obscurity laughter and strange oaths. Even Mr. Peyton, after vainly trying to fix his attention upon the construction of a sonnet to his mistress's eyebrow, succumbed to the enchantment, and sat with parted lips, drinking in wonders; but the Surveyor-General, though he listened courteously, listened with forced smiles and with an attention which was hard to preserve from wandering.

In the midst of a brilliant account of the nuptials of the Chevalier de Grammont came an interruption.

"De horses am fed an' brought roun', massa."

The Governor started up. "Rat me, if good sack and good stories make not a man forget all else beside! Colonel Verney, I wish you, as lieutenant of this shire, to ride with me to this Chickahominy village where I have promised an audience to the half king of the tribe. Plague on the unreasonable vermin! Why can they not give way peaceably? If the colony needs and takes their lands, it leaves them a plenty elsewhere. Let them fall back towards the South Sea. Sir Charles, I grieve for the necessity, but we must leave the court and come back to the wilderness. Gentlemen, will you ride with Verney and me, or shall we part now to meet at sunset in his orchard?"

"We had best ride with your Excellency," said Carrington gravely. "I like not the temper of the Chickahominies, who ever mean most when they say least. And these roving Ricahecrians, their guests, are of a strange and fierce aspect. It is as well to go in force."

"Those vagrants from the Blue Mountains have been here overlong," said the Governor. "I shall send them packing! Well, gentlemen, since we are to have the pleasure of your company, boot and saddle is the word!"

CHAPTER XX

WHEREIN THE PEACE PIPE IS SMOKED

The sun had some time passed the meridian when the party saw through the widening glades of the forest the gleam of a great river, and upon its bank an Indian village of perhaps fifty wigwams, set in fields of maize and tobacco, groves of mulberries, and tangles of wild grape. The titanic laughter of Laramore and the drinking catch which Sir Charles trolled forth at the top of a high, sweet voice had announced their approach long before they pushed their horses into the open; and the population of the village was come forth to meet them with song and dance and in gala attire. The soft and musical voices of the young women raised a kind of recitative wherein was lauded to the skies the virtue, wisdom and power of the white father who had come from the banks of the Powhatan to those of the Pamunkey to visit his faithful Chickahominies, bringing (beyond doubt) justice in his hand. The deeper tones of the men chimed in, and the mob of naked children, bringing up the rear of the procession, added their shrill voices to the clamor, which, upon the booming in of a drum and the furious shaking of the conjurer's rattle, became deafening.

The chant came to an end, but the orchestra persevered. Ten girls left the throng, formed themselves into line, and advancing one after the other with a slow and measured motion, laid at the feet of the Governor (who had dismounted) platters of parched maize, beans and chinquepins, with thin maize cakes. They were succeeded by two stalwart youths bearing, slung upon a pole between them, a large buck which they deposited upon the ground before the white men. There came a tremendous crash from the drum, and a discordant scream from a long pipe made of a reed. The crowd opened, and from out their midst stalked a venerable Indian.

"My fathers are welcome," he said gravely.

"Where is the half king?" demanded the Governor sharply. "I have no time for these fooleries. Make them stop that infernal racket, and lead us to your chiefs at once."

The Indian frowned at this cavalier reception of the village civilities, but he waved his arm for the music to cease, and proceeded to conduct the visitors through a lane made by two rows of dusky bodies and staring faces, to a large wigwam in the centre of the village. Before this hut stood a mulberry tree of enormous size, and seated upon billets of wood in the shade of its spreading branches were the half king of the tribe and the principal men of the village.

Their faces and the upper portions of their bodies were painted red—the color of peace. They wore mantles of otter skins, and from their ears depended strings of pearl and bits of copper. To the earring of the half king were attached two small, green snakes that twisted and writhed about his neck; his body had been oiled and then plastered with small feathers of a brilliant blue, and upon his head was fastened a stuffed hawk with extended wings.

To one side of this group stood a band of Indians, two score or more in number, who differed in appearance and attire from the Chickahominies. The iron had entered the soul of the latter; they had the bearing of a subject race. Not so with the former. They were men of great size and strength, with keen, fierce faces; their clothing was of the scantiest possible description; ornaments they had, but of a peculiar kind—necklaces and armlets of human bones, belts in which long tufts of silk grass were interwoven with a more sinister fibre. They leaned on great bows, and each sternly motionless figure looked a bronze Murder.

The chief of the Chickahominies raised his eyes from the ground as the Governor and his party entered the circle. "My white fathers are welcome," he said. "Let them be seated," and looked at the ground again. The "white fathers" took possession of half a dozen billets, and waited in silence the next move of the game. After a while, the half king lifted from the log beside him a pipe with a stem a yard long and a bowl in which an orange might have rested. An Indian, rising, went to where a fire burned beneath a tripod, and returning with a live coal between his fingers, calmly and leisurely lighted the pipe. The half king, still in dead silence, lifted it to his lips, smoked for five minutes, and handed it to the Indian, who bore it to the Governor. The Governor drew two or three tremendous whiffs and passed it on to Colonel Verney, who in his turn transferred it to the Surveyor-General. When the monster pipe had been smoked by each of the white men, it went the round of the savages. An Indian summer haze began to settle around the company. Through it the patient gazing throng on the outskirts of the circle became shadowy, impalpable; the face of the half king, now hidden in shifting smoke wreaths, now darkly visible, like that of an eastern idol before whom incense is burned. There was no sound save the wash of the waters below them, the sighing of the wind, the drone of the cicadas in the trees. The Indians sat like statues, but the white men were more restive. The elders managed to restrain their impatience, but Laramore began to whistle, and when checked by a look from the Governor, turned to Sir Charles with a comically disconsolate face and a shrug of the shoulders. Whereupon the latter drew from his pocket, dice and a handful of gold pieces. Laramore's face brightened, and the two, screened from observation by the Colonel's shoulders, which were of the broadest, fell to playing noiselessly, cursing beneath their breath. Mr. Peyton leaned his elbow on his knee, and his chin upon his hand, and allowed the dreamy beauty of the afternoon to overflow a poetic soul.

At length, and when the patience of the whites was well-nigh exhausted, the pipe came back to where the half king sat with lowered eyes and impassive face. He laid it down beside him and rose to his feet, gathering his mantle around him.

"My white fathers are welcome," he said in a sonorous voice. "Very welcome to the Chickahominies is the face of the white father, who rules in the place of the great white father across the sea. Their corn feast is not yet, and yet my people rejoice. Our hearts were glad when my father sent word that he would this day visit his faithful Chickahominies. Our ears are open: let my father speak."

"I thank Harquip and his people for their welcome," said the Governor coldly. "I have ever found them full of words. They profess loyalty to the great white father beyond the seas, but they forget his good laws and disobey his officers. I am weary of their words."

"Tell me," said Harquip, with a sombre face, "are they good laws which drive us from our hunting grounds? Are they good laws which take from us our maize fields? Does the great white father love to hear our women cry for food? or is his heart Indian and longs for the sound of the war whoop?"

"That is a threat," the Governor said sternly.

The Indian waved his hands. "Have we not smoked the peace pipe?" he said coldly.

"Humph!" said the Governor then, "I am not come to listen to idle complaints. Your grievances as to the land shall be laid before the next Assembly, and it will pass judgment upon them—justly and righteously, of course."

"Ugh!" said the Indian.

"I am here," continued the Governor, "to ask certain questions of the Chickahominies, and to lay certain commands upon them which they will do well to obey."

"Let my father speak," said the Indian calmly.

"Why did you shelter in your village the man with the red hair? Word was sent to all the tribes, to the Nansemonds, the Wyanokes, the Cheskiacks, the Paspaheghs, the Pamunkeys, the Chickahominies, that he should be delivered up if they found him among them. Why did the Chickahominies hide him?"

"In the night time, the red fox came to the village of the Chickahominies and burrowed there. The eyes of my people were closed: they saw him not."

"Humph! Why did you not carry your guns to the Court House when the tribes were ordered to do so, a fortnight ago, and leave them there, taking in exchange roanoke and fire-water?"

"My fathers asked much," said the half king gloomily. "My young men love their sticks-that-speak. They love to see the deer go down before them like maize before the hail storm. My fathers asked much."

"How many guns has your village?"

"Five," was the prompt reply.

"Humph! To-morrow you will deliver ten guns to the captain of the trainband at the court-house. When do these men," pointing to the stranger band, "return to their tribe?"

"They are our friends. They wait to dance the corn dance with us. Then will they return to the Blue Mountains, and will tell the Ricahecrians of the great things they have seen, and of the wisdom and power of my white fathers."

"When is your corn feast?"

"Seven suns hence."

"They must be gone to-morrow."

The face of the half king darkened, and there was a slight, instantly repressed movement among the circle of braves.

"My father asks very much," said the half king with emphasis.

"Not more than I can, and will, enforce," said the Governor sternly, and getting to his feet as he spoke. "You, Harquip, shall be answerable to me and to the Council for these men's departure to-morrow. If by sunrise of the next morning their canoes are far up the river, headed for the Blue Mountains, if by the same hour the guns which you have retained in defiance of the express decree of the Assembly, be given up to those at the Court House, then will I overlook your hiding the man with the red hair, and the Assembly will listen to your complaints as to your hunting grounds. Disobey, and my warriors shall come, each with a stick-that-speaks in his hand. I have spoken," and the Governor beckoned to the servants who held the horses.

The half king rose also. "My white father shall be obeyed," he said with gloomy dignity. "He is stronger than we. Otee has been angry with the red men for many years. He is gone over to the palefaces and helps their god against the red men. My young men shall take their guns back to the palefaces to-morrow, and shall bring back fire-water, and we will drink, and forget that the days of Powhatan are past and that Otee fights against us. Also when the Pamunkey is red with to-morrow's sunset, my brothers from the Blue Mountains shall turn their faces homewards. My father is content?"

"I am content," said the Governor.

"There is a thing which my brothers have to say to my white fathers," continued the half king. "Will they hear the great chief, Black Wolf?"

The Governor pulled out a great watch, glanced at it, and sighed resignedly. "Gentlemen, have patience a moment longer. Harquip, I will listen to the Ricahecrian until the shadow of that tree reaches the fire. What says he?"

The half king spoke to the strangers in their own tongue—their ranks broke, and an Indian stalked forward to the centre of the circle. His tall, powerful, nearly nude figure was thickly tatooed with representations of birds and beasts; he wore an armlet of a dull, yellow metal ("Gold! by the Eternal!" ejaculated the Governor to Colonel Verney); over his naked, deeply scarred breast hung three strings of hideous mementoes of torture stakes; the belt that held tomahawk and scalping knife was fringed with human hair; beside his streaming scalplock was stuck the dried hand of an enemy. The face beneath was cunning, relentless, formidable. He spoke in his own language, and the half king translated.

"Black Wolf is a great chief. In his village in the Blue Mountains are fifty wigwams—the largest is his. There are a hundred braves—he leads the war parties. The Monacans run like deer, the hearts of the Tuscaroras become soft, they hide behind their squaws! Black Wolf is a great chief. Seven moons of cohonks have passed since the Ricahecrians sharpened their hatchets and came down from the mountains to where the waters of Powhatan fall over many rocks. There they met the palefaces. The One above all was angry with his Ricahecrians. They saw for the first time the guns of the palefaces. They thought they were gods who spat fire at them and slew them with thunder. Their hearts became soft, and they fled before the strange gods. Some the palefaces slew, and some they took prisoner. Black Wolf saw his brother, the great chief Grey Wolf, fall. The Ricahecrians went back to the Blue Mountains, and their women raised the death chant for those whom they left stretched out on the bank of the great river.... Seven times had the maize ripened, when Black Wolf led a war party against a tribe that dwelt on the banks of the Pamunkey where a fallen pine might span it. The waters ran red with blood. When there were no more Monacans to kill, when the fires had burnt low, Black Wolf looked down the waters of the Pamunkey. He had heard that it ran into a great water that was salt, whose further bank a man could not see. He had heard that the palefaces rode in canoes that had wings, great and white. He thought he would like to know if these things were true, or if they were but tales of the singing birds. To find out, Black Wolf and his young men dipped their oars into the water of the Pamunkey, and rowed towards the moonrise. In the morning they met twenty men of the Pamunkeys in three canoes. The Pamunkeys lie deep in the slime of the river; the eels eat them; their scalps shall hang before the wigwams of Black Wolf and his young men. In the afternoon, they drove their canoes into the reeds and went into the forest to find meat. Black Wolf's arrow brought down a buck and they feasted. Afterwards they caught a hunter who saw only the deer he was chasing. They tied him to a tree and made merry with him. When he was dead, they drew their boats from out the reeds, and rowed on down the broadening river. The next day, at the time of the full sun-power, they came to this village. Many years before the palefaces came, the Chickahominies were a great nation, reaching to the foot of the Blue Mountains, and then were they and the Ricahecrians friends and allies. When Black Wolf showed them the totem of his tribe upon his breast, they welcomed him and his young men. That was ten suns ago. Black Wolf and his young men have seen many things. When they go back to the Blue Mountains, the Ricahecrians will think they listen to singing birds. They will tell of the great salt water, of the boats with wings, of the palefaces, of their fields of maize and tobacco, of the black men who serve them, of their temples, werowances and women. They will tell of the great white father who rules, of his power, his wisdom, his open hand—"

"I thought it would come at last," quoth the Governor. "What does he want, Harquip?"

"The Ricahecrian starts for his wigwam in the Blue Mountains to-morrow as my father commands. He says: 'Shall I not return to my people with a gift from the great white father in my hand?'"

The Governor laughed. "Let one of your young men go to the court-house. I will give him an order for beads, for a piece of red cloth, and yes, rat me! he shall have a mirror! I hope he is satisfied!"

The half king's eyes gleamed covetously. "My father gives large gifts. He has indeed an open hand. But the Ricahecrian desires another thing. He says: 'Seven years ago, at the falls of the Powhatan, Black Wolf saw his brother fall before the stick-that-speaks of the palefaces. Grey Wolf was a great chief. The village in the Blue Mountains mourned very much.

Nicotee, his squaw, went wailing into the land of shadows. His son hath seen but seven moons of corn, but he dreams of the day when he shall sharpen the hatchet against the slayers of his father.... The Chickahominies have told Black Wolf that his brother was wounded and not slain by the palefaces. They brought him captive to their great board wigwams. There they tied him not to the torture stake; they knew that a Ricahecrian laughs at the pine splinters. They tortured his spirit. They made him a woman. The great chief of the Ricahecrians no longer throws the tomahawk—the guns of the palefaces are about him. He dances the corn dance no more—his back is bowed with burdens. His arrow brings not down the fleeing deer, he tracks not the bear to his den—he toils like a squaw in the fields of the palefaces. Black Wolf says to the white father: "Give back the Sagamore to the Ricahecrians, to his son, to the village by the falling stream in the Blue Mountains. Then will the Ricahecrians be friends with the palefaces forever." To-morrow Black Wolf and his young men row towards the sunset; let the captive chief be in their midst. This is the gift which Black Wolf asks of his white fathers. He has spoken.'"

In the midst of a dead silence the half king took his seat and studied the ground. The Chickahominies, squatted round the circle, stirred not a finger, and the outer row of spectators, motionless against a background of interlacing branches patched with vivid blue, seemed a procession in tapestry. The Ricahecrians and their formidable chief maintained a stony gloom. Whatever interest they felt in the fate of their captive chief was carefully concealed. The sun, now hanging, broad and red, low in the heavens might have been the Gorgon's head and the whole village staring at it.

The Governor began to laugh. Sir Charles chimed in musically and Laramore followed suit. The Surveyor-General frowned, but the Colonel, after one or two attempts at sobriety of demeanor, succumbed, and the trio became a quartette. The glades of the forest rang to the jovial sound—it was as though there were enchantment in the golden afternoon, or in the ring of dark and frowning countenances before them, for they laughed as though they would never stop. Even the servants at the horses' heads were infected, and laughed at they knew not what.

The Surveyor-General lost patience. "I think the Jamestown weed groweth in these woods," he said dryly.

The Governor pulled himself together. "Faith! I believe you are right!" he said airily. "But rat me! if the impudence of the varlets be not the most amusing thing since the Quaker's plea for toleration!"

"The amusement seems to be on our side," said the Surveyor-General.

The Governor cast a careless glance in the direction indicated by the other. "Pshaw! a fit of the sulks! They will get over it. Is this precious captive the giant whom I have seen at Rosemead, Major Carrington?"

"Not so, your Excellency. My man is a Susquehannock."

"I believe I may lay claim to the fellow, Sir William," said the Colonel, wiping his eyes.

"Is he the Indian who was whipt the other day?" asked Sir Charles, taking snuff.

"For stealing fire-water—yes."

The Governor began to laugh again. "Of course you will release the rascal, Colonel? The Blue Mountains threaten war if you do not. Fling yourself into the breach, and so prevent a 'scandal to the community and a menace to the State,' to quote your words of this morning. Consistency is a jewel, Dick the Peacemaker. Wherefore let the savage go."

"I'll be d—d if I do!" cried the Colonel.

The Governor, shaking with laughter, got to his feet. At a signal his groom brought up his horse and held the stirrup for him to mount. His Excellency swung himself into the saddle and gathered the reins into his gauntleted hands; the remainder of the company, too, got to horse. The Governor's steed, a fiery, coal black Arabian, danced with impatience.

"Selim scents a fray!" cried his Excellency. "Come on, gentlemen! 'T will be sunset before we reach that sweet piece of earth behind Verney's orchard."

The half king rose from his seat, took three measured strides, and stood side by side with the Ricahecrian chief.

"My white father will give to the Ricahecrian the gift he asks?"

A gust of passion took the Governor. "No!" he thundered, turning in his saddle. "The Ricahecrian may go to the devil and the Blue Mountains alone!" He struck spurs into his horse's sides. "Gentlemen, we waste time!"

The Arabian dashed down one of the winding glades of the forest; the remainder of the party spurred their horses into the mad gallop known as the "planter's pace," and in an instant the whole cavalcade had whirled out of sight. A burst of laughter, made elfin by distance, came back to the village on the banks of the Pamunkey, then all was quiet again. The gold-laced, audacious company had vanished like a troop of powerful enchanters, leaving behind them a sullen throng of native genii, kept down by a Solomon's Seal which is *not* always unbreakable.

Something stirred in the midst of the great mulberry tree, a tree so vast and leafy that it might have hidden many things. A man swung himself down with a lithe grace from limb to limb, and finally dropped into the circle of Indians who stood or sat in a sombre stillness which might mean much or little. Only on the outskirts the crowd of women, children and youths, had commenced a low, monotonous, undefined noise which had in it something sinister, ominous. It was like the sound, dull and heavy, of the ground swell that precedes the storm. The man who dropped from the tree was Luiz Sebastian, and his appearance seemed in no degree to surprise the Indians. There followed a short and sententious conversation between the mulatto, the half king and the Ricahecrian chief. Beside the half king lay the still smoking peace pipe. When the colloquy was ended, he raised it. At a signal an Indian brought water in a gourd, and into it the half king plunged the glowing bowl. The fire went out in a cloud of hissing steam. The sound of the ground swell became louder and more threatening.

CHAPTER XXI

THE DUEL

The trees of the orchard stood out black against a crimson sky. "Faith! it is a color we shall see more of presently," said Laramore, divesting himself of his doublet.

His antagonist, passing a laced handkerchief along a gleaming blade, smiled politely. "A pretty tint. Wine, the lips of women, Captain Laramore's blood—Lard! 'tis a color I adore!"

"Gentlemen!" cried Colonel Verney. "Once more I beg of you to forego this foolish quarrel. William Berkeley, for the first time in your life, be reasonable!"

The Governor turned sharply, his chest, beneath his shirt of finest holland, swelling, each closely cropped hair upon his head, bared for action, stiff with injured dignity.

"Colonel Richard Verney forgets himself," he began angrily; then, "Confound you, Dick! keep your hands out of this. I don't want to fight you too! I say not that this gentleman is disloyal, but I do say, and I will maintain it with the last drop of my blood, that he strives to draw to himself a party in the State, with what intent he best knows. If he choose to pocket that assertion and withdraw, I am content."

"On guard, sir," said Carrington, raising his sword.

The Colonel shrugged his shoulders, and returned to his post beside Mr. Peyton.

"Very well, gentlemen, since you will not be ruled. Are you ready?"

The rapiers clashed together, and the game began.

The Governor fenced brilliantly, if a trifle wildly; his antagonist with a cool steadiness of manner and an iron wrist. Laramore fought with bull-like ferocity, striving to beat down his opponent's guard, making mad lunges, stamping, and keeping up a continuous rumble of oaths. Sir Charles, always smiling, and with an air as if his thoughts were anywhere but at that particular spot, put aside his thrusts with the ease with which the toreador avoids the bull.

Mr. Peyton was moved to reluctant admiration. "When I was in London, sir," he said in an excited whisper to the Colonel, "I did see Mathews fight with Westwicke, and thought I had seen fencing indeed, but your cousin—ah!"

Laramore's sword described a curve in the air, and lodged in the boughs of an apple-tree, while its owner staggered forward and fell heavily to the ground. At the same instant Carrington wounded the Governor in the wrist. Colonel Verney struck up the weapons. "By the Lord, gentlemen! you shall go no further! Jack Laramore's down, run through the shoulder! Major Carrington, you have drawn blood—it is enough."

"If Sir William Berkeley is content," began Carrington, bowing to his antagonist.

"Rat me! I've no choice," said the Governor ruefully. "You've disabled my sword arm, and the gout has the other."

"I shall be happy to wait until the wound shall have healed," said the Surveyor-General, with another bow.

"No, no," said his Excellency, with a laugh. "We'll cry quits. And rat me! if now that we have had it out, I do not love thee better, Miles Carrington, than ever I did before. In the morning when thou goest home, burn thy library, burn Milton and Bastwick, and Withers, and the rest of the rogues, forswear such rascally company forever, and rat me! if I will not maintain that thou art the honestest, as well as the longest-headed, man in the colony. There's my hand on it, and to-night we'll have a rouse such as would make old Noll turn in his grave if he had one."

Carrington took the proffered hand courteously, if coldly. "I thank your Excellency for your advice. Your Excellency should have your wound attended to at once. You are losing a deal of blood."

"Tut, a trifle!" said the Governor, airily, winding a handkerchief about the bleeding member.

"Is there ever a chirurgeon upon the place?" asked Sir Charles in his most dulcet tones. "If not, I fear that Captain Laramore will very shortly make his last voyage."

"Egad! that will never do!" cried the Colonel, dropping upon his knees beside the wounded man. "A bad thrust! Charles, thou art the very devil!"

"Shall I ride for the doctor?" cried Mr. Peyton.

"No. Anthony Nash is at the house. Run, lad, and fetch him. He is surgeon as well as divine."

Mr. Peyton disappeared; and presently there stood in the midst of the group gathered about the unconscious captain, a man clad in a clerical dress and of a very dignified and scholarly demeanor.

"Ha, gentlemen!" he said gravely, looking with bright, dark eyes from one to the other. "This is a sorry business. Shirts, drawn rapiers, trampled turf, Sir William bleeding, Captain Laramore senseless upon the ground! His Excellency the Governor; Major Carrington, the Surveyor-General; Colonel Verney, the lieutenant of the shire;—scandalous, gentlemen!"

"And Anthony Nash who would give his chance of a mitre to have been one of us," cried the Governor. "Ha! Anthony! dost remember the fight behind Paul's, three to one,—and the baggage that brought it about?"

The divine, on his knees beside Laramore, looked up with a twinkle in his eye from his work of tying laced handkerchiefs into bandages. "That was in the dark ages, your Excellency. My memory goeth not back so far. Ha! that is better! He is coming to himself. It is not so bad after all."

Laramore groaned, opened his eyes, and struggled into a sitting posture.

"Blast me! but I am properly spitted. Sir Charles Carew, my compliments to you. You are a man after my own heart. Ha, your Excellency! I find myself in good company. Dr. Anthony Nash, I shall have you out! You have torn the handkerchief Mistress Lettice Verney gave me."

The Doctor laughed. "You must be got to the house at once, and to bed, where Mistress Lettice, who is as skillful in healing as in making wounds, shall help me to properly dress this one."

Laramore staggered to his feet. "Give me an arm, Doctor; and Peyton, clap my periwig upon my head, will you? and fetch me my sword from where I see it, adorning yonder bough. Sir Charles Carew, I am your humble servant. Damme! it's no disgrace to be worsted by the best sword at Whitehall." And the gallant captain, supported by the clergyman and Mr. Peyton, reeled off the ground; the remainder of the party waiting only to assume doublets and wigs before following him to the house.

Two hours later Sir Charles Carew rose from the supper-table, and leaving the gentlemen at wine, passed into the great room, and came softly up to Patricia, sitting at the spinet.

"My heart was not there," he said, answering her smile and lifted brows. "I am come in search of it."

She laughed, fingering the keys. "Did you leave it on the field of honor? Fie, sir, for shame! Doctor Nash says that Captain Laramore will not use his arm for a fortnight."

"What—" said Sir Charles, dropping his voice and leaning over her—"what if I had been the wounded one?"

"I would have made your gruel with great pleasure, cousin."

She laughed again, and looked at him half tenderly, half mockingly. There were silver candlesticks upon the spinet and the light from the tall wax tapers fell with a white radiance over the slender figure in brocade and lace, the gleaming shoulders, the beautiful face, and the shining hair. Her eyes were brilliant, her mouth all elusive, mocking, exquisite curves.

He raised a wandering lock of gold to his lips. "The King hath written, commanding me home to England," he said abruptly.

"Yes, my father told me. He says the King loves you much."

Sir Charles left her side, twice walked the length of the room, and came back to her. "Am I to go as I came—alone?" he asked, standing before her with folded arms.

"If you so desire, sir?"

"Will you go with me?"

"Yes."

He caught her in his arms; but she cried out and freed herself.

"No, no, not yet!" she said breathlessly. "Listen to me."

She moved backwards a step or two, and stood facing him, her hand at her bosom, a color in her cheek, her eyes like stars. "I do not know that I love you, Sir Charles Carew. At times I have thought that I did; at times, not. There is an unrest here," touching her heart, "which has come to me lately. I do not know—it may be the beginning of love. Last night my father had much talk with me. It is his dearest wish that you and I should wed. He has been my very good father always. If you will take me as I am, not loving you yet, but with a heart free to learn, why—" Her voice broke.

Sir Charles flung himself at her feet, and, taking possession of her hands, covered them with kisses. A voice passed the window, singing through the night:—

"Martinmas wind, when wilt thou blow,

And shake the green leaves from the tree;

O gentle death, when wilt thou come?

For of my life I am weary."

"Margery again?" said Sir Charles, rising.

"Yes," said Patricia, with a troubled voice.

The voice began the stanza again:—

"Martinmas wind, when wilt thou blow,

And shake the green leaves from the tree?"

"What is the matter?" cried Sir Charles in alarm.

Patricia stared at him with wide, unseeing eyes. "Martinmas wind," she said in a low, clear, even voice. "Martinmas wind! The leaves drift in clouds, yellow and red, red like blood. Look at the river flowing in the sunshine! And the tall gray crags! Ah!" and she put her hands before her face.

"What is it?" cried her suitor. "What is the matter? You are ill!"

She dropped her hands. "I am well now," she said tremulously. "I do not know what it was. I had a vision—" she broke into wild laughter.

"I am fey, I think," she cried. "Let me go to my room; I am better there."

He held the door open, and she passed him quickly with lowered eyes. He watched her run up the stairs, and then threw himself into a chair and stared thoughtfully at the floor.

CHAPTER XXII

THE TOBACCO HOUSE AGAIN

The master of Verney Manor and his guests slept late, for the carouse of the night before had been deep and prolonged. The master's daughter rose with the sun, and went down into the garden, and thence through the wicket into the mulberry grove, where she found Margery sitting on the ground, tying golden-rod to her staff. "Come and walk with me, Margery," she said.

Margery rose with alacrity. "Where shall we go?" she asked in a whisper. "To the forest? There were eyes in the forest last night, not the great, still, solemn eyes that stare at Margery every night, but eyes that glowed like coals, and moved from bush to bush. Margery was afraid, and she left the forest, and sat by the water side all night, listening to what it had to say. A star shot, and Margery knew that a soul was on its way to Paradise, where she would fain go if only she could find the way.... There are purple flowers growing by the creek between the cedar wood and the marsh. Let us go gather them, and trim Margery's staff very bravely."

"I care not where we go," said her mistress. "There as well as elsewhere."

"Come, then," said Margery, and took the lead.

When they had entered the strip of cedars which lay between the wide fields and the point of land on which stood the third tobacco house, Patricia stopped beneath a great tree. "We will go no further, Margery," she said.

Margery objected. "The purple flowers grow by the water side."

"Do you go and gather them then," said Patricia wearily. "I will wait for you here."

Margery glided away, and her mistress sat down upon the dark-red earth at the foot of the tree. There was a cold and sombre stillness in the wood. The air smelt chill and dank, and the light came through the low, closely woven roof of foliage, as though it were filtered through crape, but at the end of the vista of trees shone a glory of sea and sky and gold-green marsh. Patricia gazed with dreamy eyes. "It is all fair," she said. "What was it that Dr. Nash read? 'My lines are fallen in pleasant places.' Riches and honor, and, they say, beauty, and many to love me.—O Lord God! I wish for happiness!" She laid her cheek against the cool earth, and the splendor before her wavered into a mist of rose and azure. "Why should I weep," she said, "that my lines are laid in pleasant places?"

Margery with her arms filled with flowers appeared at her side. "Here are the purple flowers," she said. "Here is farewell-summer for me and a passion-flower for you." She threw the blooms upon the ground, and sitting down at her mistress's feet, began to weave them into garlands. Presently she took up the passion-flower. "This grew beside the tobacco house, close to the wall. Margery saw it, and ran to pluck it. The door of the tobacco house was closed, but above the passion-flower was a great crack between the logs." She began to laugh. "Margery heard a strange thing, while she was plucking the passion-flower. Shall she tell it to you?"

"If you like, Margery," said Patricia indifferently.

Margery leaned forward, and laid a cold, thin hand upon her mistress' arm.

"There were seven men in the tobacco house. One said, 'When the Malignants are put down, what then?' and another answered, 'Surely we will possess their lands and their houses, their silver and their gold, for is it not written, "The Lord hath given them a spoil unto their servants."' Then the first said, 'Shall we not kill the Malignant, Verney?' Margery heard no more. She came away."

Patricia rose to her feet, pale, with brilliant eyes.

"You heard no more?"

"No."

"Margery, show me the place where you listened."

Margery took up her staff, and led the way to the outskirts of the wood. "There," she said, pointing with her staff. "There, where the elder grows."

Patricia laid her hand on the mad woman's shoulder. "Listen to me, Margery," she said in a low, distinct voice. "Listen very carefully. Go quickly to the great house, and to my father, or to Woodson, or to Sir Charles Carew give the message I am about to give you. Do you understand, Margery?"

Margery nodding emphatically, Patricia gave the message, and watched her flit away through the gloom of the cedars into the sunlight beyond; then turned and went swiftly and noiselessly across the strip of field to the tall, dark, windowless tobacco house. As she neared it, there came to her a low and undistinguishable murmur of voices which rose into distinctness as she entered the clump of alders.

Within the tobacco house were assembled the Muggletonian, the man branded upon the forehead, the youth with the hectic cheek (who acted as Secretary to the Surveyor-General), two newly purchased servants of Colonel Verney, Trail and Godfrey Landless. In the uncertain light which streamed from above through rents in the roof and crevices between the upper logs the interior of the tobacco house looked mysterious, sinister, threatening. Here and there tobacco still hung from the poles which crossed from wall to wall, and in the partial light the long, dusky masses looked wonderfully like other hanging things. The great casks beneath had the appearance of shadowy scaffolds, and the men, sitting or standing against them, looked larger than life. All was dusk, subdued, save where a stray sunbeam, sifting through a crack in the opposite wall, lit the ghastly face and shaven crown of the Muggletonian.

Landless, leaning against a cask, addressed a man of a grave and resolute bearing—one of the newly acquired servants of Verney Manor.

"Major Havisham, you are a wise and a brave man. I will gladly listen to any counsel you may have to give anent this matter."

Havisham shook his head. "I have nothing to say. The spirit of the father lives in the son. Skillful in planning, bold in action was Warham Landless!"

"I am but the tool of Robert Godwyn," said Landless. "You approve, then, of our arrangements?"

"Entirely. It is a daring enterprise, but if it succeeds—" he drew a long breath.

"And if it fails," said Landless, "there is freedom yet."

The other nodded. "Yes, death hath few terrors for us."

"What is death?" cried the hectic youth. "A short, dim passage from darkness into light; the antechamber of the white court of God; the curtain that we lift; the veil that we tear—and SEE! My soul longeth for death, yea, even fainteth for the courts of God! But He will not call His servants until His work is done. Wherefore let us haste to rise up and slay, to work the Lord's work, and go from hence!"

"Yea!" cried the Muggletonian. "I fear not death! I fear not the Throne and the Judgment seat. The Two Witnesses will speak for me! But Death is not upon us; he passeth by the weak, and seizeth upon the strong. The Malignants shall die, for the word of the Lord has gone out against them. 'Thy foot shall be dipped in the blood of thy enemies, and the tongue of thy dogs into the same! They shall fall by the sword, they shall be a portion for foxes; as smoke is drawn away so shall they vanish, as wax melteth before the fire so shall they perish! He that sitteth in the heavens shall have them in derision. And the righteous shall rejoice in His vengeance!'"

"Amen," drawled Trail through his nose. "Verily, we will fatten on the good things of the land, we will spend our days in ease and pleasantness! The Malignants shall work for us. They shall toil in our tobacco fields, their women shall be our handmaidens, we will drink their wines, and wear their rich clothing, and our pockets shall be filled with their gold and silver—"

"Silence!" cried Landless fiercely. "Once more I tell you, mad dreamers that you are, that there shall be no such devil's work! Major Havisham, there are not among us many of this ilk. Two thirds of our number are men of the stamp of Robert Godwyn and yourself. These men rave."

"I heed them not," said Havisham with a slighting gesture of the hand; then, "Let us recapitulate. Upon this appointed day we whom they call Oliverians, and the great majority of the redemptioners, are to rise throughout the colony. We—"

"Are to do no damage to property nor offer any unnecessary violence to masters and overseers," said Landless firmly.

"We are simply to arm ourselves, seize horses or boats, and resort to this appointed place."

"Yes."

"Calling upon the slaves to follow us?"

"Which they will do. Yes."

"And when all are assembled, to oppose any force sent against us?"

"Yes."

"And if we conquer, then—"

"Then the Republic,—Commonwealth,—anything you choose—at any rate, freedom."

"It is a desperate plan."

"We are desperate men."

"Yes," Havisham said thoughtfully; "it is the best chance for that escape of which we all dream, and which two of our number, I see, have attempted in vain. I had set to-morrow night for my own attempt. This promises better."

"Yea," said Porringer, "the stars in their courses fight against the refugee! Four times have I tried, to be retaken, and handled, as you see. Twice has this man tried and failed. And the murderer of Robert Godwyn failed."

"That remains to be seen," said Trail. "Roach has broken gaol."

The Muggletonian exclaimed, and Landless turned upon the forger. "How do you know?" he asked sternly.

"I heard," was the smooth reply.

"I am sorry for it," said Landless grimly, and stood with a sternly thoughtful countenance.

There was a silence in the tobacco house broken by Havisham.

"And now—for time passes and the overseer may come and find us not at our tasks—tell me the day upon which we are to rise, and the place to which all are to resort."

"Both are close at hand," said Landless slowly. "The day is—" he broke off and leaned forward, staring through the dusk.

"What is it?" cried Havisham.

"My eyes met other eyes. There, behind that great crack between the logs!"

The Muggletonian rushed to the door, flung it open, and vanished; the branded man followed. The remaining occupants of the tobacco house started to their feet, and Havisham picked from the floor a pole and broke from it a stout cudgel. Godfrey Landless strode forward into the broad shaft of sunshine that entered through the opened door and met the eavesdropper face to face, as, with either arm in the rude grasp of the fanatics, she crossed the threshold.

The conspirators, recognizing the lady of the manor, were stricken dumb. In the three minutes of dead silence which ensued they saw their plans defeated, their hopes ruined, their cause vanquished, their lives lost. The graceful figure with white scorn in the beautiful face was death come upon them. The shadow fell heavy and cold upon their souls, the very air seemed to darken and grow chill around them The figure of the woman in their midst gathered up the sunshine, became ethereal, transplendent, a triumphant white and gold Spirit of Evil.

Landless was the first to speak. "Unhand her!" he said in a suppressed voice.

The men obeyed, but the Muggletonian placed himself between his prisoner and the door. She saw the movement and said scornfully, "You need not fear; I shall not run away." Upon her bare, white arms, where they had been clasped too rudely, were fast darkening marks. She glanced from them to the scarred face of the Muggletonian. "*They* will wear out," she said.

"Madam," said Landless hoarsely, "how long were you in that place?"

She flashed upon him a look that was like a blow. "Liar! be silent!" she said, then turned to the row of faces that frowned upon her from out the shadow. "To you others I address myself. Traitors, rebellious servants, base plotters! I hold your lives in my hand."

"And your own?" said Trail.

"Cursed daughter of the mother of evil!" cried the Muggletonian, a baleful light burning in his eyes. "Scarlet woman, whose vain apparel, whose uncovered hair and bared bosom, whose light songs and laughter have long been an offense and a stumbling-block to the righteous—thy cup of iniquity is full, thy life is forfeit, thy hour is come!" He drew a knife from his bosom and with an unearthly cry flourished it above his head, then rushed upon her, to be met by Landless, who hurled himself upon the would-be murderer with a force that sent them both staggering against the wall. A struggle ensued, which ended in Landless securing the knife. With it in his hand he sprang to the side of the girl, who stood unflinching, a pride that was superb in her still white face and steadfast eyes.

"Who touches her dies," he said between his teeth.

Havisham came to his aid. "Men, are you mad? You cannot murder a defenseless woman! Moreover such a deed would prove our utter ruin."

"If her body were found, yes!" cried the hectic youth. "But the water is near, and who is to know that the devil sent her hither?"

"It is her death or ours," cried the branded man.

The Muggletonian tossed his arms into the air.

"The cause! the cause! Cursed be he that putteth his hand to the plough and finisheth not the furrow! Ride on! Ride on! though it were over the bodies of a thousand painted Jezebels such as this!"

"Time presses!" cried the branded man. "Woodson may come!"

They closed in upon the three who stood at bay. In their dark faces were a passion and an exaltation—they saw in the woman fallen into their hands, a sacrifice bound to the altar. Trail alone looked uneasy and held back, muttering between his teeth.

Landless stepped in front of Patricia and faced them with a still and deadly eye, and with the hand that held the knife drawn back against his breast. Knowing them, he saw no use in any appeal; also he saw that it was indeed her life or theirs. On the one hand, the downfall of all their hopes, the death or perpetual enslavement of many, and for himself surely the gibbet and the rope; on the other—

He made a gesture of command. "Thou shalt do no murder!" he cried.

"It is not murder; it is sacrifice."

"There must be another way!" cried Havisham.

"Find it!"

Havisham turned to the prisoner. "Madam, will you swear to be silent concerning what you have heard?"

The Muggletonian laughed wildly. "Who trusts a woman's oath!"

"You shall have no need," said the lady of the manor calmly. She paused and her eyes went to the door in an intent and listening gaze, then came back to the faces about her with a strange light in their depths. "Rebel servants," she said in a clear, low voice, "I defy you! And you, false slave, stand from before me. I need not your hateful aid." In the moment of ominous silence that followed, she swayed towards the door, her hand at her throat, her soul in her eyes. Suddenly she cried out, "My father! Charles! help!"

From without came an answering cry, followed by a rush of men through the door, and in an instant the room was filled with struggling forms as the two parties threw themselves upon each other. The newcomers were half a dozen blacks, the two overseers and Sir Charles Carew. The overseers had pistols and Sir Charles his sword. With it he met the rush of the youth with the hectic cheek, who came towards him in long, hound-like leaps, brandishing a piece of wood above his head, and drove the blade deep into the chest of the fanatic. The wretched man staggered and fell, then rose to his knees. Flinging his arms above his head, he turned his worn face towards the flood of sunshine pouring in through the door, and cried in a loud voice, "I see!" A stream of blood gushed from his lips, his arms dropped, and without a groan he fell back, dead.

Landless, wrestling with the slave Regulus, at length succeeded in hurling the powerful figure to the ground, where it lay stunned, and turned to find himself confronted by Woodson's pistol and the point of Sir Charles's rapier. A glance showed him the remaining conspirators, overpowered, and in the act of being bound with the ropes that had lain, coiled for use in packing, in the corners of the tobacco house. The hectic youth lay, a ghastly spectacle, in a pool of blood across the doorway. At his feet was the branded man, a bullet through his brain, and near him the groaning figure of Havisham's mortally wounded companion. The woman who had brought all this to pass stood unharmed, white, with tragic, exultant eyes.

Sir Charles, serene and debonair, lowered his point. "Your hand is played," he said with a fine smile. Landless's stern, despairing gaze passed him and went on to the overseer. "I surrender to you," he said briefly.

Woodson chuckled grimly and stuck his pistol in his belt. He was in high good humor, visions of reward and thanks from the Assembly dancing before his eyes. "I've had my eye on you for some time, young man," he said almost genially. "I've suspected that you were up to something, but Lord! to think that a woman's wit should have trapped you at last! Haines, bring that rope over here."

Sir Charles went over to Patricia and offered her his arm. "Dearest and bravest of women!" he said in a caressing whisper. "Come with me from this place, which must be dreadful to you."

She did not answer him at once, but stood looking past him at the picture of laughing water and waving forest framed in the doorway.

"I thought I should never see the sunshine again," she said dreamily. "Did Margery give *you* the message?"

"Yes, she met me under the mulberries. I would not wait to rouse your father, but calling the overseers and the blacks from the fields, came at once."

"I owe you my life," she said. "You and—"

Her eyes left the summer outside and came back to the shadowy forms within the tobacco house. "I will go with you directly, cousin," she said quietly, "but first I wish to speak to that man."

He shot a swift glance at her face, but drew back with a bow, and she walked with a steady step up to Landless. "Fall back a little," she said with an imperious wave of her hand to the men about him. They obeyed her. Landless, left standing before her, his arms bound to his sides, raised his head and looked her in the face. She met his eyes. "You lied to me," she said in a low, even voice.

"Once, madam, and to save others," he said proudly,

"Not once, but twice. Do you think that now I believe that tale you told me that night, that fairy tale of persecuted innocence? When I think that I ever believed it I hate myself."

"Nevertheless, it is true, madam."

"It is false! Yesterday I thought of you as a gallant gentleman, greatly wronged ... and I pitied you. To-day I am wiser."

He held her eyes with his own for a moment, then let them go. "Some day you will know," he said.

She turned from him and held out her hands to Sir Charles. He hurried to her and she clung to him. "Take me away," she said in a whisper. "Take me home."

He put his arm about her. "You are faint," he said tenderly. "Come! the air will revive you."

Supporting her on his arm, he guided her from the house. As they passed the body stretched across the threshold, the skirt of her robe touched the blood in which it was lying. She saw it and shuddered.

"Blood is upon me!" she said. "It is an omen!"

"A good one, then," said her companion coolly, "for it is the blood of a fanatic traitor. Think not of it." He turned at the threshold and cast a careless glance back into the tobacco house. "Woodson, get rid of this carrion, and bring these men quietly to the great house, where your master will deal with them."

CHAPTER XXIII

THE QUESTION

"We know all but two things, but those are the most important of all," said the Governor, tapping his jeweled fingers against the table.

"It is much to be regretted," said the Surveyor-General, "that the presence of the young lady was so soon discovered. Otherwise—"

"Otherwise we might have had further information on more than one subject," said the Governor dryly.

"We must make the best of what we have," continued Carrington calmly. "After all, it is enough."

The Governor rose and began to pace the floor, his head thoughtfully bent, his unwounded hand tugging at the curls of his periwig. "It is not enough," he said at length, pausing before the great table around which the company were seated. "Thanks to the gallant daughter of the gallant Verneys,"—a bow and smile to Patricia, sitting enthroned in the great chair in their midst,—"we know much, but it is not enough. These rogues have set a day upon which to rise; they have appointed a place to which they are to resort. That day may be to-morrow, that place any point in any one of a dozen counties."

"I apprehend that the cockatrice was to be hatched near by," said Sir Charles.

"It is the likeliest thing," answered the Governor, "seeing that their ringleader belongs to this plantation. But we do not know. And there may not be time to reach the planters, to give them warning, to arrest these d—d traitors, scattered as they are from the James to Rappahannock, and from Henricus to the Chesapeake. It might be best to assemble the trainbands at this cursed spot if it can be found, and to await their coming in force. But to know neither time nor place—to start a hue and cry and have the storm burst before it reaches ten plantations—to guard one point and see fire rise at another a dozen leagues away—impossible! Gentlemen, we must come at the heart of this matter!"

"It is most advisable," said Colonel Verney gravely. "Examine the prisoners again," suggested Sir Charles.

"One of them is no wiser than we. You are certain as to this, Mistress Patricia?"

"Yes, your Excellency."

"Humph! one does not know; three are dead; there remain, then, that shaven and branded runaway and the two convicts."

"You will learn naught from the runaway, your Excellency!" called out the overseer from where he stood at a respectful distance from the company. "He's one of them crazy fanatics that wild horses couldn't draw truth from. No Indian torture stake could make him speak if he didn't want to,—nor keep him from it if he did."

"I know that kind," said the Governor, with a short laugh, "and we will not waste time upon him, but will try if the convict—he who seems to have been their leader—be not more amenable. Bring him in, Woodson."

When the overseer had gone, a silence fell upon the company gathered in the master's room. The Governor paced to and fro, perplexity in his face; the Colonel knit his grizzled brows and studied the floor; Dr. Anthony Nash brought the writing materials displayed upon the table, closer to him, and held a quill ready poised for dipping into the ink horn, while the Surveyor-General with a carefully composed countenance toyed with a pink which he took from the bowl of flowers before him. Sir Charles leaned back in his seat and looked at Patricia who, seated between him and her father, stared before her with hard, bright eyes. Her lips were like a scarlet flower against the absolute pallor of her face; her hair was a crown of pale gold. In the great chair, her white arms resting upon the dark wood, her feet upon a carved footstool, she looked a queen, and the knot of brilliantly dressed gentlemen her attendant council.

The door opened and the two overseers appeared with Landless, who advanced and stood, silent and collected, before the ring of hostile faces.

"What is your name, sirrah?" said the Governor, throwing himself into his chair and frowning heavily.

"Godfrey Landless."

"I am told that you are son to one Warham Landless, a so-called colonel in the rebel army and hand in glove with the usurper himself."

"I am the son of Colonel Warham Landless of the forces of the Commonwealth, and friend to his Highness the Lord Protector."

"Humph! And did you fight in these same forces yourself?"

"At Worcester, yes."

"Humph! the son of a traitor and rebel—traitor and rebel yourself—and convict to boot! A pretty record! On what day was this rising to occur?"

No answer. The Governor repeated the question. "On what day was this precious mine to be sprung? And to what place were you to resort?"

Landless remaining silent, the Governor's face began to flush and the veins in his forehead to swell. "Have you lost your tongue?" he said fiercely. "If so, we will find a way to recover it."

"I shall not answer those questions," said Landless firmly.

"It is your one chance for life," said the Governor sternly. "Answer me truly, and you may escape the gallows. Refuse, and you hang, so surely as I sit here."

"I shall not answer them."

"Sink me if I ever knew a Roundhead so careless of his own interests," drawled Sir Charles. The Governor whispered to the master of the plantation, then turned again to the prisoner.

"I give you one more chance," he said harshly. "When is this day? Where is this place?"

"I shall not tell you."

"We will see about that," said his Excellency with compressed lips. "Verney, send your daughter from the room. Woodson, you understand this gear, having been in the Indies. This man is to tell us all that he knows of this business. Call in a trustworthy slave or two to help you."

Patricia uttered a low cry, and the Surveyor-General crushed the flower between his fingers and turned upon the Governor. "Your Excellency! I protest! This that you would do is not lawful! Surely such harsh measures are not needed."

The Governor's fury exploded. "Not needful!" he exclaimed in a high voice. "Not needful, when upon these questions hang the fortunes of the Colony! when if we fail, to-morrow may usher in a blacker forty-four! And not lawful! I am the law in this. State, Major Carrington; I am the King's representative, and this is my prerogative! and I say that by fair means or foul this information must be gained. This is no time to prate of humanity. We are to show humanity to ourselves; we are to stamp out this lit fuse. Or does Major Carrington wish it to burn on?"

"No," said Carrington coldly. "I spoke hastily. You are right, of course, and I will interfere no further."

An hour later Patricia stood before the hall window looking out upon the dazzling water and the green velvet of the marshes with wide, unseeing eyes. Her hands were clenched at her sides and upon each cheek burned a crimson spot. Beside her crouched Betty Carrington who, upon the first rumor of trouble at Verney Manor, had ridden over from Rosemead. Their strained ears caught no sound from the room opposite other than the occasional sound of the Governor's voice, raised in interrogation. There came no answering voice. Patricia stood motionless, with eyes that never wandered from the rich scene without, and with lips pressed together, but Betty hid her face in the other's skirts and shivered. The door of the master's room opened and both started violently. The overseer strode down the hall and had laid his hand upon the latch of the door leading to the offices, when his mistress called him to her. "Do they know? Has the man told?" she asked with an effort.

Woodson shook his head. "He's as dumb as an oyster. Might as well try to get anything from an Indian. They're going to try t' other—Trail."

He left the hall, but was back in five minutes' time with the forger. They entered the master's room, and Patricia, seized by a sudden impulse, followed them, leaving Betty trembling in the window seat.

Unnoted by all but one of the company, she slipt to a seat in the shadow of her father's burly shoulders. He was leaning forward, talking to the Governor, who sat very erect, his features fixed in an expression of dogged determination. The Surveyor-General sat well behind the table, and upon the polished wood before him lay a little heap of torn petals and broken stems. At the far end of the room and leaning heavily against the wall was the prisoner whose examination was just finished.

Sir Charles had seen the entrance of the lady of the manor, and he now rose from his seat and came to her. "Not a syllable," he whispered in answer to the question in her eyes. "Roundhead obstinacy! But I think that this fellow will prove more malleable."

His prediction was verified. Ten minutes later the Governor rose to his feet triumphant. "So!" he said, drawing a long breath. "We are, I think, gentlemen, at the very core at last. The time, day after to-morrow; the place, Poplar Spring in this county. And now to work! Those of these d—d Oliverians whom we can reach must be arrested at once. Swift messengers must be sent to all plantations far and near. The trainbands must be called out. Time presses, gentlemen!"

"And these men?" said the Colonel.

"Must go to Jamestown gaol, where the one shall hang as surely as my name is William Berkeley. For the other—"

"Your Excellency has promised me my life," said Trail cringingly, but with an inscrutable something that was not fear in his sinister green eyes.

"An escort must be gotten together," said the Colonel, "and the day is far advanced. I advise keeping them here until the morning."

"See that you keep them straitly then," said the Governor.

"Trust me for that, your Excellency," said the overseer grimly.

"Then to work, gentlemen," cried the Governor, "for there is much to do and but little time to do it in. Major Carrington, you with Mr. Peyton will ride with me to Jamestown. Colonel Verney, you will know what measures to take for the safety of your shire. Woodson, have the horses brought around at once."

The Council broke up in haste and confusion, and its members, talking eagerly, streamed into the hall. Carrington was the last in line, and he paused before Landless. The under overseer and the slave Regulus were at a little distance replacing the cords about Trail's arms. The Surveyor-General cast a quick glance towards the door, saw that the last retreating figure was that of Mr. Peyton, and approached his lips close to Landless's ear.

"You are a brave man," he said in a low and troubled voice. "From my soul I honor you! I would have saved you, would save you now if I could. But I am cruelly placed."

"I have no hope for this life—and no fear," said Landless calmly.

Carrington paused irresolute, and a flush rose to his face. "I would like to hear you say that you do not blame me," he said at last with an effort.

"I do not blame you," said Landless.

Woodson appeared in the doorway. "The Governor is waiting, Major Carrington."

"If I can do ought to help you, I will," said Carrington hastily, and left the room. A moment later came the jingling of reins and the sound of rapid hoofs quickening into the planter's pace as the Governor and the Surveyor-General whirled away.

CHAPTER XXIV

A MESSAGE

In an unused attic room of the great house lay Godfrey Landless, cords about his ankles, and his arms bound to his sides by cords and by a thick rope, one end of which was fastened to a beam on the wall. He was alone, for the Muggletonian, Havisham and Trail were confined in the overseer's house. Opposite him was a small window framing a square of sky. He had watched light clouds drift across it, and the sun pass slowly and majestically down it, and the sunset turn the clouds into floating blood-red plumes. He had been there since noon. Thick walls kept from him all sound in the house below—it might have been a house of the dead. Through the closed window came the low, incessant hum of the summer world without, but no unusual noise. He had heard the sunset horn, and the song of the slaves coming from the fields, and as dusk began to fall, the cry of a whip-poor-will.

When the door had closed upon the retreating figures of the men who brought him there, he had thrown himself upon the floor where he lay, faint from physical anguish, in a stupor of misery, conscious only of a sick longing for death. This mood had passed and he was himself again.

As he lay with his eyes following the fiery, shifting feathers of cloud, he remembered that the gaol at Jamestown faced the south, and he thought, "This is the last sunset I shall ever see." He had the strong abiding faith of his time and party, and he looked beyond the clouds with an awe and a light in his eyes. Verses learnt at his mother's knee came back to him; he said them over to himself, and the tender, solemn, beneficent words fell like balm upon his troubled heart. He thought of his mother who had died young, and then of scenes and occurrences of his childhood. All earthly hope was past, there could be no more struggling; in a little while he would be dead. Dying, his mind reverted, not to the sordid misery from which death would set him free, but to the long past, to the child at the mother's knee, to the boy who had climbed down great cliffs in search of a smuggler's cave. The unearthly light that rests upon that time so far behind us shone strong for him—he saw every twig in the rooks' nests in the lofty elms, every ivy leaf about a ruined oriel, black against a gold sky; the cool, dark smell of the box alleys filled his nostrils; the sound of the sea came to him; he heard his mother singing on the terrace. He bowed his face with a sudden rain of tender, not sorrowful, tears.

Something crashed in at the window, splintering the coarse glass and falling upon the floor at a little distance from him. It was a large pebble, to which was tied a piece of paper. He started up and made for it, to be brought up within two feet of it by the tug of the rope which bound him to the wall. He thought a moment, then lay down upon the floor and found that he could touch the end of the string that tied the paper to the pebble. He took it between his teeth and slowly drew it towards him, then, rising to his knees, he strained with all his might at the cords that bound his arms. They were tightly drawn, but when at length he desisted, panting, he had so loosened them that he could move one hand a very little way. With it and with his teeth he disengaged the paper from the pebble and spread it upon his knee. There was just light enough to read the sprawling schoolboy hand with which it was covered. It ran thus:—

"I don't know as this will ever reach you. I am doing all I can. Luiz Sebastian has not let me get at arm's length from him since I overheard him and the Turk, and a sailor from Captain Laramore's ship and *Roach* at the hut on the marsh, two hours ago. They would have killed me there, but I ran, and he did not catch me until I was almost to the quarters. He will kill me though in a little while, I know; he has a knife and he is sitting on the doorstep, and the Turk is with him, and I can not pass them. He held his hand over my mouth and the knife to my heart when Woodson went the rounds, and I couldn't make no sound—Lord have mercy upon me! I write this with my blood, on a leaf from your Bible, while he sits there whispering to the Turk. He goes to his own cabin directly and he will take me with him and kill me there, I know he will. He goes to the stables first and I must go with him. If we pass close enough, and if I can do it without his seeing me I will throw this in at the window of the room where I know you are, if not—the Lord help us all!... Landless, for God's sake! before moonrise to-night the Chickahominies and the Ricahecrians from the Blue Mountains will come down on the plantation. With them are leagued Luiz Sebastian, the Turk, Trail, Roach, and most of the slaves.... When all is over, the Indians will take the scalps and Grey Wolf and will make for the Blue Mountains; Luiz Sebastian and the others will seize the boats and put off for the ship at the Point. Her crew will give her up and they will all turn pirate together. The women go with them if they can keep them from the Indians; the men are all to be killed.... I have told you all I heard. For God's sake, save them if you can,—and remember poor Dick Whittington."

Dropping the paper, Landless strained with all his might, first at the cords which bound his arms, and then at the rope which fastened him to the wall. Again and again he put forth the strength of despair—his muscles cracked, great beads stood upon his forehead—but the ropes held. As well as he could with his shackled feet he stamped upon the floor; he called aloud, but there came no answering voice or sound from below. He was at the end of the house over unused chambers, and the walls and flooring were very thick. He clenched his teeth and began again the battle with the cords which held him. All in vain. He shouted until he was hoarse—it was crying aloud in a desert. With a groan he leaned against the wall, gathering strength for another effort. It was dark now and the moon rose at eleven.... There was a piece of glass upon the floor, one of the splinters from the shattered window. He remembered noticing it—a long narrow piece like the blade of a knife. Sinking to his knees he felt for it, and after a long time found it. He now had a knife, but he could not move the hand that held it six inches from his side. Stooping, he took the splinter between his teeth, and making the rope taut, drew the sharp edge of the glass across it. Again and again he drew it across, and at length he perceived that a strand was severed. With a thrill of joy he settled to the slow, laborious and painful task. Time passed, a long, long time, and yet the rope was but half severed. As he worked he counted the moments with feverish dread, his heart throbbed one passionate prayer: "Lord, let me save her!" Now and then he glanced at the blackness of the night outside with a terrible fear—though he knew it could not be yet—that he should see it waver into moonlight. Another interval of toil, and he stood erect, gathered his forces, made one supreme effort—and was free! There was not time for the cords about his arms, but he must get rid of those which fettered his ankles. An endless task it seemed, but hand and friendly splinter accomplished it at last; and he sprang to the door. It was locked. He dashed himself against it, once, twice, thrice, and it crashed outwards, precipitating him into a large, bare room. He crossed this, managed to open its unlocked door with his free hand, descended a winding stair and came into the upper hall. It was in darkness, but up the wide staircase streamed the perfumed light of many myrtle candles, and with it laughter, and the sound of a man's voice singing to a lute.

CHAPTER XXV

THE ROAD TO PARADISE

The family and guests of Verney Manor were assembled in the great room. The day had been one of confusion, haste and anxiety; but it was past, and the stillness and forced inaction of the night was upon them. With the readiness of those to whom danger is no novelty they seized the hour and made the most of it. Sufficient unto the morrow was the evil thereof.

The Colonel, weary from hard riding, but well satisfied with his afternoon's work, had sunk into a great chair and challenged Dr. Anthony Nash to a game of chess. "Everything is in train," he told them, "and all quiet upon the plantations in this shire at least. I believe the danger past. God be thanked!" Upon a settle piled with cushions lay Captain Laramore, with a bandaged shoulder, a long pipe between his teeth, and at his elbow a tankard of sack and an elderly Hebe in the person of Mistress Lettice Verney. Patricia, sumptuously clad and beautiful as a dream, sat in the great window with Betty and Sir Charles. Her eyes shone with a feverish brilliancy, her white hands were never still, she laughed and jested with her lover, touching this or that with light wit. Once or twice she broke into song, rich, passionate, throbbing through the night. The gentle Betty looked at her in wonder, but Sir Charles was enchanted.

Steps sounded on the stairs and in the hall. "Who is that?" cried the master, taking his hand from his rook.

"The overseer, probably," said Dr. Nash. "Check to your king."

A loud scream from Mistress Lettice. The master leaped to his feet, knocking over the chess-table and sending the pieces rattling into corners. Sir Charles, drawing his rapier, sprang to his side, the wounded Captain started up from amidst his pillows and the divine snatched a brass andiron from the fireplace.

Framed in the doorway, looking larger than life against the blackness of the space behind him, stood the arch plotter, the Roundhead, the convict, the rebellious servant whom the Governor had sworn to hang. Blood dropped from his face, cut by the glass with which he had severed the rope, to meet the blood upon his arms and chest, lacerated by his savage straining at his bonds. For a moment he stood, blinded by the light, then advanced into the room. His master seized him. "Still bound!" he cried with an oath. "He is alone then! How did you get here? What are you doing here? Speak, scoundrel!"

"I bring you this paper, sir," said Landless hoarsely. "Will you take it from me. I cannot raise my hands."

The Colonel snatched the paper, glanced at it, read it with a face from which all the ruddy color had fled, and held it out to Sir Charles with a shaking hand. "Read it," he gasped. "Read it aloud," and sank into his chair breathing heavily.

Sir Charles read. "Damnation!" he cried, crushing the paper in his hand. Laramore started up with a roar of "My ship!" and then broke into a torrent of oaths. Mistress Lettice's screams filled the room until her brother roughly silenced her by clapping his hand over her mouth. "By the Lord Harry, Lettice, I will throw you out to them if you do not hush! Gentlemen, in God's name, what are we to do?"

"Barricade door and window and hold the house against them," said the baronet.

"Send for help to Rosemead and to Fitzhugh and Ludwell!" cried the divine.

"Five men and three women to hold this house against a hundred Indians and negroes! And no help could come for hours and it is now nearly ten! Moreover, the messenger would have to pass through the savages lying in the woods,—he would never reach Rosemead with his scalp on!"

"I will be your messenger," said Nash rising, "and as every moment is more precious than rubies, I had best start at once."

"You, Anthony! God forbid!" cried the Colonel "You would go to certain death."

"I would stay to certain death, would I not?" retorted the other. "But my mare, Pixie, and I can shew clean heels to the red villains, were they as thick as chinquepins. Give me the stable-key, Verney. I know the way to the jade's stall, and she will follow her master through fire and water without a whinny. I don't want a light. Not a soul on the place must know that I have left Verney Manor."

"Anthony, Anthony, I am loth to see you go, old friend!" cried the Colonel.

"Tut, tut, as well leave my scalp in the woods as in Dick Verney's parlor! but I shall do neither. Hold the house as long as you can, and look for Carrington, and Fitzhugh, and Ludwell, and myself with a hundred men at our heels before the dawn. Until then *vale*."

He was gone. "And now the doors and windows," said Sir Charles.

"The windows, save those in this room, are secured as they always are at night. The shutters are heavy and strongly barred, and we have but to draw the chains across the doors. They will find it hard work to fire the house, for the logs are wet from this morning's shower. There is ammunition enough, and the shutters are loopholed. If we were in force, we might hold out, but, my God! what can we do? Even with the overseers whom we must manage to call to us, if we can do so without arousing suspicion, we are not enough to defend one face of the house."

"Are there no honest servants?"

"How can I tell the true men from the knaves? To rouse the quarters would be to show that we know, and to ourselves spring the mine which is to destroy us. And if we brought men into the house, who are leagued with the fiends outside, then would their work be done for them. There are a very few whom I know to be faithful, but how to secure them without giving the alarm—my God! how helpless we are!"

"Perhaps I can help you, Colonel Verney," said Landless.

In the midst of a dead silence the eyes of each occupant of the room,—the master, the courtier, the wounded captain, the women, trembling in each other's arms,—were turned upon the speaker who stood before them, haggard, torn and bleeding, but with a quiet power in his dark face and steadfast eyes.

"You?" said the master sternly, "What can you do?"

"I will tell you," said Landless, "but I must be freed from these bonds first."

Another pause, and then Sir Charles, responding to a nod from his kinsman, walked over to Landless, and with his rapier cut the ropes which bound him.

"Now speak!" said the Colonel.

The quarters lay, to all appearance, wrapt in the profoundest slumber—no movement in the low-browed cabins, or in the lane or square; no sound other than the croak of the frogs in the marshes, the wail of the whip-poor-wills, and the sighing of the night wind in the pines. All was dark save in the east, where the low stars were beginning to pale. Below them glowed a dull red spark, shining dimly across a long expanse of black marsh and water, and coming from Captain Laramore's ship, anchored off the Point.

One moment it seemed the only light in the wide landscape of darkness; the next the flame of a torch, streaming sidewise in the wind, cast an orange glare upon the dead tree in the centre of the square and upon the windowless fronts of the cabins surrounding it. The torch was in the hand of the overseer, who went the rounds, striking upon each door, and summoning the inmates of the cabin to the square. "The master wants a word with you," was all the answer he vouchsafed to startled, sullen, or suspicious inquiries. In five minutes the square was thronged. White and black, servant and slave, rustic, convict, Jew, Turk, Indian, mulatto, quadroon, coal black, untamed African—the motley crowd pressed and jostled towards that end of the square at which stood the master, his kinsman, the overseer, and Godfrey Landless. Behind them on the steps of the overseer's house were the Muggletonian, Havisham, and Trail. They had been unbound. In the Muggletonian's scarred face was stolid indifference, but Trail looked furtively about until he spied Luiz Sebastian, when he signaled "What is it?" with his eyes. The mulatto shook his head, and continued to shoulder his way through the press until he stood in the front row, face to face with the party from the great house. On one side of him was the Turk, on the other an Indian.

The master stepped a pace or two in front of his companions, and held up his hand for silence. When the excited muttering had sunk into a breathless hush, he beckoned to Landless, and the young man stepped to his side. There were many streaming lights by now, and men saw each other, now clearly, now darkly, as the fitful glare rose and fell.

"Now, my man," said the master in a loud, slow voice, "you will point out to me, as you have agreed to do, every man concerned in the plot discovered this morning. And you whom he designates, I command you, in the name of the King, to surrender peaceably. Your hope of pardon depends upon your doing so. Now, Landless!"

"John Havisham," said Landless.

"Taken redhanded," quoth the master. "Place him here, Woodson, in front of us. When all are in line, I shall have a word to say to them."

Havisham advanced with quiet dignity, passing Landless as if unaware of his presence. "I surrender," he said, raising his voice, "because I have no choice. And I advise those of our number here present to do the same. Our plans known, our friends taken, betrayed and deserted by the man in whom we trusted most, whom we called our leader, we have, indeed, no choice."

"Win-Grace Porringer," said Landless.

The Muggletonian threw up his arms. "Iscariot!" he cried wildly. "Woe, woe to him by whom offenses come! Well for thee, son of Warham Landless, hadst thou never been born! By the power given to the Two Witnesses and to their followers I curse thee! Thou shalt be anathema maranatha! Famine, thirst, and a violent death be thy portion in this life, and in the world to come mayest thou burn forever, howling! Amen and amen!" With a wild laugh he stalked to the side of Havisham, leaving Trail standing alone upon the doorstep. The eyes of the forger met the eyes of Luiz Sebastian in another puzzled inquiry, but the latter shook his head with a frown. Not doubting that his name would be the next called, Trail had already taken a step forward, but Landless's eyes passed him over, and rested upon the face of a man standing near Luiz Sebastian.

"John Robert!" he cried.

The man, a Baptist preacher suffering under the Act of Uniformity, turned a gentle, reproachful face upon him, and stepping from the crowd, joined himself to Havisham and the Muggletonian.

"James Holt!" said Landless.

A rustic, standing behind Luiz Sebastian, uttered a dreadful imprecation. "You may hang me and welcome, your Honor," he cried as he took his place, "if you'll just let me see this d—d Judas hung first!"

Luiz Sebastian fixed his great eyes upon Landless. "If he calls my name," said the wicked brain behind the blandly smiling face, "shall I, or shall I not—? It is many minutes to moonrise yet."

But Landless did not call him. He passed him by as he had passed Trail, and named another rustic at some little distance from the mulatto, then a Fifth Monarchy man, then a veteran of Cromwell's, then the plantation miller and the carpenter, then two more Oliverians, then more peasants. Each man, as his name was called, stepped forward into the lengthening line that faced the master and his party, standing with pistols leveled and cocked; and each man bestowed upon Godfrey Landless a curse, or a look that was bitterer than a curse.

"Humfrey Elder!" called Landless.

The old butler shot from out the crowd, as though impelled from a catapult. "Your Honor!" he screamed, "the man as says *I* plot against a Verney, lies! I that fought with your Honor at Naseby! I that you brought from home with you when Mistress Patricia was a baby, and that has poured your wine from that day to this! I plot with these rapscallions and Roundheads! Your Honor, he lies in his throat!"

"Fall into line, Humfrey," said his master quietly; "I will hear you out later, but now, obey me."

The watchful eyes of Luiz Sebastian were growing very watchful indeed.

"Regulus!" cried Landless.

Under cover of a burst of protestation from Regulus, the Turk whispered to the mulatto, "By Allah! this is the slave you would not approach! You said he would die for his master."

"He is not of them," returned the other. "St. Jago! if I understand it! But what can it matter? The moon will rise in less than an hour."

"Dick Whittington!" cried Landless.

There was a moment's silence, broken by the mulatto, who had stepped out of line, and now stood facing the party from the great house. "I grieve to say, señors," he said in his silkiest tone, "that the poor Dick was but now taken with the fever, and lies in a stupor within his cabin. To-morrow, perhaps, he will be better, and will answer when you call."

"That is your cabin, just beyond you there, is it not?" demanded Landless.

"Assuredly," with a quick glance. "And what then?"

Landless raised his voice to a shout. "Dick Whittngton!"

"Mother of God! what do you mean?" exclaimed the mulatto. "Your voice cannot reach him, deaf and dumb from the fever, lying in his cabin at the far end of the lane."

"Dick Whittington!" again loudly called Landless.

A cry arose from the crowd behind the mulatto and between him and his cabin. The next instant there broke through them the figure, bound and gagged, of young Dick Whittington. As he rushed past the mulatto, the latter, with a snarl of fury, grappled with him, but animated with the strength of despair, the boy, bound as he was, broke from him and rushed to Landless, at whose feet he dropped in a dead faint. Upon the crowd fell a silence so intense that nature herself seemed to have ceased to breathe. Luiz Sebastian, darting glances here, there, and everywhere, from eyes in which doubt was last growing into certainty, came upon something which told its own tale. The women's cabins were at some distance from the square, and nearer to the great house, and from the one to the other was passing a hurried line of women and children with the under overseer at their head.

With the sight vanished the last remnant of doubt from the mind of the mulatto.... Landless saw that he saw; saw the intention with which he slipped out of range of the pistols; saw the wicked light in his face; saw him beckon to the Indian and point to the forest; saw the glistening and rolling eyeballs and the working lips of the throng of slaves who had by imperceptible degrees separated from the whites, and were now massing together at one side of the square; saw the Turk with a knife in his hand;

saw Trail edging away from the group before the overseer's cabin—and sprang forward, his powerful figure instinct with determination, the set calm of the face with which he had met Havisham's quiet disdain and the imprecations of the other conspirators, broken up into fire and passion, high and resolved. Blood was upon it still, and upon his arms and half naked breast; his eyes burned; and as he threw up his arm in a gesture of command, he looked the very genius of war, and he seized and held every eye and ear.

"Men!" he cried, addressing himself to the line he had called into being. "Havisham, Arnold, Allen, Braxton! we fought in the same cause once, fought for God and the Commonwealth! To-night we will fight again, and together; fight for our lives and for the honor of women! Comrades, I am no traitor! I have not sold you! You have cursed me without cause. Listen! Colonel Verney, will you repeat the oath you swore to me an hour ago?"

The master stepped to his side. "I swear," he cried, in his loud, manly voice, "by the faith of a Christian, by the honor of a gentleman, that not one of you whose names have been given by this man, shall in any way suffer by having been privy to this plot. I will so work with the Governor and Council that your bodies shall not be touched, nor your time of service increased. Bygones shall be bygones between us. This applies to all save this man, the head and front of the conspiracy. Him I cannot save. He must pay the penalty, but he shall be the scapegoat for the rest of you. You have my promise, the promise of a man who never breaks his word for good or evil."

"In the woods yonder are Indians," cried Landless. "They wait but for moonrise, for the appointed hour, to fall upon the plantation. You called me traitor! It is Luiz Sebastian and Trail who are the traitors, the betrayers! They are leagued with the Indians and with the slaves. Look at them, and see that I speak truth!"

The look was sufficient. The dusky mass of slaves had swayed forward with one low, deep, bestial growl. Crouched for the spring, they were yet held in leash by the menace of the pistols, leveled upon them and gleaming in the torchlight, and by the restraining gesture and voice of Luiz Sebastian. In the crowd of servants, now quite separated from the slaves, was noise and confusion, and behind the Turk, standing midway between the parties, was forming a phalanx of villainous white faces—the dissolute, the convict, the refuse of the plantation,—and at his side, suddenly as though sprung from the earth, appeared the evil face and red hair of the murderer of Robert Godwyn.

The silence of the Oliverians, stricken dumb by this new turn of affairs, was broken by Havisham's crying to Landless,—

"What are we to do, friend?"

"Make for the house and defend it and our lives," answered Landless, "but first I call upon all true men among you yonder to leave those murderers and join yourselves to us."

"In the name of the King!" cried the Colonel.

"In the name of God!" said Landless.

Some seven or eight broke from the opposite throng and with lowered heads ran to them across the open space. Landless stooped, and lifting the senseless figure at his feet swung it over his shoulder.

"We are ready, Colonel Verney. Steady, men! Follow me!" He turned to the great house, rising vast and dark, two hundred yards away.

A gigantic, coal black Ashantee chief broke from the throng opposite and, uttering his war cry, bounded across the space between them. Another instant and he would have been upon them, and close after him a yelling pack of hell hounds—the overseer's pistol cracked, and the black giant fell dead. A yell arose from the crowd, but they stood irresolute. For firearms, so strictly kept from servants and slaves, so preeminently pertaining to the dominant class, they had a superstitious dread. Four pistols meant four lives picked from the foremost to advance.

"Let them go," cried the mulatto, with a taunting laugh. "Let them go! Let them go cage themselves in wooden walls where we will take them all together—rats in a trap. We will wait for the Chickahominies who have guns, señors, and for the Ricahecrians whose scalping knives are very bright. Until moonrise, señors from the great house, and you others who go with them! Mother of God! look well upon it, for it is the last you will ever see!"

Fifteen minutes later saw the house of Verney Manor garrisoned by some thirty desperate men. They had entered to find a scene of confusion—the hall and lower rooms filled with frightened women and crying children. Patricia with white cheeks and brilliant eyes had come forward to meet her father, carrying a three days' child in her arms. Beyond her was Betty, bending her sweet, pale face over the mother, caught up from her pallet and carried to the house in the arms of the under overseer. Mistress Lettice was alternately wailing that they were all undone and murdered, and wringing her hands over the obstinacy of Captain Laramore who, rapier in left hand, would stand guard at the door, instead of keeping quiet as the Doctor had said he must. The master's stern command for silence reduced the clamor of women and children to an undertone of lamentation. "We must to work at once," he said, "and apportion our forces. There are about thirty men, are there not, Woodson? I shall take the front with ten; Charles, thou shalt have one side, Woodson the other, and Haines the back. Laramore, thou must let us fight for thee, man, though I know thou findest it a bitter pill. Do you marshal the men, Woodson, and divide them into four parties, one for each face, and tell the women to leave off their whimpering and prepare to load the muskets. Haines, have the arms taken down from the racks and distribute them. Men and women, one and all, you are to remember that you are fighting for your lives and for more than your lives. You know what you have to expect if you are taken."

Sir Charles, followed by Landless, the Muggletonian and some three or four others, entered the great room, which, with the master's room, occupied that side of the house allotted to the baronet. The wax candles still burned upon the spinet, and upon the high mantel, and in the middle of the floor lay the overturned chess table. Three of the four windows were closely shuttered, but the fourth was open, and before it stood a graceful figure, looking out into the darkness.

Sir Charles strode hurriedly over to it. "Cousin! this is madness! You know not to what danger you may be exposing yourself. Come away!"

"I am watching for the moonrise," she said dreamily. "It is very near now. Look at the white glow above the water, and how pale the stars are! How beautiful it is, and how cool the wind upon your forehead! Listen! that was the cry of a jay, surely! and yet why should we hear it at night?"

"It is the cry of a jay, sure enough," said the overseer, pausing in his hurried passage through the room, "but it was made by Indian lips."

"Come away, for God's sake!" cried the baronet.

"Look! there is the moon!" she answered.

Above the level of marsh and water appeared a thin line of silver. It thickened, rounded, became a glorious orb. The marshes blanched from black to gray, and across the water, from the dim land to the great silver globe, stretched a long, bright, shimmering path.

A knot of women appeared in the doorway, laden with powder-flasks and platters filled with bullets. One, with only a stick wound with faded flowers in her hand, left them and glided to the open window.

"Margery!" said Patricia softly.

The mad woman, pressing in front of her mistress, looked out into the night and saw the white shining road cutting through the darkness and stretching endlessly away. She threw up her arms with a cry of rapture.

"The road to Paradise! the road to Paradise!"

An arrow whistled through the window and struck into her bosom—into her heart—the staff dropped from her hand, and she swayed forward and fell at her mistress's feet.

The night, so placid, still and beautiful, was rent and in an instant made hideous by a sound so long, loud, and dreadful, that it might have been the shriek of a legion of exultant fiends. It rose to the stars, sunk to the earth and rose again, unearthly, menacing, curdling the blood and turning the heart to stone.

"The war-whoop," said Woodson. "Close the window, quick."

CHAPTER XXVI

NIGHT

That terrible cadence preluded pandemonium, the hush of horror that followed it being broken by one deep and awful roar of voices as the insurgents, red, white, and black, joined forces and swept down upon the devoted house.

"They will try the front first," quoth the master from his loophole. "Steady, men, until I give the word! Now, let them have it with a wannion!"

The muskets cracked and a louder yell arose from without.

"Two," said the master composedly, receiving a fresh musket from his daughter's hand.

"They will try to dash in the door, your Honor!" cried the overseer from his post of observation. "They have the trunk of a pine with them."

"Let them come," said his master grimly. "They will find a warm welcome."

A double line of savages raised the great trunk from the ground and advanced with it at a run, yelling as they came. They had reached the steps leading up into the porch when from the loopholed door and window within there poured a deadly fire. Three fell, but the battering-ram came on and struck against the door with tremendous force. The door held, and but twelve of the twenty who had entered the porch returned to their fellows.

"They won't try that again," said the master with a short laugh.

"They are dividing," cried the overseer. "They will surround the house. Every man to his post!"

Around the corner of the house to the moonlit sward beneath the great room windows swept a tide of Indians and negroes with Luiz Sebastian and the two Ricahecrian brothers at their head. A few of the Indians had guns; the slaves were armed with axes, scythes, knives—the plunder of the tool house—or with jagged pieces of old iron, or with oars taken from the boats and broken into dreadful clubs. They came on with a din that was terrific, the savages from the eastern hemisphere howling like the beasts within their native forests, those from the western uttering at intervals their sterner, more appalling cry.

Within the great room Sir Charles, languidly graceful as ever, stood beside the small square opening in the door that led down into the garden, and fired again and again into the mob without. He fought with an air as became the fine gentleman of the period, but underneath the elaborate carelessness of demeanor was a cool precision of action. The hand that so nonchalantly brushed away the grains of powder from his white ruffles, was steady enough at the trigger; the eye that turned from the red death without to cast languishing glances at his mistress where she stood directing the women, was quick to note the minutest change in savage tactics. He jested as he fought—once he drew a tremulous wail of laughter from Mistress Lettice's lips.

A bullet sung through the aperture and grazed his arm. "The first blood," he said, with a laugh.

"There's a man killed in the master's room and two in the hall!" cried young Whittington, from his post at the far window.

"And Margery," said Patricia, coming forward with the kerchief from her neck in her hand. "Let me bind up your wound, cousin."

He held out his arm with a smile and a few low, caressing words, and she wound the lawn that was not whiter than her face about it; then moved back to where the women worked, loading and passing the muskets to the men who kept up an incessant fire upon the assailants.

The whole house filled with smoke through which the figures of the besieged loomed large and indistinct, and the noise—the crack of the muskets, the loud commands and oaths, the scream of a frightened woman or child, the groans of the wounded, of whom there were now many—became deafening. The attack was now general, and the men on each face had their hands full. Without was horrible clamor, oaths, shots, yells, crashing blows against door and window; within was noise and confusion, and fear, stern and controlled, but blanching the lip of the men and showing in the agony of the women's eyes.

Sir Charles, turning for a fresh musket, after a highly successful shot as the yell outside had testified, found Patricia at his elbow. "There are very few bullets left, cousin, and this is all the powder."

The baronet drew in his breath. "Peste! we are unfortunate! One of you men go beg, borrow, or steal from the others."

Landless left his loophole in charge of the Muggletonian and went swiftly into the hall, where he found the master, his wig off, his shirt torn, his face and hands blackened with powder, now firing with his own hand, now shouting encouragement to the panting men.

"Powder and shot!" he cried. "God help us! are you out? Not a grain or a bullet can we spare, for if we keep them not from the great door we are dead men!"

Landless went to the overseer. "Two more rounds and *we* are out," said Woodson coolly, firing as he spoke.

"There is no sign that they have had enough," said Landless, as the clamor outside redoubled, and a man fell heavily back from his loophole with a bullet through his brain.

"Enough! Damn them, no!" said the overseer. "When they've had our lives they will have had enough—not before! They're paying dearly for their fun though."

Landless went back to the great room with empty hands.

"They are all in like case," he said, in answer to Sir Charles's lifted eyebrows.

The other shrugged his shoulders. "What will be, will be. If we could have saved our fire—but we had to keep them from the door! Get to your post, and we will hold them back as long as may be. Then a short passage to eternal nothingness!"

"A short passage!" muttered the Muggletonian at Landless's ear. "Well for those who find that at the hands of the uncircumcised heathen. Eternal nothingness! The fool hath said in his heart There is no God—and he is being dashed headlong upon the judgment bar of the God who saith, I will repay. Cursed be the Atheist! May he find the passage, fiery though it be, as nothing to the flames of the avenging God; may he go to his appointed place where the worm dieth not and the fire is not quenched; may—"

The trunk of a tree was dashed against the door with a force that shook the room. "Dey're comin'!" shouted Regulus, who stood behind Sir Charles, and raised the axe with which he was armed above his head. Another crash and the wood splintered. Through the ragged opening was thrust a red hand—the axe, wielded by Regulus's powerful arms, flashed downwards, and the hand, severed at the wrist, fell with a dull thud upon the floor. A yell from without, and another blow, widening the opening. Landless fired his last bullet into the crowd, and clubbing his musket sprang to the door, in front of which were now massed all the defenders of that side of the house. Sir Charles threw down his useless musket and drew his sword. "Cousin," he said over his shoulder to Patricia, standing white and erect in the midst of the cowering women, "you had best betake yourselves to the hall, and that quickly. This will be no ladies' bower presently."

"Come," said Patricia to the women, and led the way towards the door leading into the hall. As she passed Sir Charles she put out her hand, and he caught it, sunk to his knee, and pressed his lips upon it.

"I am going to my father," she said steadily, "and I shall pray him as he loves me to pass his sword through my heart when they break into the hall. So it is farewell, cousin."

She drew her hand away and moved towards the door, passing Landless so closely that her rich skirts brushed him, but without a change in the white calm of her face. The terrified women had pressed before her into the hall, only Betty Carrington keeping by her side. Her foot was upon the threshold, when with loud screams they surged back into the great room. A thundering crash in the hall was followed by a babel of oaths, screams, triumphant yells. The voice of the master made itself heard above all the hubbub, "Charles, Woodson, Haines, they are upon us! Defend the women to the last, as you are men, all of you!"

The splintered plank between them in the great room and the murderers without was dashed inwards. An Indian, naked, horribly painted, brandishing a tomahawk, sprang through the opening, and Sir Charles ran him through with his sword. A second followed, and Landless dashed his brains out with the butt of his musket. A third, and the Muggletonian struck at him through the wildly flaring light and the drifting smoke wreaths, and missed his aim. The knife of the savage gleamed high in air, then, descending, stuck quivering in the breast of the fanatic. He sunk to his knees, flung up his skeleton arms, and raised his scarred face, into which a light that was not of earth had come, then cried in a loud voice, "Turn ye, turn ye to the Stronghold, ye prisoners of Hope!" His eyes closed and he fell forward upon his face, his blood making the ground slippery about the feet of the others.

Landless closed with the Indian, finally slew him, and turned to behold a stream, impetuous, not to be withstood, of Indians and negroes pouring through the doorway. From the hall came the clash of weapons and a most terrific din, and presently there burst into the great room the Colonel, Laramore, Woodson, and Haines, followed by some fifteen men—making, with the five in the great room, all that were left of the defenders of Verney Manor.

CHAPTER XXVII

MORNING

The women crouched in a far corner of the room behind a barricade of chairs and tables; the men stood between them and the thirsters for blood, and fought coolly, desperately, with such effect that, fearful as were the odds, a glimmering of hope came to them. The ammunition on both sides was exhausted, and it had become a hand to hand struggle in which the advantage of position and weapons was with the assailed.

"Damme, but we will beat them yet!" cried Laramore, panting, and leaning heavily upon his rapier. "They're drawing off; we've tired them out!"

"They'll never tire while that hellhound of an Indian whoops them on and that yellow devil, Luiz Sebastian, backs him up," said the overseer.

"They are gathering for a rush," said Landless.

The assailants had fallen back to the opposite wall, leaving a space, cumbered with the dead and slippery with blood, between them and the defenders of the house. In this space now appeared the lithe figure, and the watchful, large-eyed, amber countenance of Luiz Sebastian.

"Ohè!" he cried, "slaves, all of you! Ashantees, Popoes, Angolans, Fidas, Malimbe, Ambrice! you who are all black! think of the jungle and the village; think of the wives and the children! think of the slaver and the slave ship! You from the Indies, you who are like me, Luiz Sebastian, think of the blood which is the white man's blood and yet the blood of a slave—and hate the white man as I, Luiz Sebastian, hate him! Kill them and take the women!"

The swollen figure and dreadful face of Roach appeared at his side. "Ay!" cried the murderer, with a tremendous oath. "Kill them! Smash them, batter them, hear them scream! In the old man's pocket is the key of his money chest. It is filled with bright yellow gold. Kill him and get the money, and away to turn pirate and get more!"

"It grows late!" cried Trail. "We must up sail, and away before the dawn!"

The gigantic, horribly painted form of the Ricahecrian chief stalked into the open space and commenced a harangue in his own tongue. It was short, but effective.

"God!" said the Colonel, under his breath, and grasped his bloodstained sword more closely.

With one shrill and horrible cry Indians, negroes, mulattoes, and villainous whites were upon them, breaking their line, forcing them apart into knots of two and three away from the frail barrier, behind which cowered the screaming women, striking with knife and tomahawk, axe and club. Two of the Colonel's men fell, one under the knife of the seven-year-captive Ricahecrian, the other beaten down by the jagged and knotted club with which Roach, foaming at the mouth, and swearing horribly, struck madly to left and right. The Ricahecrian, drawing the knife from the heart of his victim, rushed on to where Landless and Sir Charles still maintained, by dint of desperate fighting, their position before the women, but Luiz Sebastian with Roach and half a dozen negroes swept between him and his prey. He swerved aside, and, bounding into the midst of the women, seized the one who chanced to be in his path,—a young and beautiful girl, newly come over from Plymouth, and a favorite with the ladies of Verney Manor. The despairing scream which the poor child uttered rang out above all the tumult. Landless turned, saw, and darted to her aid—but too late. With one hand the savage gathered up the loosened hair, with the other he passed the scalping knife around the young head—when Landless reached them, she who so short time before had been so fair to see, lay a shocking spectacle, writhing in her death agony. With white lips and burning eyes Landless swung his gun above his head, and brought it down upon the shaven crown of Grey Wolf. It cracked like an egg shell, and the Indian dropped across the body of his victim.

Landless, springing back to the post he had quitted, found Sir Charles in desperate case, but as coolly composed as ever, and with the air of the Court still about him despite his bared head and torn and bloodstained clothing, treating those who came against him to an exhibition of swordsmanship such as the New World had probably rarely witnessed. Landless, striking down a cutpurse from Tyburn, saw him run the Turk through, and saw behind him the nightmare visage and the raised club of Roach. He uttered a warning cry, but the club descended, and the handsome, careless face fell backwards, and the slender debonair figure swayed and fell. Landless caught him, saw that he was but stunned, and letting him drop to the floor at his feet, wrenched the sword from his hand, and stood over him, facing Roach with a stern smile.

The murderer raised his club again.

"We've met at last!" he cried with a taunting laugh. "Do you remember the tobacco house, and what I said? I says: 'Every dog has its day, and I'll have mine.' It's my day now!"

"And I said," rejoined Landless, "'I let you go now, but one day I will kill you.' And *that* day has come."

With an oath Roach brought down the club. Landless swerved, and the blow fell harmlessly; before the arm could be again raised, he caught it, held it with a grasp of steel, and shortened his sword. The miscreant saw his death, and screamed for mercy. "Remember Robert Godwyn!" said Landless, and drove the blade home.

The sword was a more effective weapon than the gun, and with it he kept the enemy at bay, while he glanced despairingly around. There were as many dead as living within the room by this. The floor was piled with the slain; they made traps for the living who in the wild surging to and fro stumbled over them, and fell, and were slain before they could rise. Three fourths of the dead belonged to the insurgents, but the attacked had suffered severely. Of the thirty men with whom the defense had commenced there now remained but twelve, and of that number several were wounded. The Colonel was bleeding from a cut on the head, the under overseer had a ball through his arm, Sir Charles still lay without movement at Landless's feet.

Forced, together with almost all of his party, by the mad rush of the assailants to the further end of the room, the master had seen with agony the women left well-nigh defenseless. Followed by Woodson, Havisham, Regulus, and young Whittington, he had all but cut his way back to them, when a fresh influx from the hall of slaves and whites who had been engaged in plundering the house, drove them apart again.

The newcomers came fresh to the work, maddened, moreover, by the master's wines. They advanced upon the Colonel and his party with drunken shouts, some brandishing rude weapons, others silver salvers and tankards, the spoil of the plate chest. The voice of Luiz Sebastian rang through the room. "Quick work of them, friends; I smell the morning!" With a laugh and a scrap of Spanish song upon his lips he came at Landless with a knife, but a turn of the white man's wrist sent the weapon hurling through the air.

"Curse you!" cried the mulatto, springing out of reach of the deadly point, and holding his arm from which the blood was flowing. "Mother of God! but I will have you yet!" and bounded towards his weapon. Landless, steadily watchful, and pointing that fatal sword this way or that against all comers, cleared for himself and the still senseless man at his feet a circle into which few cared to intrude, for the fame of that blade had gone through the room. "Leave him until we have dealt with the others," said the mulatto between his teeth. "Then will we give him reason to wish that he had never been born."

A touch upon his arm, and Landless turned to find Patricia standing beside him. "Go back," he cried. "Go back!"

"They are murdering them all over there," she said steadily. "My father is dead. I saw him fall."

"Not so, madam. He did but stumble over the dead. See, Woodson fights them back from him. For God's sake, get back behind the barricade!"

She shook her head. "He is dead. They will all be dead directly, my cousin and all. My father cannot help me, and he who lies here cannot help me. I will not be taken alive by these devils, and I have no knife. Will you kill me?"

"My God!"

"Quick!" she said in the same low, steady tones. "They are coming; they will beat us down in a moment. Kill me!"

For answer Landless raised his voice until it rang high above the uproar, and arrested the attention of the combatants on both sides. "Fight with a will, men," he cried, "for help is at hand! Do you not hear the hoofs of the horses?"

"By God! you are right!" cried the Colonel, suddenly struggling to his feet. "Hold out, men! Anthony Nash reached Rosemead, and has brought us aid!"

"The dog priest!" the mulatto cried fiercely to Trail. "Was he here? Then they have sent for help, and Mother of God! it is here!"

"And coming at the planter's pace," answered Trail. "They will be upon us before we reach the boats."

The mulatto glanced at the friend with whom he had fled the Indies with a sinister smile. "Ay," he muttered to himself. "They will be upon us indeed, before we reach the boats, wherefore Luiz Sebastian goes not to turn pirate this time. He throws in his lot with the Ricahecrians whose canoes are close at hand in the inlet that winds into the Pamunkey. They are very swift, and in the Blue Mountains there is safety. But one thing first."

He gave a shrill and peculiar whistle which brought to him half a dozen Indians. He pointed to the body of Grey Wolf and then to Landless. A yell burst from the lips of the savages, and they rushed upon the latter. He met them, ran his sword through the heart of the first, of the second: Sir Charles moaned, stirred, and struggled to his knees. A third raised his knife; it would have descended, but Landless darted between the savage and the half-dazed, utterly helpless man at whom the blow was aimed, struck up the arm, and plunged his sword into the dark breast. A broken oar, snatched from the floor by the mulatto, descended upon his head, and with a woman's scream sounding in his ear, he fell heavily to the floor, and lay as one dead.

When he came to himself, it was to find the great room still crowded with men, and filled with noise and confusion, but the thronging figures and the excited voices were those of friends—of servants from the neighboring plantations, of small planters and tenants of Colonels Ludwell and Fitzhugh, the Surveyor-General, and Dr. Anthony Nash. He saw the master, panting, bleeding, but exultant, seize Dr. Nash's hands in his own. He saw Sir Charles smile and extend his box of richly scented snuff to Colonel Ludwell, and the women leaving their corner of refuge with hysterical laughter and tears; saw Betty Carrington in her father's arms, and Mistress Lettice being helped across a heap of dead by Captain Laramore. Indians, negroes, mulatto, scoundrel whites, were gone.

"They got off clear—the d—d villains," said Dick Whittington, appearing beside him, "just before the horses came up. But Woodson has gone after the slaves and the convicts with a party of Carrington's men. He'll catch them, I'm thinking, and they'll come to a pirate's end—that's all the pirating they'll get. The Indians will get clean away; they're most to the Pamunkey by now, I reckon."

Landless staggered to his feet, and put his hand to his head, which was bleeding. "The women are all safe?" he demanded.

"All but poor Annis," said the boy. "When I saw the poor maid fall, I thanked the Lord that Joyce Whitbread was safe in her mother's cottage at Banbury. But none of the others were hurt. There is Mistress Lettice and Mistress Betty Carrington—I do not see Mistress Patricia."

The master of Verney Manor, pouring forth a rapid account of the late affair to the gentlemen who crowded around him, was brought to a dead stop by the appearance of a man who had burst through the throng, and now stood before him, half naked, bleeding, with white, drawn face and wild eyes.

"What is it? Speak!" cried the master, terror of he knew not what growing in his eyes.

"Your daughter, Colonel Verney!" cried Landless. "She is not here. The Ricahecrians have carried her off."

With a sound between a groan and a scream the Colonel staggered, and would have fallen had not Carrington caught him. "Gone! Impossible!" cried Sir Charles vehemently, all his studied insouciance thrown to the winds. "She was with the women behind the barrier that we made. She is here."

He began to call her by name, loudly, appealingly, but there came no answering voice.

"She will not answer," said Landless hoarsely. "She is not here. She was with the women until just before the last. She saw her father fall, and thought him dead, and you dead, too, Sir Charles Carew, and she came to me, and prayed me to kill her. Then we heard the sound of the horses, and six Indians—Ricahecrians—with Luiz Sebastian, came against me. She stood at my side while I killed three. Then I was struck down, and I heard her scream as I fell."

The master freed himself from Carrington's supporting arm, and raised from his hands a face that had suddenly become that of an old man. But the voice was steady with which he said quietly,—

"Let them search the room thoroughly, for the child may be laying in a faint beneath these dead, though my soul doth tell me that it is as this man says, and that she is gone. But we will after them at once, and, please God, we will have her back, safe and sound. They have but an hour's start."

"Ay," muttered young Whittington to Havisham. "Only an hour. But the Chickahominies build the swiftest canoes in this corner of the world, and I have heard that the canoes of the Ricahecrians are to the canoes of the Chickahominies as swallows are to cranes."

CHAPTER XXVIII

BREAD CAST UPON THE WATERS

Great trees, drooping from the banks of the Pamunkey, shadowed into inky blackness the water below them; but between the lines of darkness slept a charmed sheet, glassy, fiery red from the sunken sun. Three boats moved silently and swiftly up the crimson stream, until, rounding a low point, they came upon an Indian village, nestling amidst vines and mulberries, and girt with a green ribbon of late maize, when they swung round from the middle stream and made for the bank. They were rowed by stalwart servants, and in the foremost sat the master of Verney Manor and Sir Charles Carew. In the second boat was the Surveyor-General and Dr. Anthony Nash, and in the third the overseer, and among the rowers of this last was Godfrey Landless.

As they neared the bank their occupants saw that the usual sleepy evening stillness was not upon the village above them. A shrill sound of wailing from women and children rose and fell through the gathering dusk, and in the open space round which the bark wigwams were built, dark figures moved to and fro in a kind of measured dance, slow and solemn, and marked at intervals by dismal cries. As the boats touched the shore and the white men sprang out, a boy, stationed as scarecrow upon the usual scaffold in the midst of the maize fields, raised a shrill whoop of warning which brought the lamentation of the women and the dance of the men to a dead stop. The latter rushed down to the river side, brandishing their weapons, and yelling; but there seemed little strength in the arms that flourished the tomahawk; the voices sounded cracked and shrill, and the weak fury and noise died away when a nearer approach showed the newcomers to be white. A very aged man, with a face all wrinkles and a chest all scars, stepped from out the throng which was now augmented by the women and children.

"My white fathers are far from the salt water. Seldom do the Pamunkeys see their faces coming up the narrowing stream or through the forest. They are welcome. Let my fathers tarry and my women shall bring them chinquepin cakes and tuckahoe, pohickory and succotash, and my young men—"

He paused, and a low wailing murmur like the sound of the wind in the forest rose from the women.

"Where are your young men, your braves?" demanded the Surveyor-General. "Here are only the very old and the very young—they who have not seen a Huskanawing."

The Indian pointed to the crimson flood below. "There are my young men; there are my braves. Among them were a werowance and a sagamore. They two have strings of pearl thicker than the stem of the grape vine; they are painted with puccoon, and the feathers of the bluebird and the red-bird are upon them. They have hills of hatchets and of arrow heads, sharp and clean, and very much tobacco, and they sing and dance in the great wigwam of Okee, in the home of Kiwassa, in the land beyond the setting sun. But the rest—they lie deep in the slime of the river; it is red with their blood; their wives wail for them; their village is left desolate.... When the time of the full sun power was past the smoking of three pipes, came up the Pamunkey, swift as the swallow that skims its waters, the Ricahecrian dogs who, passing down towards the salt water twelve suns ago, slew the young men of a village that lieth below us. My young men went out against them, but a cloud came up and Kiwassa hid his face behind it. They came not back, their boats were sunk, the Ricahecrians laughed and went their way, swift as swallows."

"Ask him," said the Colonel huskily.

"Had they a captive with them—a woman, a paleface woman?" demanded Carrington.

"With hair like the sunshine and a white robe. And a man, the color of the falling sycamore leaf, one of those who work in the fields of the white fathers. The arms of the woman were bound, but his were not—he fought with the Ricahecrian dogs."

"Luiz Sebastian!" said the overseer with a muttered oath. "I thought as much when we found that he was not with the drunken scoundrels whom we took before they reached the Point. And we had better have killed him than all the rest put together, for he is the devil incarnate."

"Let us get on!" Sir Charles cried impatiently. "We waste time when every moment is precious."

The Colonel, who had been speaking to the Surveyor-General, came over to him. All the jovial life and fire was gone from his face, his eyes were haggard and bloodshot, he stooped like an old man, but the voice with which he spoke was steady and authoritative as ever.

"Ay," he said. "We must on at once, but not all of us. Richard Verney must not forget the danger of the state, in the danger of his child, nor let his private quarrel take precedence. I had hoped when we left the Manor at dawn to have been up with the villains ere now, but it was not to be. This will be a long chase and a stern one, and how it will end God only knows. We go into a wilderness from which we may never return. Behind us in the settlement is turmoil and danger, a conspiracy to be put down, the Chickahominies to be subdued, the strong hand needed everywhere. Every man should be at his post, and Richard Verney, Lieutenant of his shire, and Colonel of the trainbands, is many leagues from the danger which threatens the colony, and with his face to the west. He must on, but Major Carrington must go back to do his duty to the King, and Anthony Nash must not desert his flock. And you, Woodson, I send back to the Manor to do what you can to repair the havoc there, and to protect Mistress Lettice. My kinsman will go on with me; is it not so, Charles?"

"Assuredly, sir," said the baronet quietly.

"I'd a sight rather go with your Honor," growled the overseer, "but I'll do my best both by the plantation and by Mistress Lettice, and I look for your Honor and Mistress Patricia back in no time at all. We are to take the small boat, I reckon?"

"Yes, with four men to row you. We will press a boat and a crew from the next Pamunkey village. Pick out your men, and let us be gone."

"Humph! There's one that I reckon had best go back with us. Does your Honor know that you've got with you the head of all this d—d Oliverian business, the man that Trail swore was their general—that they all obeyed as though he were Oliver himself?"

"No! How came he here?" cried the master, staring at Landless, who stood at some distance from them with folded arms and compressed lips, gazing steadily up the glowing reaches of the river.

"Found him in the boat when I stepped into it myself. I didn't say anything then, for we were in a mortal hurry and he's a good rower. But I reckon your Honor will send him back with me? He'll give you the slip the first chance he gets."

"Of course he must go back," the master said peremptorily. "He should never have been brought thus far. A dozen or so of these Oliverians must swing as an example to the rest, and he, their leader, and a felon to boot, at their head. The service he did us last night can not help him—he fought for his own life. The Governor has sworn to hang him, and I am accountable for his safe delivery at Jamestown. Bind him and take him back with you, and send him at once to Jamestown under a strong escort." He turned from the overseer to the two gentlemen who were to go down the river. "Carrington, Anthony Nash, old friends, farewell—it may be forever. Anthony, pray that I may find my child safe and spotless."

They embraced, and he wrung their hands, and, stepping hastily into the boat, sank down and covered his face with his cloak. The Surveyor-General stood with a pale and troubled face, and Dr. Anthony Nash prayed aloud. The rowers took their places and the boat shot out into the middle stream.

Landless, seeing the second boat filling, and supposing that the third would receive its load in a moment, stepped towards it. As he passed the overseer, standing a little to one side with two servants belonging to Colonel Fitzhugh, a tenant of Colonel Verney, and an Indian from Rosemead, Woodson put forth an arm and stopped him.

"No, no, my man," he said with a grim smile but with a watchful eye, and nodding to the men to close in around them. "Your way's down, not up."

"What do you mean?" cried Landless, recoiling.

"I mean that the Doctor and the Major and I and these men go back to the settlements to look after things there, and that you are going to renew your acquaintance with Jamestown gaol."

For a moment Landless stood, turned to stone, within the other's grasp, then with a cry he broke from him and rushed to the water's edge. The boat containing the master had turned her head up stream and was beyond call; in the second boat the men held the oars poised while Sir Charles, with one foot upon the gunwale, gave a gravely courteous farewell to the Surveyor-General and the divine.

"Sir Charles Carew!" cried Landless. "I pray you to take me with you!"

Without moving, Sir Charles looked at him coldly, a peculiar smile just curling his lip.

"I remember a day," he said, "when you said that I might wait until doomsday and not hear favor asked of me by you."

"You are not generous," Landless said slowly, "but I ask the favor. I ask it on my knees. Let me go with you."

Sir Charles stepped into the boat and took the seat reserved for him. "I regret," he said politely, "that it comports not with my duty as a gentleman and an officer of the King to assist you in your very natural endeavors to escape the gibbet. Push off, men."

The boat shot from the shore and up the darkening stream, hastening to overtake its consort. Sir Charles raised his Spanish hat and fluttered a lace handkerchief. "To a happier meeting, gentlemen!" The Surveyor-General and the divine returned the salute, and stood in silence watching the canoe with its brawny rowers and the slender, elegant figure in the stern. It caught up with the Colonel's boat and the two grew smaller and smaller, until they became mere black dots and the dusk swallowed them up.

Landless watched them too with a face set like a stone. The overseer, backed by two of the servants, approached him with caution, but there was no need,—he submitted to be bound without a word, or struggle, or change in the expression of his face. He turned mechanically towards the boat, but the overseer plucked him back. "Not yet," he said. "We are all dead beat, and we have not the need to hurry that have those who are gone on. The Major's commander now, and he says sleep here a few hours. I'll fasten you so that you can't get away, I promise ye! Fegs! it's a pity that a man who can fight as you fought last night should have to die a dog's death after all! But you've only yourself to thank for it."

The red glow died from the river like the scarlet from cooling iron, and it lay dark and silent, dimly reflecting a myriad of stars. The sloping bank, the maize fields, tobacco patch and mulberry grove, the plateau upon which were ranged the wigwams of the Indians, the dark and endless forest—all the wide, sombre earth—had their stars also—myriads on myriads of fireflies, restlessly sparkling lanterns swung by legions of fairies. There was no wind; the cataracts of wild grape descending from the tops of the tallest trees stirred not a leaf; the pines were soundless. But the whip-poor-wills wailed on, and once a catamount screamed, and the deer, coming to a lick close by, made a trampling over the fern.

Landless, tightly bound to a great bay tree with thongs of deerskin, watched the night grow old with hard, despairing eyes. The stars paled and the moon rose softly above the tree-tops, silvering the world beneath. By her light he saw the little glade of which the tree to which he was bound marked the centre, and the recumbent forms of those who were to return to the settlements stretched on Indian mats laid upon the short grass. Worn out with the toil of the day and the storm and stress of the night before, they slumbered heavily. The watcher in their midst thought, "If I could sleep!" and resolutely closed his eyes, but the vision of a flying canoe and a brightness of golden hair, which had vexed him, passing up the reaches of the river over and over and over again, was with him still, and he opened them and raised them to the stars, thinking, "She may be above them now."

How still it was! no air, no breath, no sound—the thongs, that, wound many times around his body, bound him to the tree, fell at his feet, a figure slipped from behind the trunk, laid a hand, in which was a knife that gleamed in the moonlight, upon his arm, and whispering, "Follow," glided over the grass, past the sleepers and into the forest.

Swiftly but cautiously Landless went after it. The overseer lay within ten feet of him; he passed him, passed the unconscious servants, crossed a strip of moonlight, entered the shadow of a locust, and all but stumbled over a man lying asleep beneath it. He recoiled, and a twig snapped beneath his foot. The sleeper stirred, turned upon his side, and opened his eyes. The moon, now high in the heavens, shone so brightly that there was soft light even beneath the heavy branches of the trees, and by this light his Majesty's Surveyor-General and his Majesty's rebellious, convicted, and condemned servant recognized each other. For one long minute they stared each at the other, then, without a word or sign to denote that he was aware that aught stood between him and the moonlight, Carrington lay down again, pillowed his head upon his arm and closed his eyes. Landless was passing on with a light and steady step and the ghost of a smile upon his lips when the apparently slumbering figure put forth an arm and laid something long and dark across his pathway. He glanced quickly around, but the Surveyor-General lay motionless, with closed eyes. Stooping, he took up the object, which proved to be a richly inlaid musket with flask and pouch. He paused again, but no sign coming from the quietly breathing form on the grass he lightly and silently left it and the tiny encampment and entered the forest, where he found a dark figure leaning against a tree, waiting for him. Without a word it moved forward into the dense shadow of the forest, and in the same silence he followed it. They were now in thick woods, moving beneath interlocking branches and a vast canopy of wild grape that, stretching from the summit of one lofty tree to that of another, formed a green and undulating roof upon which beat the moonbeams that could not penetrate the close darkness of the world below. They came to a small and sluggish stream, flowing without noise between the towering trees, and stepping into the water, walked up it for a long while with giant blacknesses on either hand and above them the moon.

All this time the figure had stalked along before Landless without speaking or turning its head, but now, the trees thinning, and they coming upon a field of wild flax that lay fair and white beneath the moon, it quitted the lazy stream, and turning upon Landless as he too stepped upon the bank, showed him the bronze countenance and the gigantic form of the Susquehannock to whom he had once done a kindness, and with whom he had fought on such a night as this, in such a moonlight space.

"Monakatocka, I thought it had been you," said Landless quietly.

With the never failing "Ugh!" the Indian took Landless's hand and with it touched his own dark shoulder.

"I too am grateful, and with far more reason," said Landless smiling. "I will be yet more so if you will bring me out upon the bank of the river at some distance above yonder encampment."

"What will my brother do then?"

"I will go up the river."

"After the canoes in which sit the palefaces from whom my brother flees?"

"After the canoe which those canoes pursue."

"If my brother wishes to take the warpath against the Algonquin dogs," said the Indian quietly, "he must not follow the Pamunkey, but the Powhatan."

"They passed this village yesterday, going up the Pamunkey!" cried Landless.

"A false trail. Let my brother come a little further and I will show him."

He stepped in front of the white man, and moving rapidly across the field of flax, dived into the forest again. Following the stream in its windings they came to where it debouched into a wide and muddy creek, which, in its turn, flowed into an expanse of water that lay like molten silver beyond the fringe of trees.

"The Pamunkey!" exclaimed Landless.

The Indian nodded and led the way to a thicket of dwarf willow and alder that grew upon the very brink of the creek.

"While the palefaces slept, Monakatocka was busy. Look!" he said, parting the bushes and pointing.

Within the thicket, drawn up upon the sloping mud, were two large canoes, quite empty save for a debris of broken oars.

Landless gasped. "How do you know them to be the same?"

The Indian stooped and pointed to dark stains. "Blood. They had wounded among them. And this." He put something into the other's hand. Landless looked at it, then thrust it into his bosom. "You are right. It is a ribbon which the lady wore. But why have they left their boats, and where are they?"

The Indian pointed to the side of the larger canoe. "The hatchets of the Pamunkeys were sharp. They fought like real men. This canoe could go no further. See, it is wet within—they had to ply the gourd very fast to keep afloat so far. One canoe would not hold them all, so they hid both here. They knew the palefaces would follow up the river, so they cared not to stay upon its banks; the Pamunkeys, too, are their enemies. They have gone through the forest towards the Powhatan. My brother cannot see their trail, for the eyes of the palefaces are clouded, but Monakatocka sees it."

Landless turned upon him. "Will Monakatocka go with me against the Ricahecrians?"

"Monakatocka has dreamt of the village on the pleasant river where he was born. The arm of the white men cannot reach him here, in these woods, far from their wigwams and warriors and guns; it cannot pluck him back to be beaten. He toils no more in their fields. He is a real man again, a warrior of the long house, a chief of the Conestogas. Let my white brother go with him, across the great rivers, through the forest, until they come to the Susquehanna and the village of the Conestogas. There will the maidens and the young men welcome Monakatocka with song and dance, and my brother shall be welcome also and shall become a great chief and shall take the warpath against the Algonquin and against the paleface at the side of Monakatocka. In the Blue Mountains is Death. Let us go to the pleasant river, to the hunting grounds of the Conestogas."

Landless shook his head. "My thanks and good wishes go with you, friend, but my path lies towards the Blue Mountains. Farewell."

He put out his hand, but the Indian did not touch it. Instead, he stooped and examined the ground about him with attention, then, beckoning the other to follow, he moved rapidly and silently along the border of the creek. Landless overtook him and laid his hand upon his arm. "This is my path, but yours lies across the river, to the north."

"If my brother will not go with me, I will go with my brother," said the Conestoga.

CHAPTER XXIX

THE BRIDGE OF ROCK

For twenty days they had followed the Ricahecrians. At times the trail lay before them so plain that even Landless's unaccustomed eyes could read it; at times he saw nothing but untrodden ways—no sign to show that man had been in that wilderness since the beginning of the world—but the Susquehannock saw and went steadily onward; at times they lost it altogether, to find it hours, days afterwards.... It had led them westward, then south to the banks of the Powhatan, then westward again. At first they had to avoid an occasional clearing with the cabin of a pioneer rising from it, or some frontier post, or the village of one of the Powhatan tribes, but that time had long past. The world of the white man was far behind them, so far that it might have been another planet for all it threatened them; the Indian villages were few and far between and inhabited by tribes whose tongue the Susquehannock did not know. For the most part they gave these villages a wide berth, but sometimes in the quiet of the evening they entered one, and were met by the eldest man and conducted to the stranger's lodging, where slim brown maidens came to them with platters of maize cakes and nuts and broiled fish, and the warriors and old men gathered around, marveling at the color of the one and conversing with the other in stately gesture. Sometimes, crouched in a tangle of vines or behind the giant bole of some fallen tree they watched a war party file past, noiseless, like shadows, disappearing in the blue haze that filled the distant aisles of the forest. Once a band of five attacked them, coming upon them in their sleep. Three they killed and the others fled. They dipped into the next stream that crossed their path and swam up it a long distance, then emerged and went their way, tolerably confident that they had covered their trail. Sometimes they struggled for hours through coverts of wild grape, thick with fruit; sometimes they walked for miles down endless colonnades of pine trees, where the needle-strewn ground was like ice for slipperiness, and the blue sky gleamed faintly through the far away tree tops. The wind in the pines rose and fell in long, measured cadences. It made the only sound there, for the birds forgot to sing and the insect world kept silence in those vast and sombre cathedrals.

On the afternoon of the twentieth day they came to a halt upon the bank of a small stream that fell purling over a long, smooth slide of limestone into the river. Mountains had loomed into existence in the last few days. In the distance they made a vast blue rampart which seemed to prop the western skies. When the sun sank behind them it was as though a mighty warrior had entered his fortress. Nearer at hand they fell into lofty hills, over which the forest undulated in unbroken green. In front the river made a sudden turn and was lost to sight, disappearing through a frowning gateway of gray cliffs as completely as though it had plunged into the bowels of the earth.... Landless sat down on the bank of the stream above the fall and, chin in hand, gazed at the mountain-piled horizon. The Indian, leaning against a great sycamore whose branches trailed in the water, watched him attentively.

"My brother is tired," he said at last.

Landless shook his head. The Susquehannock paused, still with his eyes upon the other's face, and then went on, "We have searched and have found nothing. There have been five suns since the great rains blotted out the trail. My brother has done very much. Let him say so and we will go back to the falls of the far west and thence to the northward, to the pleasant river, to Monakatocka's people, to the graves of his fathers. And my brother will be welcome to the Conestogas, and he shall be made one of them, and become a great warrior, and both he and Monakatocka will forget the evil days when they were slaves—until they meet a paleface from the great water. My brother has but to speak."

"If these hills in front of us," said Landless with gloomy emphasis, "were higher than the Alps, I would climb them. If behind them there were another range, and then another, and another, if we looked upon the nearest wave of an ocean of mountains, I would climb them all. If they are before us, sooner or later I shall find them. But not to know that they are before us! To know that they may be to the north of us, may be to the south of us! that we may even have passed them! it is maddening!"

"We have not passed them," said his companion slowly, "for—" he stopped abruptly, broke off a bough from a sumach bush beside him, and falling on his knees, leaned far out over the stream. There were many tiny cascades in the brook with little eddies below them where sticks and leaves circled gaily around before they were drawn on to the next miniature fall, and into one of these eddies the Indian plunged the bough. The next moment he drew it carefully towards him, something white clinging to one of its twigs. It proved to be a fragment of lace—not more than an inch or two—and it might have been torn from a woman's kerchief. Landless's hand closed over it convulsively.

"It came down the stream!" he cried.

The other nodded. "Monakatocka saw it slip over that fall. It has not been in the water long."

"Then—my God!—they are close at hand! They are up this stream!"

The Indian nodded again with a look of satisfaction upon his bronze features. Landless raised his eyes to the cloudless blue, and his lips moved. Then, without a word he turned his face up the mountain stream, and the Indian followed him.

For an hour they crept warily onward, following the stream in its capricious wanderings. A broken trailer of grapevine, a pine cone that had been crushed under foot, the print of a moccasin on a bit of muddy ground told them that they had indeed recovered the long lost trail. They moved silently, sometimes creeping on hands and knees through the long grass where the bank was barren of bushes, sometimes gliding swiftly through a friendly covert of alder or sumach. The hills closed in upon them, and became more precipitous. The stream made another bend, and they were in a ravine where the water flowed over a rocky bed between banks too steep to afford them secure foothold. The Susquehannock swung himself down into the shallow water, and motioned to his companion to do likewise. "Monakatocka smells fire," he whispered.

A moment later they rounded an overhanging, fern-clad rock, and came full upon that at which Landless stared with a sharp intake of his breath, and which even his impassive guide greeted with a long-drawn "Ugh!" of amazement.

Towards them brawled the impetuous stream through a wonderful gorge. The precipitous hillsides, clothed with a stately growth of oak and chestnut, changed suddenly into a sheer and awful mass of rock. On either side of the stream towered up the mighty walls until, two hundred feet above the water, they swept together, spanning the chasm with a majestic arch. Great trees crowned it; trailers of grape and clematis made the span one emerald; below, through the vast opening, shone the evening sky with little, rosy clouds floating across it. A bird, flashing downwards from the far-off trees, showed black against the carnation of the heavens.

The Indian uttered another "Ugh!" then stole forward a pace or two, stood still, and waited for the other to come up. "My brother sees," he said simply.

From a covert of arbor-vitae they looked directly up the creek and through the archway. Beneath it, and for a few yards on the hither side, the water flowed in a narrower channel, leaving a little strip of boulder-strewn shore. With a leap of his heart Landless saw, rising from this shore, the blue smoke of a newly kindled fire, and squatting about it, or flitting from place to place, a dozen or more dark figures. At a little distance from the fire, close against the wall of rock, had been hastily constructed a rude shed or arbor. As he gazed at this frail shelter, he saw the flutter of a white gown pass the opening which served as door.

"Night soon," said Monakatocka at his ear. "Then will my brother see one Iroquois cheat all these Algonquin dogs."

They drew further back into the dense shade of the overhanging boughs. A large flat boulder afforded them a secure resting-place, and drawing their feet from the stream, the two curled themselves up side by side upon its friendly surface. The Indian took some slices of venison from his wallet, and they made a slender meal, then set themselves patiently to await the night and the time for action. The tiny encampment was hidden from them by the thick boughs, but through the screen of delicate, aromatic leaves they could see the bridge of rock. Around them was the stir and murmur of the summer afternoon—the wind in the trees, the whir of insects, the song of birds, the babble of the water—but far above, where the great arch cut the sky, the world seemed asleep. The trees dreamed, resting against the crimson and gold of the heavens. The Indian's appreciation of the wonders of nature was limited—with a grunted, "All safe: wake before moonrise," he turned upon his side, and was asleep.

His Anglo-Saxon neighbor watched the pensive beauty of the evening with a softened heart. The glory behind the tremendous rock faded, giving place to tender tints of pearl and amethyst. Above the distant tree tops swam the evening star. In the half light the shadowy forest on either hand blended with the great bridge carved by some mysterious force from the everlasting hills. Together they made a mountain of darkness pierced by a titanic gateway through which one looked into heavenly spaces. The chant of the wind swelled louder. It was like the moan of distant breakers. The night fell, and the stars came out one by one until the blue vault was thickly studded. Up and down the sides of the ravine flickered millions of fireflies. Their restless glimmer wearied the eyes. Landless raised his to the one star, large, calm and beautiful, and prayed, then thought of all that star shone upon that night—most of the white town of his boyhood, lying fair and still like a dream town, above a measureless, slumberous sea. A great calm was upon him. Toil and danger were past; passionate hope and settled despair were past. That he would do what he had come this journey to do, he now had no doubt,—would not have doubted had there been encamped between him and the frail shed built against the rock all the Indians this side of the South Sea.

The stars that shone through the great archway slowly paled, the stream became dull silver, and down the towering darkness on either hand fell a soft and tremulous light like a veil of white gauze. Landless put out his hand to waken the sleeping Indian, and touched bare rock. A moment later the branches before him parted. He had heard no sound, but there, within three feet of him, were the high features and the bold eyes of the Susquehannock.

"Monakatocka has been to the great rock," he said in a guttural whisper. "The Algonquin dogs sleep sound, for they do not know that a Conestoga is on their trail. They have camped beneath the rock three days, and they will move on the morrow. They have built a shed for the maiden against the rock. About it lie the Ricahecrians, the moccasins of one touching the scalp lock of another. They keep no watch, but they have scattered dried twigs over all the ground. Tread on them, and the god of the Algonquins will make them speak very loud. But a Conestoga is cunning. Monakatocka has found a way."

"Then let us go," said Landless, rising.

As they crept from out their leafy covert, the moon appeared over the tree-tops far above them, flooding the glen with light, and making a restless shimmer of diamonds of the rushing brook. The two men moved warily up the stream, setting their feet with care upon the slippery stones. Once Landless stumbled, but caught at a huge boulder, and saved himself from falling, sending, however, a stone splashing down into the water. They drew themselves up within the shadow of the rock, and listened with straining ears, but there came no answering sound save the cry of a whip-poor-will, and they went on their way. When they were within a hundred feet of the encampment, the Indian left the stream, crossed the strip of earth between it and the cliff, and pointed to a broken and uneven line that ran at a height of some five feet from the ground along the face of the cliff. Landless looked and saw a very narrow ledge, a mere projection here and there of jagged and broken rock, a pathway perilous and difficult as might well be imagined. So narrow and insignificant it looked, such a mere seam along the vast wall, that a white man passing through the ravine might never have noticed it.

"It is our path," said the Susquehannock. "It leads above the heads of these dogs and their crackling twigs, straight to where lies the maiden."

Without a word Landless caught at the stem of a cedar projecting from a fissure in the rock, and swung himself up to the cleft. The Indian followed, and with silence and caution they commenced their dangerous journey. Landless was no novice at such work. When a boy, he had often rounded the face of frowning white cliffs with the sea breaking in thunder a hundred feet below. Then a bird's nest had been the prize of high daring, death the penalty of dizziness or a misstep. Now, although not two yards below him was the solid earth, a misstep would send him crashing down to a more fearful doom—but the prize! A light was in his eyes as he crept nearer and nearer to the shed built against the rock.

They passed the smouldering embers of a large fire, and came full upon the circle of sleeping Indians. They lay in the moonlight like fallen statues, their bronze limbs motionless, their high, stern features impassive as death. From their belts came the glint of tomahawk and scalping knife, and beside each warrior lay his bow and quiver of arrows. Only one man had a gun. It lay in the hollow of his arm, its barrel making a gleaming line against his dark skin. The skin was not so dark as was that of the other recumbent figures, and the face, flung back and pillowed on the arm, was not the face of an Indian. It was Luiz Sebastian. He lay somewhat nearer to the shed than did the Ricahecrians, and directly in front of the doorway; as Landless paused above him, he turned and laughed in his sleep.

Slowly and cautiously Landless swung himself down from the ledge, his moccasined feet touching ground that was clear of pebbles and beyond the line of twigs. He glanced back to see the gigantic figure of the Susquehannock, standing upright against the rock, knife in hand, and watchful eyes roving from one to the other of the sleeping warriors, then stepped lightly across the body of the mulatto, and entered the hut.

Within it the darkness was gross. Pausing a moment to accustom his eyes to the blackness, there came to him from without the hoot of an owl. It was the signal agreed upon between him and his companion, and he wheeled to face the danger it announced.

The lithe, yellow figure that had lain in front of the doorway had waked. As Landless gazed, it rose to its knees, then with a quick, cat-like grace to its feet, stretched itself, cast a listening look around the sleeping circle, and laid its gun softly down, then with a noiseless step and a smile upon its evil face, it too entered the hut.

Landless waited until the mulatto was well across the threshold, and then sprang upon him, dragging him to the ground, where he held him with his knee against his chest. He writhed and struggled, but the white man was the stronger, and held him down; he tried to cry out, but the other's hands were at his throat choking the life from him. Putting all his strength into one hand, Landless felt with the other for his knife. The movement brought his face forward into the shaft of moonlight that trembled through the opening. "You!" said the eyes of the mulatto, and his clutching hands tore at the hand about his throat. The hand pressed closer, and with the other Landless struck the knife into the yellow bosom. When the writhing form was quite still, he rose from his knees, and looked down upon the evil face flung back to meet the moonlight. The struggle had lasted but a minute, and had been without sound—not a sleeping savage had stirred. But he now heard frightened breathing within the hut. By this time his eyes were accustomed to the darkness, and he made out something white niched into the corner opposite. As he advanced towards it, it started away, and would have brushed past him, but he seized it. "Madam!" he whispered. "Do not scream. It is I, Godfrey Landless."

In the darkness he felt the rigor of terror leave the form which he held. It swayed against him, and the head fell back across his arm. He raised the fainting figure, and stepping across the body of the mulatto issued from the shed, to find Monakatocka standing beside the entrance, knife in hand, and watchfully regardful of the sleeping Ricahecrians.

CHAPTER XXX

THE BACKWARD TRACK

Landless turned to the pathway by which they had come, but the Indian shook his head, and pointing to the stream which, making a sudden turn, brawled along at their very feet, stepped noiselessly down into the water, first, however, possessing himself of Luiz Sebastian's gun, which lay upon the ground beside the hut. Landless, following him in silence, would have turned his face towards the river, but again the Susquehannock shook his head and began to make his way slowly and warily up stream.

The other knew how to obey. Holding with one arm the unconscious form of the woman he had come so many leagues to seek, and with the other steadying himself by boulder and projecting cliff, he followed his companion past the sleeping Ricahecrians, out of the shadow of the great arch, into the splendor of the moonlight beyond. It was not until they had gone a long distance, past vast, scarred cliffs, through close, dark, scented tunnels formed by the overarching boughs of great arbor-vitæs, up smooth slides where the water came down upon them in long, unbroken, glassy green slopes, that Landless said, in a low voice:

"Why do we go up this stream instead of back to the river? It is their road we are traveling."

The faint, reluctant smile of the Indian crossed the Susquehannock's face. "The white man is very wise except when he is in the woods. Then he is as if every brook ran fire-water and he had drunk of them all. A pappoose could trick him. When these Algonquin dogs wake and find the fawn fled and the yellow slave killed, they will cast about for our trail, and they will find that we came up from the river. Then, when they find no backward track, but only that we entered the water there, before the maiden's hut, they will think that we have gone down the stream, back to the river. They will go down to the river themselves, but when they have reached it they will not know what to do. They will think, 'They who come after the Ricahecrians into the Blue Mountains must be many, with great hearts and with guns.' They will think, 'They came in boats, and one of their braves and one Iroquois, stealing up this stream, came upon the Ricahecrians when Kiwassa had closed their eyes and their ears, and stole away the fawn that the Ricahecrians had taken, and killed the man who fled with them from the palefaces.' And it will take a long time for them to find that there were no boats and that but two men have followed them into the Blue Mountains, for I covered our trail where this stream runs into the river very carefully. After a while they will find it, and after another while they will find that the chief of the Conestogas and his white brother and the maiden have gone up the stream, and they will come after us. But that will not be until after the full sun power, and by then we must be far from here."

"It is good," said Landless briefly. "Monakatocka has the wisdom of the woods."

"Monakatocka is a great chief," was the sententious reply.

"Do you think they will follow us when they find how greatly we have the start of them?"

"They will be upon our track, sun after sun, keen-eyed as the hawk, tireless as the wild horses, hungry as the wolf, until we reach the tribes that are friendly to the palefaces. And that will be many suns from now. I told my brother that we followed Death into the Blue Mountains. Now Death is upon our trail."

They came to a rivulet that emptied itself into the larger stream, and the Susquehannock led the way up its bed. Presently they reached a gently sloping mass of bare stone, a low hill running some distance back from the margin of the stream.

"Good," grunted the Susquehannock. "The moccasin will make no mark here that the sun will not wipe out."

They clambered out upon the rock and stood looking down the ravine through which they had come. "My brother is tired," said the Indian. "Monakatocka will carry the maiden."

"I am not tired," Landless answered.

The Indian looked at the face, thrown back upon the other's shoulder. "She is fair, and whiter than the flowers the maidens pluck from the bosom of the pleasant river."

"She is coming to herself," said Landless, and laid her gently down upon the rock.

Presently she opened her eyes quietly upon him as he knelt beside her. "You came," she said dreamily. "I dreamt that you would. Where are my father and my cousin?"

"Seeking you still, madam, I doubt not, though I have not seen them since the day after you were taken. They went up the Pamunkey and so missed you. Thanks to this Susquehannock, I am more fortunate."

She lay and looked at him calmly, no surprise, but only a great peace in her face. "The mulatto," she said, "I feared him more than all the rest. When I saw him enter the hut I prayed for death. Did you kill him?"

"I trust so," said Landless, "but I am not certain, I was in too great haste to make sure."

"I do not care," she said. "You will not let him hurt me—if he lives—nor let the Indians take me again?"

"No, madam," Landless said.

She smiled like a child and closed her eyes. In the moonlight which blanched her streaming robe and her loosened hair that, falling to her knees, wrapped her in a mantle of spun gold, she looked a wraith, a creature woven of the mist of the stream below, a Lörelei sleeping upon her rock. Landless, still upon his knee beside her, watched her with a beating heart, while the Susquehannock, leaning upon his gun, bent his darkly impassive looks upon them both. At length the latter said, "We must be far from here before the dogs behind us awake, and the Gold Hair cannot travel swiftly. Let us be going."

"Madam," said Landless.

She opened her eyes and he helped her to her feet. "We must hasten on," he said gently. "They will follow us and we must put as many leagues as possible between us before they find our trail."

"I did not think of that!" she said, with dilating eyes. "I thought it was all past—the terror—the horror! Let us go, let us hasten! I am quite strong; I have learned how to walk through the woods. Come!"

The Indian glided before them and led the way over the friendly rocks. They left them and found themselves upon a carpet of pine needles, and then in a dell where the fern grew rankly and the rich black earth gave like a sponge beneath their feet. Here the Indian made Landless carry Patricia, and himself came last, walking backwards in the footprints of the other, and pausing after each step to do all that Indian cunning could suggest to cover their trail. They came to more rocky ledges and walked along them for a long distance, then found and went up a wide and shallow stream. Slowly the pale light of dawn diffused itself through the forest. In the branches overhead myriads of birds began to flutter and chirp, the squirrels commenced their ceaseless chattering, and through the white mist, at bends of the stream, they saw deer coming from the fern of the forest to drink. A great hill rose before them, bare of trees, covered only with a coarse growth of grass and short blue thistles in which already buzzed a world of bees; they climbed it and from the summit watched a ball of fire rise into the cloudless blue. The morning wind, blowing over that illimitable forest, fanned their brows, and a tide of woodland sound and incense swept up to them from the world below. Around them were the Blue Mountains—gigantic masses, cloudy peaks, vast ramparts rising from a sea of mist—mysterious fastnesses, scarcely believed in and never seen by the settlers of the level land—a magic country in which they placed much gold and the wandering colonists of Roanoke, the South Sea, and long-gowned Eastern peoples.

"Oh, the mountains!" said Patricia. "The dreadful, frowning mountains! When will we be quit of them? When will we reach the level land and the blue water?"

"Before many days, I trust," said Landless. "See, our faces are set to the east—towards home."

She stood in silence for a moment, her face lifted, the color slowly coming back to her cheeks and the light to her eyes, then said suddenly:—

"Did my father send you after me?"

"No, madam."

"Then how are you here?"

He looked at her with a smile. "I broke gaol—and came."

A shadow crossed her face, but it was gone in a moment. "I am very grateful," she said. "You have saved me from worse than death."

"It is I that am thankful," he answered.

They descended the hill in silence and found the Susquehannock, who had preceded them, squatted before a fire which he had kindled upon a flat rock beside one of the innumerable streamlets that wound here and there over the land.

"The dogs yonder will need Iroquois eyes to spy out this trail," he said with grim satisfaction, as they came up to him. "Let my brother and the Gold Hair rest by the fire, and Monakatocka will go into the forest and get them something to eat."

He was gone, his gigantic figure looking larger than life as he moved through the mist which still filled the hollow between the hills, and Landless and Patricia sat themselves down beside the fire. Landless piled upon it the dead wood with which the ground was strewn, and the flames leaped and crackled, sending up thin blue smoke against the hillside and reddening the bosom of the placid stream. When he had finished his task and taken his seat, there fell a silence and constraint upon the man and woman, brought through so many strange and wayward paths, through lives so widely differing, to this companionship in the heart of a waste and savage world. They sat opposite each other in the ruddy light of the fire, and each, looking into the dark or glowing hollows, saw there the same thing—the tobacco house and what had there passed.

"I wish to believe in you," said Patricia at last, lifting appealing eyes to the opposite face. "But how can I? You lied to me!"

Landless raised his head proudly. "Madam, will you listen to me—to my defense if you will? You are a Royalist: I am a Commonwealth man. Can you not see, that as ten years ago, in the estimation of you and yours, it was all that was just and heroic for a Cavalier to plot the downfall of the Government which then was, both here and at home, so they of the Commonwealth saw no disgrace in laboring for their cause, a cause as real and as high and as holy to them, madam, as was that of the Stuart and the Church to the Cavalier.... And will not the slave fight for his liberty? Is it of choice, do you think, that men lie rotting in prison, in the noisome holds of ships, are bought and sold like oxen, are chained to the oar, to the tobacco field, are herded with the refuse of the earth, are obedient to the finger, to the whip? We—they who are known as Oliverians, and they who are felons, and I who am, if you choose, of both parties, were haled here with ropes. What allegiance did we owe to them who had cast us out, or to them who bought us as they buy dumb beasts? As God lives, none! We were no longer regarded as men, we were chattels, animals, slaves, caged, and chained. And as the caged beast will break his bars if he can, so we strove to break ours. You have been a captive, madam. Is not freedom sweet to you? We also longed for it. We staked our lives upon the throw—and lost. That dream is over,—let it go!... There is honor among rebels, madam, as among thieves. That morning after the storm, I had the choice of lying to you or of becoming a traitor indeed.... But as to what I had before asked you to believe, that was the truth, is the truth. I know that in your eyes I am still the rebel to the King, well deserving the doom which awaits me, but if, after what I say to you, by the faith of a gentleman, before the God who is above the stillness of these hills, you still believe me criminal in aught else, you wrong me much, you wrong yourself!"

He ceased abruptly, and rising, began to heap more wood upon the fire. The figure of the Indian, with something dark upon its shoulder, emerged from the spectral forest, and came towards them through the mist.

"Monakatocka has found our breakfast," said Landless, forcing himself to speak with indifference, and without looking at his companion. "I am glad of it, for you must be faint from hunger."

"I am very thirsty," she said in a low voice.

"If you will come to the water's edge, that at least can be quickly remedied."

She rose from the rock upon which she had been seated and followed him down to the brink of the little stream. "I would I had a cup of gold," he said, "and here is not even a great leaf. Will you drink from my hands, madam?"

"Yes," she said; then deliberately, after a pause, "for I well believe them to be clean hands."

Her own hand touched his as she spoke, and he put it to his lips in silence. Kneeling upon the turf by the stream, he raised the water in his hands and she stooped and drank from them, and then they went back to the fire and sat beside it without speaking until the arrival of Monakatocka, laden with a wild turkey. An hour later the Susquehannock carefully extinguished the fire, raked all the embers and ashes into the stream, hid beneath great rocks the debris of their morning meal, obliterated all moccasin prints, and having made the little hollow between the hills to all appearance precisely as it was a few hours before, when the foot of man had probably never entered it, stepped into the stream and announced that they were ready to pursue their journey. Before midday, the stream winding to the south, they left it, and plunging into the dark heart of the forest pushed rapidly on with their faces to the east.

CHAPTER XXXI

THE HUT IN THE CLEARING

Five days later saw the wayfarers some thirty leagues to the eastward of the hollow in the hills. They had traveled swiftly, sleeping but a few hours of each night and in the daytime pausing for rest only when Landless, quietly watchful, saw the weariness growing in the eyes of the woman beside him, or noted her lagging footsteps. They had left the higher mountains behind them, but still moved through what seemed an uninhabited territory. No Indian village crowned the hills above the streams; they encountered no roving bands; no solitary hunter met them; nowhere was there sign of human life. If their enemies were upon their track, they knew it not—perfect peace, perfect solitude seemed to encompass them. Still the Indian was vigilant; covering their trail with unimaginable ingenuity, taking advantage of every running stream, every stony hillside, building a fire only in some hidden hollow or fold of the hills, using his bow and arrow to bring down the deer or wild fowl which furnished them food—he stalked behind them, or sat bolt upright against the tree or rock beneath which they had made their resting place, tireless, watchful, the breathing image of caution. If he slept, it was a sleep from which the sound of a falling acorn, the sleepy stir of a partridge in the fern was sufficient to awaken him. Sometimes they rested by fires, for they heard the wolves through the darkness; upon the nights when this was necessary the Susquehannock sat with his gun across his knees, piercing the darkness in every direction with keen and restless eyes. Nothing worse than the wolves—cowardly as yet, for though drawing swiftly nearer, winter and famine were still distant—threatened them; no sound other than the forest sounds disturbed them; through the scant undergrowth or over the moss and partridge berry brushed nothing more appalling than bear or badger. But the Indian watched on.

Day after day Landless and Patricia walked side by side through the reddening forest. His hands steadied her over crags or down ravines, or broke a way for her through vast beds of sassafras or mile-long tangles of wild grape, and when their way lay along the bed of streams he carried her. She had no need to complain of fatigue, for he saw when she was weary, and called a halt. At their rustic meals he waited upon her with grave courtesy, and when they halted for the night he made her couch of fallen leaves and wove for it a screen of branches. They spoke but little and only of the needs of the hour. She bore herself towards him kindly and gently, thanking him with voice and smile for all that he did for her, and there was no mistrust in her eyes; but he saw, or fancied he saw, a shadow in their depths, and thinking, "She does not forget, and neither must I," he set a watch upon himself, and bounds, across which he was not to step.

Upon the afternoon of the sixth day they were passing through a deep and narrow ravine—a mere crack between two precipitous, heavily wooded mountains—when the Indian stopped short in his tracks and uttered a warning "Ugh!" then bent forward in a listening attitude.

"What is it?" asked Landless in a low voice. "I hear nothing."

"It is a sound," said the other in the same tone. "I do not know what yet, for it is far off. But it is in front of us."

"Shall we go on?" demanded Landless, and the Indian nodded.

It was late afternoon, and the hills which closed in behind them as the gorge writhed to left and right hid the sun. Great trees, too, pine and chestnut, walnut and oak, leaned towards each other from the opposing banks, and together with the overhanging rocks, mantled with fern, made a twilight of the pass beneath. Here and there the silver stem of a birch stood up tall and straight, and looked a ghostly sentinel. "Do you hear it still?" demanded Landless when they had gone some distance in dead silence.

"Yes."

"And still in front of us?"

"Yes."

"Ah, what can it be?" cried Patricia, turning her white face upon Landless.

A cold wind, blowing from open spaces beyond, rushed up the ravine. "I hear a very faint sound," said Landless, "like the tapping of a woodpecker in the heart of the forest."

"It is the sound of the axe of the white man," said the Indian. "Some one is cutting down a tree."

"There can be no ranger or pioneer within many leagues of us!" exclaimed Landless. "No white man hath ever come so far. It must be an Indian!"

The Susquehannock shook his head. "Why should an Indian cut down a tree? We kill them and let them stand until they are bare and white like the bones of a man when the wolves have finished with him, and they fall of themselves."

"If my father still searches for me," said Patricia in a low voice, "may it not be his party that we hear? There may be a stream there. They may make canoes."

"With all my heart I pray that it be so, madam," said Landless. "But we will soon know. See, Monakatocka has gone on ahead."

She did not answer, and they walked on through the gloom of the defile. Presently their path became rough and broken, blocked with large stones and heavily shadowed by cedars projecting from the rocks above and draped with vines. He held out his hands and she took them, and he helped her across the rough places. He felt her hands tremble in his, and he thought it was with the ecstasy of the hope which inspired her.

"If it is indeed so," she said once in a voice so low that he had to bend to catch the words, "if it is indeed my father, then this is the last time you will help me thus."

"Yes," he answered steadily. "The last time."

They passed the rocks and came to where the ravine widened. The sound that had perplexed them was now plainly audible; there was no mistaking the quick, ringing strokes of the axe. They rounded a jutting cliff and abruptly emerged from the chill darkness of the gorge upon a noble landscape of hill and valley, autumn woods and flowing water, all bathed in the golden light of the sinking sun and inestimably bright and precious of aspect after the gloom through which they had been traveling. But it was not the beauty of the scene which drew an exclamation from them both. At a little distance rose a knoll, covered with short grass and fading golden-rod, and with its base laved by a crystal stream of some width, and upon the knoll, shaded by a couple of magnificent maples, and covered with the pale and feathery bloom of the wild clematis, stood a small, rude hut. Smoke rose from its crazy chimney, and upon the strip of greensward before the door rolled a little, half-naked child—a white child. As the travelers stared in amazement, a woman's voice rang out, freshly and sweetly, in an English ballad. The trees had been cleared away from around the knoll, and in their place rose the yellowing stalks of Indian corn. The little mound, feathered with the gold of the golden-rod and girt with the gold of the maize, rose like a fairy isle from the limitless sea of forest, and the apparition of a troop of veritable elves would have astonished the wanderers less than did the tiny cabin, the romping child, and the clear song of the woman.

The Indian glided to their side from behind the trunk of an oak. "Ugh," he said with emphasis. "He is mad and so he has his scalp still." As he spoke he pointed to where, at a little distance, a man, with his back turned to the forest, was busily felling a tree.

"He dares much," said Landless. "We did not think to see the face of a white man—pioneer, ranger, trapper or trader—for many a league yet. He has built his house in the jaws of the wolf."

Patricia gazed at the hut with wistful eyes. "There is a woman there," she said, and Landless heard her voice tremble for the first time in their long, toilsome and painful journey. "There is no need to pass them by, is there? It looks very fair and peaceful. May we not rest here for this one night?"

"Yes," said Landless gently, reading, as he read all her fancies and desires, her longing for the companionship of a woman, though for so short a time. The Indian, too, nodded assent. "Good! but Monakatocka will watch to-night."

They moved through the checkered light and shade towards the man who worked at the foot of the knoll. They were quite near him when the woman, whose voice they had heard, came to the door of the cabin, shaded her eyes with her hand, looked towards the ravine, and saw the three figures emerging from it. With a loud cry she snatched up the child at her feet and rushed down the knoll towards the man, who at the sound of her voice dropped his axe, caught up a musket which leaned against a stump beside him, and wheeling, presented the gun at the newcomers.

"Give me your kerchief, madam," said Landless, and advanced with the white lawn in his hand.

"Halt!" cried the man with the gun.

"We are friends," called Landless. "This lady and I are from the Settlements. This Indian is not Algonquin, but Iroquois—a Susquehannock, as you may tell by his size. You need have no fear. We are quite alone."

The man slowly lowered his gun. "What, in the name of all the fiends, do you here?" he said, wiping away with the back of his hand the cold sweat that had sprung to his forehead. He was a tall man with a sinewy frame and a dare-devil face, tanned to well-nigh the hue of the Indian.

"I might ask the same question of you," said Landless, coming up to him with a smile. "This lady was captured and carried off by a band of roving Ricahecrians who bore her into the Blue Mountains. We ask your hospitality for to-night. The lady is very weary, and she has not seen the face of a woman for many weeks. Your good wife will entreat her kindly, I know."

The woman, who now stood beside the man, smiled, but doubtfully; the man's face too was clouded, and there was an uneasy light in his eyes.

Landless, looking steadily at him, saw upon his forehead a mark which served to explain his evident perturbation.

"You need not fear me," he said quietly. "'Tis none of our business how you come to be here in this wilderness, so far from what has been counted the furthest outpost."

The man, feeling his gaze upon him, raised his hand with an involuntary motion to his forehead, then dropped it, awkwardly enough.

"I see," said Landless. "I understand. I have been—I am—a servant. A runaway, too, if you like. I have been in trouble. I would not betray you if I could: that I cannot, goes without saying. Now, will you shelter us for this night?"

"Yes," said the man, his face clearing. "As you say, you couldn't do us harm if you would, seeing that masters, and d—d overseers, and bloodhounds are at the world's end for us. We are beyond their reach. Bring up the lady. Joan, here, will see to her."

An hour later the woman and Patricia sat side by side upon the doorstep in the long mountain twilight. At their feet the little child crowed and clapped its hands, and plucked at the golden-rod growing about the door. Below them, beside the placid stream, the owner of the hut and Godfrey Landless paced slowly up and down, now disappearing into the shadow of the trees, now dimly seen in the open spaces, while the Indian lay at full length beneath the maples, with his eye upon the blackness of the ravine down which they had come.

"It is fair to look upon, and peaceful," Patricia said dreamily, "but Danger lives in these dreadful mountains. Why did you come here?"

"We came because we loved," the woman said simply.

"But why into the very land of the savages, so far from safety, so far from the Settlements?"

The woman turned her eyes upon the beautiful face beside her and studied it in silence.

"I will tell you," she said at last, "for I believe you are as good as you are beautiful, and you are as beautiful as an angel. And, though I can see that you are a lady, yet you are woman too, as I am, and you have suffered much, as I have, and have loved too, I think, as I have loved."

"I have never loved," said Patricia.

The woman smiled, and shook her head. "There is a look in the eyes that only comes with that. I know it." She gathered the child to her, and beating its little hand against her bosom, began her story:—

"It is four years since I signed to come to the Plantations, to become the servant of an up-river planter—and to better myself. It was a hard life, my lady, a hard life—you cannot guess how hard.... One day a neighboring planter sent a message to my master, and I (for I served in the house) took it from the messenger. The messenger was one that I had known in the village at home, in England. He had left home to make his fortune, and I had not heard of him for a long time. They used to call me his sweetheart. When I saw him I cried out, and he caught my hands in his.... After that we met whenever we could, on Sundays, on Instruction days, whenever chance offered. He had tried to run away twice before we met, but he never tried afterwards. His master was a hard man—mine was worse.... After a while we began to meet in secret—at night.... You are a lady—that is different—you cannot understand; but I loved him, loved him as well as any lady in the land could love; better, maybe.... There came a night when I was followed, and taken, and he with me." She broke off to smell at the scentless spear of golden-rod which the child held up, and to say, "Yes, my darling, pretty, pretty, pretty," then went on with her eyes following the figures walking up and down beside the stream. "The next night found us in the sheriff's hands, in the gaol at the court-house. Oh that blank, dreadful, heavy night! I felt the lash already—I did not mind that—but I saw the platform and the post, and the gaping crowd beneath. I thought of him, and my heart was sick; I thought of my mother, and my tears fell like rain.... There was a noise at the window, and I stood upon my stool to see what it was. It was he! He had a knife and he worked and wrenched at the bars until he had wrenched them away, then dragged me through the window and we stood together beneath the stars—free! Another moment and we were down at the water side and into a boat which was fastened there. We loosed it and rowed with all our speed up the river. He had killed the gaoler and gotten away, bringing with him a musket and an axe. All that night we rowed, and when morning broke we were well-nigh past the settlements, for we had been far up river to begin with. That day we hid in the reeds, but when night came we sped up the stream. We came to the falls of the far west and left our boat there. For many days we walked through the woods, hurrying on, day after day, for when we lay down at night, I saw in my dreams the flash of the torches and heard the baying of the hounds. After a long while we came to an Indian village not many leagues from here, and there we found the mercies of the savage kinder than the mercies of the white man. They may have thought us mad—I do not know—but they did not harm us. There we dwelt for a time, in the stranger's wigwam, and there the child was born." She pressed the little hand which she held, and which she had never ceased to beat against her bosom, to her lips. "He would have stayed in the village, but in sleep I still heard the bloodhounds, and we left the friendly Indians and pressed on. We came upon this knoll on just such an evening as this—the light in the west, and the stream very still, with a large white star shining down upon it. We lay down beside it, and that night I slept without a dream.... We have been here ever since, and here we shall stay until we die."

"It is fair now," said Patricia, "but in a little while it will be winter and very cold."

"Bitterly cold," said the woman. "The snow lies long in these hills, and the wind howls down the ravine."

"And the wolves are bold in winter."

"Very bold. This scar upon my arm is from the teeth of one which I fought here, on the very threshold."

"The Indians threaten always, summer or winter."

"Ay, sooner or later they will come against us. We shall die that way at last. But what does it matter—so that we die together?"

The lady of the manor turned her pure, pale face upon the other with wonder, and yet with comprehension, written upon it.

"You are happy!" she said, almost in a whisper.

"Yes, I am happy," the woman answered, a light that was not from the faintly crimson west upon her face.

CHAPTER XXXII

ATTACK

About midnight, Landless, lying upon the dirt floor of the lean-to attached to the one room of the cabin, felt a hand upon his shoulder and opened his eyes upon a shadowy figure, blocking up the starlight that came faintly in at the open door.

"Hist!" said the figure. "Ricahecrians!"

Landless sprang to his feet. "My God! You are sure?"

"They are coming out of the ravine. You will hear the whoop directly."

The owner of the hut, stirred by the Susquehannock's foot, started up. Such an alarm being about the least surprising thing that could happen, he kept his wits, and after the first intake of the breath and exclamation of, "Indians!" he went about his preparations coolly enough. Rushing into the cabin where Landless had already waked the women, he groped for his tinder box, and with a steady hand struck a light and fired a pine knot which he stuck into a block of wood pierced to receive it; then jerked from the wall his musket and powder horn.

"You both have guns," he said coolly. "Good! We'll die fighting." The woman had flown to the door, had seen that the heavy wooden bars were drawn across it, and now stood beside him with a resolute face, and an axe in her hands.

A moment of silence, and then the quiet night was cleft by the war whoop—dreadful sound, forerunner of death and torture, concentrating in its savage cadence all ideas of terror! A moment more, and there came the sound of many moccasined feet and the hurling of many bodies against the door. The door held, and the man put the muzzle of his gun in one of the cracks between the logs and fired. The explosion was followed by a yell. Shot and cry preluded pandemonium. Without were demoniacal cries, quick crashing blows against the door, stealthy feet, clambering forms; within were smoke and the noise of the muskets, the crying of the child, and a red and flickering light which now brought out each detail of the rude interior, now plunged all into shadow.

"We are making it hot for them," cried the owner of the hut, reloading his musket. "There's some shall go to hell before we do. Joan, my girl—"

An arrow, whistling through a crack, pierced his brain and he fell to the ground with a crash. The shriek that the woman set up was answered from without by a triumphant yell, and then one voice was heard speaking.

"It is the mulatto!" cried Patricia, clasping her hands.

"Yes," answered Landless grimly. "I thought I had done for that devil, but it seems not. May I have better luck this time!"

"Ugh!" said the Indian, and pointed to the roof, which was low and thatched with dried grass and moss.

"I see," said Landless. "The cabin is on fire. We must leave it in five minutes, come what may."

"We will never leave it alive," the Indian said calmly. "The dogs have us fast. The Chief of the Conestogas will die in a strange land; his bones will be a plaything for the wolves of the mountains; his scalp will hang before the wigwam of an Algonquin dog. He will never see the village and the pleasant river, never will he smoke the peace pipe, he and his braves, with the Wyandots and the Lenni Lenape, sitting beneath the mulberries in front of the lodge. He will never see the cornfeast. He will never dance the war dance again, nor will he lead the war party. The sagamore dies, and who will tell his tribe? He falls like a leaf in the forest, like a pebble that is cast into the water. The leaf is not seen: the stream closes above the pebble—it is gone!" His voice rose into a chant, stern and mournful, and his vast form appeared to expand, to become taller. He threw down his gun and drew his long, bright knife.

"They are upon us!" cried Landless, and thrust Patricia behind him.

The rude door, constructed of the trunks of saplings, bound together with withes, crashed inwards, coming to the floor with a tremendous noise, and a dozen savages precipitated themselves into the cabin. Landless fired, bringing one to his knee; then clubbed his musket and swung it over his shoulder. Between him and the Susquehannock, standing beside him with bent body and knife drawn back against his breast, and the invaders, was a space some few feet in width, and in this space something dreadful now happened.

On one side lay the body of the man with the woman crouched above it, on the other a pile of skins upon which lay the little child. It had sobbed itself into exhaustion and quiet, but terrified afresh by the savage forms pouring through the doorway, the increased and awful clamor, the flames which had now seized upon the walls, and the choking smoke which filled the hut, it now scrambled from the pallet, and with a weak cry started across the space towards its mother. It crossed the path of the Ricahecrian chief—he glanced downwards, saw the tiny tottering figure with its outstretched arms, caught it up, and holding it by its feet, dashed its head against the ground. The cry which the child uttered as he raised it reached the until then deaf ears of the mother. She started up with a shriek that rang high above the yelling of the savages, and darted forward, only to receive at her very feet the mangled form of the baby she had sung to sleep but a few hours before. She caught it to her breast and with another dreadful cry rushed upon the savage. He met her, seized her free arm, raised it, and plunged his knife into her bosom. Still clasping the child to her bosom, she fell without a groan, while the Indian bounded on towards the three who yet remained alive.

The Susquehannock met him. "A chief for a chief," he said with a cold smile, and the two locked together in a deadly embrace. When the Ricahecrian was dead, the Susquehannock turned to find Landless—one Indian dead before him, another writhing away like a wounded snake—confronting across the body at his feet the graceful figure and the amber-hued, evil, smiling face of Luiz Sebastian. So strong were the flames by now, and so dense and stifling the smoke, that of the score or more who had broken into the cabin but few remained within its walls, which were fast becoming those of a furnace, the majority retreating to the fresh air outside, whence they whooped on to their devil's work the bolder spirits within.

These now bore down *en masse* upon the devoted three. One threw his tomahawk; it whistled within half an inch of Landless's head, and stuck into the wall behind him. Another struck at him with his knife, but he beat him down with his musket, and turned again to the mulatto, who, knife in hand, watched his chance to run in upon him.

"Look to the yellow slave, my brother," cried the Susquehannock, "I will care for these dogs," and hurled his gigantic form upon them. One went down before his knife; he broke the back of another, bending him like a reed across his knee; a third fell, cleft to the brain by his tomahawk—there was a fresh influx from without, and he was borne down and knives thrust into him. Struggling to his feet, with one last superhuman exertion of his vast strength, he shook them off as a stag shakes off the dogs, and stretching out his arm, cried to Landless, dimly seen through the ever thickening smoke;—

"My brother, farewell! I said we should find Death in the Blue Mountains.... The Iroquois laughs at the Algonquin dogs, laughs at Death—dies laughing."

He broke into wild, unearthly, choking laughter, his figure swaying to and fro like a pine in a storm. The laughter, an indescribable and most dreadful sound, became low, choked, a mere rattle in the throat, died into silence, and the laugher crashed to the ground like a pine for which the storm has been too much.

Landless drew a breath that was like a moan, but kept his eyes upon the yellow menace before him.

"The Ricahecrians are my good friends," said Luiz Sebastian. "They promise me a wigwam in their village in the Blue Mountains. I shall lead to it a bride, and she shall be no Indian girl."

Landless struck at him over the dead body between them, but the mulatto, springing back, avoided the blow.

"It is my hour," he said, still with a smile.

A portion of the roof fell in, making a barrier of flame between them. A volume of smoke arose, and through it Landless and Patricia dimly saw Indians and mulatto making for the doorway, driven forth by the intolerable heat and the imminent danger of the burning walls and the remainder of the roof caving in upon them. Beyond Landless was the square opening leading into the tiny shed in which he had been sleeping when this midnight visitation came upon them. Raising Patricia in his arms, he made for it, and they presently found themselves in temporary security. It was but for a moment, he knew, for the flames were already taking hold upon the shed, but as he set his burden down he whispered encouraging words.

"I know," she answered. "We are in God's hands. I would rather die than to come into that man's power. But the door to the shed is open and the way seems clear. Could we not escape even now?"

"Alas! madam, the flames make it as light as day around the cabin. They would certainly see us. And yet if we stay, we burn. When the fire reaches this straw above our heads we will try it."

"I would rather stay here," said Patricia.

Behind them the flames roared and crackled, the cabin burning like a torch, and with the flames rose and fell the triumphant cries of the savages, who, unaware of the existence of the tiny shed, so covered with the vines that draped the cabin that it seemed one with it, congregated in front of the gap in the wall where had been the door, and waited for their still living victims to emerge from it.

"Look!" breathed Patricia, grasping Landless's arm.

They stood facing the open door of the shed, and gazing through it down the lit slope of the knoll. Into the light, out of the darkness at the foot of the hill, now glided a man, naked save for the loin cloth, and painted with horrible devices; in the figure, noiseless and bent forward, savage cunning; in the eyes, the lust for blood. In his footsteps came his double, then a third, in all points exactly similar, then a fourth, a fifth—a long line, creeping as silently as shadows—a nightmare procession—up through the lurid light.

Landless drew Patricia further into the shadow.

"Wait," he said. "They may prove our deliverance."

The stealthy line reached the summit of the knoll, then broadened into a disc, and swept past the frail shelter in which stood the fugitives. A moment, and the war whoop rang out, to be answered by a burst of yells from the Ricahecrians, and then by prolonged and awful clamor.

"Now is our time," said Landless.

Hand in hand they ran from the shed that was now in a light flame, and down the slope up which had come the band of unconscious Samaritans.

"The stream!" said Landless. "There is a small raft upon it if they have not destroyed it."

They made for the water, found the raft hidden in a clump of reeds and uninjured, and stepped upon it. In ten minutes' time from the appearance of the new factor in the sum they were moving steadily, if slowly, down a stream so wide that in Europe it would have been called a river. The glare from the burning cabin faded, the flaming mass itself shrunk until it looked a burning bush, then dwindled to a star. The noise of the struggle upon the mount was with them longer, but at length it, too, died away.

"Which will conquer?" said Patricia at last, from where she crouched at the feet of Landless, who stood erect, poling.

"The Ricahecrians were the stronger," he answered. "But they may be so handled that they will not come at us again. That must be our hope."

There followed a long silence, broken by Patricia.

"The baby," she said in a quivering voice, "the poor, pretty, innocent little thing!"

"It is well with it," said Landless. "It is spared all toil and suffering. It is better as it is."

"The man and woman went together," said Patricia, still with the sob in her voice. "They would have chosen it so, I think. But the poor Indian—"

"He was my friend," said Landless slowly, "and I brought him death."

"It is I that brought him death!" cried Patricia, tossing up her arms. "I that shall bring you death!"

Her voice rose into a cry that echoed drearily from the hills about them, and she beat her hands against the raft with a sudden passion.

"You would bring me no unwelcome gift," said Landless steadily, "provided only that the time when I could serve you with my life were past."

She did not answer, and they floated on in silence down the little river, between banks lined with dwarf willows and sighing reeds. With the dawn they came to rapids through which they could not pilot their frail craft. Leaving the water, they turned their faces towards the rising sun, and pursued their journey through the forest that seemed to stretch to the end of the world.

CHAPTER XXXIII

THE FALL OF THE LEAF

Days passed, and the forest put on a beauty, austere, yet fantastic, bizarre. Above it hung a pale blue sky; within it, a perpetual, pale blue haze, through which blazed the scarlet and gold of the trees—great bonfires which did not warm, flaming pyres which were never consumed. Morning and evening a shroud of chill, white mist fell upon them, or they would have mocked the sunrise and the sunset. Along the summit of low hills ran a comb of fire—the scarlet of the sumach, leaf and berry; underfoot were crimson vines like trails and splashes of blood; into the streams from which the wanderers stooped to drink, fell the gold of the sycamore. From the hills they looked down upon a red and yellow world, a gorgeous bourgeoning and blossoming that put the spring to shame, a sea of splendor with here and there a dark-green isle of cedar or of pine. Day after day saw the same calm blue sky, the same blue haze, the same slow drifting of crimson and gold to earth. The winds did not blow, and the murmur of the forest was hushed. All sound seemed muffled and remote. The deer passed noiseless down the long aisles, the beaver and the otter slipped noiseless into the stream, the bear rolled its shambling bulk away from human neighborhood like a shapeless shadow. At times vast flocks of wild pigeons darkened the air, but they passed like a cloud. The singing birds were gone. Only at night did sound awake, for then the wolves howled, and the infrequent scream of the panther chilled the blood, and the fires which the wanderers must needs build roared and crackled through the darkness. In the daytime beauty, vast and melancholy; in the night, shadows and mysteries, the voice of wild beasts and the stillness of the stars; at all times an enemy, they knew not how far away or how near at hand, behind them.

Through this world which seemed more a phantasm than a reality, Landless and Patricia fared, and were happy. All passion, all fear, all mistrust and anger slept in that enchanted calm. They never spoke of the past, they had well-nigh ceased to think of it. When they knelt upon the turf beside some crystal brook, and drank of the water which seemed red wine or molten gold according to the nature of the trees above it, it might have been the water of Lethe.

In the illimitable forest, too, in the monotony of sunshine and shade, of glade and dell, of crystal streams and tiny valleys, each the counterpart of the other, in dense woods and grassy savannahs; in the yesterday so like to-day, and the to-day so like to-morrow, there was no hint of the future. It was enchanted ground, where to-morrow must always be like to-day. They kept their faces to the east, and they walked each day as many leagues as her strength would permit, and Landless, imitating as best he could the dead Susquehannock, took all precautions to cover their trail; but that done all was done, and they put care behind them. Landless, walking in a dream, knew that it was a dream, and said to himself, "I must awaken, but not yet. I will dream and be happy yet a little while." But Patricia dreamt and knew it not. She kept her wonted state, or, rather, with a quiet insistence he kept it for her. He never addressed her save as "Madam," and he cared for her comfort, and in all things bore himself towards her with the formal courtesy he would have shown a queen. He said to himself, "Godfrey Landless, Godfrey Landless, thou mayst forget much, perhaps, for a little while; but not this! If thou dost, thou art no honorable man."

Master of himself, he walked beside her, cared for her, tended her, guarded her, served her as if he had been a knight-errant out of a romance, and she a distressed princess. And she rewarded him with a delicate kindliness, and a perfectly trustful, childlike dependence upon his strength, wisdom, and resource. All her bearing towards him was marked by an inexpressible charm, half-playful, wholly gracious and womanly. The lady of the manor was gone, and in her place moved the Patricia Verney of the enchanted forest—a very different creature.

Thus they fared through the dying summer, and were happy in the present of soft sunshine, tender haze, fantastic beauty. Sometimes they walked in silence, too truly companions to feel the need of words; at other times they talked, and the hours flew past, for they both had wit, intelligence, quick fancy, high imagination. Sometimes their laughter rang through the glades of the forest, and set the squirrels in the oaks to chattering; sometimes in the melancholy grace of the evening when the purple twilight sank through the trees, and the large stars came out one by one, they spoke of grave things, of the mysteries of life and death, of the soul and its hereafter. She had early noticed that he never lay down at night without having first silently prayed. There had been a time when she would have laughed at this as Puritan hypocrisy, but now, one dark night, when the noises of the forest were loud about them, and the wind rushed through the trees, she came close to him and knelt beside him. Thenceforward each night, before they lay down beside their fire, and when from out the darkness came all weird and mournful sounds, when the owl hooted, and the catamount screamed, and the long howl of the wolf was answered by its fellow, he stood with bared head, and in a few short, simple words commended them both to God. "I will both lay me down in peace and sleep, for Thou, Lord, only makest me to dwell in safety."

There came a day when they sat down to rest upon the dark, smooth ground in a belt of pines, and looked between rows of stately columns to where, in the distance, the arcade was closed by a broken and confused glory of crimson oak and yellow maple. Landless told her that it was like gazing at a rose window down the long nave of a cathedral.

"I have never seen a cathedral," she said; "I have dreamed of them, though, of your Milton's 'dim religious light,' and of the rolling music."

"I have seen many," he answered. "But none of them are to me what the abbey at Westminster is. If you should ever see it—"

Something in her face stopped him; there was a silence, and then he said quietly:—

"When you shall see it, is perhaps better, madam?"

"Yes," she answered, gazing before her with wide fixed eyes.

He did not finish his sentence, and neither spoke again until they had left the pines and were forcing their way through the tall grass and reeds of a wide savannah. They came to a small, clear stream, dotted with wild fowl and mirroring the pale blue sky, and he lifted her in his arms as was his wont and bore her through the shallow water. As he set her gently down upon the other side, she said in a low voice, "I thought you knew. Had it not been for that night, that night which sets us here, you and me,—I should be now in London, at Whitehall, at some masque or pageant perhaps. I should be all clad in brocade and jewels, not like this—" She touched her ragged gown as she spoke, then burst into strange laughter. "But God disposes! And you—"

"I should be in a place which is never mentioned at Court, madam," said Landless grimly. "The grave, to wit. Unless indeed his Excellency proposed hanging me in chains."

She cried out as though she had been struck. "Don't!" she said passionately. "Don't speak to me so! I will not bear it!" and ran past him into the woods beyond the savannah.

When he came up with her he found her lying on a mossy bank with her face hidden.

"Madam," he said, kneeling beside her, "forgive me."

She lifted a colorless face from her hands. "How far are we from the Settlements?" she demanded.

"I do not know, madam. Some twenty leagues, probably, from the frontier posts."

"How far from the friendly tribes?"

"Something less than that distance."

"Then when we reach them, sir," she said imperiously, "you are to leave me with them at one of the villages above the falls."

"To leave you there!"

"Yes. You will tell them that I am the daughter of one of the paleface chiefs, of one whom the great white chief calls 'brother,' and then they will not dare to harm me or to detain me. They will send me down the river to the nearest post, and the men there will bring me on to Jamestown, and so home."

"And why may not I bring you on to Jamestown—and so home?" demanded Landless with a smile.

"Because—because—you *know* that you are lost if you return to the Settlements."

"And nevertheless I shall return," he said with another smile.

She struck her hands together. "You will be mad—mad! If you had not been their leader!—but as it is, there is no hope. Leave me with the friendly Indians, then go yourself to the northward. Make for New Amsterdam. God will carry you through the Indians as he has done so far. I will pray to him that he do so. Ah, promise me that you will go!"

Landless took her hand and kissed it. "Were you in absolute safety, madam," he said gently, "and if it were not for one other thing, I would go, because you wish it, and because I would save you any pang, however slight, that you might feel for the fate of one who was, who is, your servant—your slave. I would go from you, and because it else might grieve you, I would strive to keep my life through the forest, through the winter—"

"Ah, the winter!" she cried. "I had forgotten that winter will come."

"But to do that which you propose," he continued, "to leave you to the mercy of fierce and treacherous Indians, but half subdued, friends to the whites only because they must—it is out of the question. To leave you at a frontier post among rude trappers and traders, or at some half savage pioneer's, is equally impossible. What tale would you have to tell Colonel Verney? 'The Ricahecrians carried me into the Blue Mountains. There your servant Landless found me and brought me a long distance towards my home. But at the last, to save his own neck, forfeit to the State, he left me, still in the wilderness and in danger, and went his way.' My honor, madam, is my own, and I choose not so to stain it. Again: I must be the witness to your story. You have wandered for many weeks in a wilderness, far beyond the ken of your friends. To your world, madam, I am a rebel, traitor and convict, a wretch capable of any baseness, of any crime. If I go back with you, throwing myself into the power of Governor and Council, at least I shall be credited with having so borne myself towards my master's daughter as to fear nothing from their hands on that score. The idle and censorious cannot choose but believe when you say, 'I am come scatheless through weeks of daily and hourly companionship with this man. Rebel and traitor and gaol-bird though he be, he never injured me in word, thought, or deed....' For all these reasons, madam, we must be companions still."

She had covered her face while he was speaking, and she kept it hidden when he had finished. The slowly lengthening shadows of the trees had barred the little glade with black when he spoke again. It was only to ask in his usual voice if she were rested and ready to continue their journey.

She raised her head and looked at him with swimming eyes, then held out two trembling hands. He took them, helped her to her feet, and before releasing them, bent and touched them with his lips. Then side by side and in silence they traveled on through the halcyon calm of the world around them.

CHAPTER XXXIV

AN ACCIDENT

It was early morning, and the mist lay heavy upon the forest and on the bosom of the James. Landless and Patricia raked together the dying embers of their fire and heaped fresh wood upon them. The flames leaped up, warming their chilled bodies and filling the hollow that had been their camping place with a cheerful light, in which the moisture that clothed tree bole and fallen log and withered fern glistened like diamonds. Their breakfast of deer meat and broiled fish, nuts and a few late clusters of grape, with coldest water from a spring hard by, was eaten amidst laughter and pleasant talk. When they had lingered through it and when Landless had carefully extinguished their fire and had seen to the priming of his gun, they addressed themselves to their journey.

A bowshot away was the river, and Patricia willed that they walk along its banks that they might see the white mist lift, and the silver flash of fish rising from the water, and the swoop of the kingfisher. Landless agreeing, they went down to the river, and standing upon a rocky spit of ground which ran far out into the stream, they looked down the misty expanse, then turned involuntarily and looked up. At that moment the fog lifted.

"Ah!" cried Patricia, and shrunk back, cowering almost to the ground.

Landless seized her in his arms and ran with her across the shingle and up the bank. Plunging into the woods he made for the little stream which flowed past their camping place, and entering the water, walked rapidly up it.

"Did they see us?" Patricia asked in a low, strained voice.

"I am afraid so."

"They turned their boats towards the land. They are in the forest by now."

"Yes."

"And there is no doubt that they are the same. I saw the scarlet handkerchief upon the head of the mulatto."

"Yes, they are the same."

"They were such a little way from us. Oh, they may be upon us at any moment!"

"We are in great danger," he answered gravely, "but it is not so imminent as that. They were nearly a mile above us, and they have to land, to hide their boats and to find our trail, all of which will take time. We may count on having an hour's start of them, and we will do all in our power to increase it by breaking our trail as we are doing now. Then we cannot be many leagues from the falls, and the post below them, or we may stumble at any moment upon some Monacan village which will not need our urging to fly out against the Ricahecrians. Please God, we will win through them yet."

Somewhat comforted, she lay within his arms without speaking until they left the stream, when he set her down, and giving her his hand, ran with her over the fallen leaves down the long aisles of the forest.

Red gold showers fell upon them; fiery vines clutched at their feet, or, swinging from the trees, struck at their faces with vicious tendrils; the pines made the ground beneath like ice; rotting logs covered with gorgeous fungi barred their way; dark and poisonous swamps appeared before them, and had to be skirted—the forest leagued itself with its children and did them yeoman service.

The two aliens hastened breathlessly on. The sun climbed above the tree tops and looked down upon them through the half denuded branches. Midday came, and the short bright afternoon, and still they went fast through the woods, and still they heard no other sound than the rustle and sough of the leaves and the beating of their own hearts. They came to rising ground, and mounting it, found themselves upon a chinquepin ridge, and before them an abrupt descent of rain-washed, boulder-strewn earth. It was so nearly a precipice that Patricia shrunk back with an exclamation of dismay.

"I will go first," said Landless. "Give me your hands. So!"

Half way down, the earth began to slip. Patricia, looking up and over her shoulder, uttered a cry. A great boulder, imbedded in the earth directly above them, was dislodging itself, was falling! At her cry Landless raised his eyes, saw the threatening mass, caught her around the waist, and with one supreme effort swung her out of the path of the avalanche which descended the next moment, bearing him with it to the ground beneath.

He was recalled to consciousness by the dash of water against his face, and opened his eyes to behold Patricia bending over him, very white, with tragic eyes, and lips pressed closely together. She had run to the river, flowing through the sunshine a hundred yards away, for water, which she had brought back in his cap, and she had taken the kerchief from her neck, wet it, and laid it upon his forehead. Her hands were torn and bleeding. He saw them and uttered an exclamation. "It is nothing," she said; "I had to move the rock." Scarcely fully conscious as yet, his eyes glanced from her to the great rock which lay upon one side, and upon which there were bloodstains. "I have had a bad fall," he said unsteadily, but with an attempt to speak lightly because of the trouble in her eyes, "but it is over. Come! we must hurry on. We have no time to lose."

As he spoke he strove to rise, but with the effort came a pang of anguish, and he sank back, faint and sick, upon the ground.

"Ah! you cannot!" cried Patricia with a great sob in her voice. "It is your foot. The rock fell upon it."

After a moment of lying with closed eyes, he sat up and with his knife began to cut away the moccasin from the wounded limb. Presently he looked up. "Yes, it is badly crushed. There is no doing anything with it."

For many moments they gazed at each other in a despairing silence, broken by Patricia's low, "What are we to do now?"

"We must go on," answered Landless. "It is death to stay here."

Holding by the bank against which he had leaned, he dragged himself up and stood for an instant with eyes dark with pain; then, setting his lips, took a step forward. The bronze of his face paled, and beads of anguish stood upon his brow, but he took another step. Patricia, the tears running down her cheeks, came to him and put his arm around her shoulder. "I will be your crutch," she said, striving to smile. "I will carry the gun, too."

Before them was a steeply sloping, grass-grown ascent rising to a broken line of cliffs, scarred and gray, crowned with cedars and hung here and there with crimson creepers, and with a chance medley of huge gray boulders scattered about their base. Up this ascent they labored, so slowly that the crags seemed like the mountain in the Arabian tale, ever receding as they advanced. Twice Landless staggered and fell to his knee, but when, after what seemed an eternity of pain and distress, they reached the summit and Patricia would have had him rest, he shook his head and motioned with his hand towards the narrow, boulder-strewn plateau at the foot of the crags.

With her accustomed unquestioning obedience she turned towards the rocks, and after another interval of painful toil they found themselves in a sort of rocky chamber, a natural blockhouse, of which the sheer cliff formed one wall and boulders of varying height and shape the others.

Above them gleamed the blue sky; through the gaps between the rocks they looked down upon the shining river and the parti-colored woods, and behind them towered the cliffs. A strong wind was blowing and it sent red leaves from the vines that draped the rock whirling down upon them.

"The tall gray crags," said Patricia in a strange voice, "and the Martinmas wind. The river flowing in the sunshine too."

Landless sank upon the rocky floor. "I can go no further," he said. "God help me!"

"I do not think another man could have come so far," she answered. "What are we to do now?"

"You must go on without me."

She cried out angrily, "What do you mean? I don't understand you."

"Listen," he said earnestly, dragging himself closer to her. "We can be but a very few leagues from the falls, still fewer from the Indian villages above them. Reach one of those villages and you are safe from these devils at least. We have kept the start of them. They may not reach this spot for several hours, and when they come, I will keep them here, God helping me, for more hours than one. This place is a natural fortress, and they have no guns. They will not take me until my ammunition is exhausted, and you know there is store of bullets and powder. They will think that you are with me, hidden behind the rocks—"

"And I shall be with you!" she cried vehemently.

"No, no. You must go through this pass in the cliff to the right of us, and thence down the river with all your speed. Please God, to-morrow will find you in safety. It is the only way. To stay here is to fall into their hands. And you must not delay. You must go at once."

"And you—" she said in a whisper.

"What does it matter if I lose my life to-day instead of a few weeks hence? I grieve for this," with a glance at his foot, "because it keeps me from being with you, from guarding you into perfect safety. Otherwise it does not matter. You lose time, madam."

She stood with heaving bosom and foot tapping the ground, an expression that he could not read in her wonderful eyes. "I am not going," she said at last.

CHAPTER XXXV

THE BOAT THAT WAS NOT

"You will not go?" cried Landless.

"No, I will not!" she answered passionately. "Why should you think such a thing of me? See! we have been together, you and I, for long weeks! You have been my faithful guide, my faithful protector. Over and over again you have saved my life. And now, now when you are the helpless one, when it is through me that you lie there helpless, when it is through me that you are in this dreadful forest at all, you tell me to go! to leave you to the fate I have brought upon you! to save myself! I will not save myself! But the other day it was dishonor in you to leave me below the falls—almost in safety. Mine the dishonor if I do what you bid me do!"

"Madam, madam, it is not with women as with men!"

"I care not for women! I care for myself. Never, never, will I leave, helpless and wounded, the man who dies for me!"

"Upon my knees I implore you!" Landless cried in desperation. "You cannot save me, you cannot help me. It is you that would make the bitterness of my fate. Let me die believing that you have escaped these fiends, and then, do what they will to me, I shall die happy, blessing with my last breath the generous woman who lets me give—how proudly and gladly she will never know—my worthless life in exchange for hers, so young, bright, innocent. Go, go, before it is too late!"

He dragged himself a foot nearer, and grasping the hem of her dress, pressed it to his lips. "Good-bye," he said with a faint smile. "Keep behind the rocks for some distance, then follow the river. Think kindly of me. Good-bye."

"It is too late," she said. "I can see the river through this crack between the rocks. One of those two canoes has just passed, going down the river. In it were seven Ricahecrians and the mulatto. I saw him quite plainly, for they row close to the bank with their faces turned to the woods. They will land at some point below this and search for our trail. When they do not find it, they will know that we are between them and the rest of the band, and they will come upon us from behind. If I go now, it will be to meet them. Shall I go?"

"No, no," groaned Landless. "It is too late. God help you! I cannot."

The large tears gathered in her eyes and fell over her white cheeks. "Oh, why," she said plaintively, "why did He let you hurt yourself just now?" She turned her face to the rock against which she was standing, and hiding it in her arm, broke into a low sobbing. It went to the heart of the man at her feet to hear her.

Presently the weeping ceased. She drew a long tremulous sigh, and dashed the tears from her eyes. Her hands went up to her disheveled hair in a little involuntary, feminine gesture, and she looked at him with a wan smile.

"I did not mean to be so cowardly," she said simply. "I will be brave now."

"You are the bravest woman in the world," he answered.

Below them waved the painted forest flaunting triumphant banners of crimson and gold. A strong south wind was blowing, and it brought to them a sound as of the whispering of many voices. The shining river, too, murmured to its reeds and pebbles, and in the air was the dull whirr of wings as the vast flocks of wild fowl rose like dark smoke from the water, or, skimming along its surface, broke it into myriad diamond sprays. Around the horizon towered heaped-up masses of cloud—Ossa piled on Pelion—fantastic Jack-and-the-Beanstalk castles, built high above the world, with rampart and turret and bastion of pearl and coral. Above rose the sky intensely blue and calm.

All the wealth, the warmth and loveliness of the world they were about to leave flowed over the souls of the doomed pair. In their hearts they each said farewell to it forever. Patricia stood with uplifted face and clear eyes, looking deep into the azure heaven. "I am trying to think," she said, "that death is not so bitter after all. To-day is beautiful—but ours will be a fairer morrow! After to-day we will never be tired, or fear, or be in danger any more. I am not afraid to die; but ah! if it could only come to us now, swiftly, silently, out of the blue yonder; if we could go without the blood—the horror—" she broke off shuddering. Her eyes closed and she rested her head against the rock. Landless watched the beautiful, pale face, the quivering eyelids, the coral underlip drawn between the pearly teeth, in a passion of pity and despair. Horrid visions of torture flashed through his brain; he saw the delicate limbs writhing, heard the agonized screams.... If he killed the mulatto, it might come to that; if the mulatto lived, he knew that she would kill herself. He had given her the knife that had been Monakatocka's, and she had it now, hidden in her bosom.... The glory of the autumn day darkened and went out, the bitter waters of affliction surged over him, an immeasurable sea; it seemed to him that until then he had never suffered. A cold sweat broke out upon him, and with an inarticulate cry of rage and despair he struck at his wounded foot as at a deadly foe. The girl cried out at the sound of the blow.

"Oh, don't, don't! What are you doing? You have loosened the bandage, and it is bleeding afresh."

Despite his effort to prevent her she readjusted the kerchief which she had wound about the torn and crushed foot, very carefully and tenderly. "It must hurt you very much," she said pityingly.

He took the little ministering hands in his and kissed them. "Oh, madam, madam!" he groaned. "God knows I would shed every drop of my blood a thousand times to save you. Death to me is nothing, nor life so fair that I should care to keep it. The grave is a less dreadful prison than those on earth, and I think to find in God a more merciful Judge. But you—so young and beautiful, with friends, love—"

She stopped him with a gesture full of dignity and sweetness. "That life is gone forever,—it is thousands of miles and ages on ages away. It is a world more distant than the stars, and we are nearer to Heaven than to it.... It is strange to think how we have drifted, you and I, to this rock. A year ago we had never seen each other's faces, had never heard each other's names, and yet you were coming to this rock from prison and over seas, and I was coming to meet you.... And it is our death place, and we will die together, and to-morrow maybe the little birds will cover us with leaves as they did the children in the story. They were brother and sister.... When our time comes I will not be afraid, for I will be with you ... my brother."

Landless covered his face with his hands.

The shadows grew longer and the cloud castles began to flush rosily, though the sun still rode above the tree tops. A purple light filled the aisles of the forest, through which a herd of deer, making for some accustomed lick, passed like a phantom troop. They vanished, and from out the stillness of the glades came the sudden, startled barking of a fox. A shadow darted across a sunlit alley from gloom to gloom, paused on the outskirts of the wood below the crags while one might count ten, then turned and flitted back into the darkness from whence it came. They beneath the crags did not see it.

Suddenly Landless raised his head. Upon his face was the look of one who has come through much doubt and anguish of spirit to an immutable resolve. He looked to the priming of his gun and laid it upon the rock beside him, together with his powderhorn and pouch of bullets. Raising himself to his knees he gazed long and intently into the forest below. There was no sign of danger. On the checkered ground beneath two mighty oaks squirrels were playing together like frolicsome kittens, and through the clear air came the tapping of a woodpecker. The forest was silent as to the shadow that had flitted through it. It can keep a secret very well.

Landless sank back against the rock. He had lost much blood, and that and the pain of his mangled foot turned him faint and sick for minutes at a time. He clenched his teeth and forced back the deadly faintness, then turned to the woman who stood beside him, her hands clasped before her, her eyes following the declining sun, her lips sometimes set in mournful curves, sometimes murmuring broken and inaudible words of prayer. He called her twice before she answered, turning to him with eyes of feverish splendor which saw and yet saw not. "What is it?" she asked dreamily.

"Come back to earth, madam," he said. "There is that that I wish to say to you. Listen to me kindly and pitifully, as to a dying man."

"I am listening," she answered. "What is it?"

"It is this, madam: I love you. For God's sake don't turn away! Oh, I know that I should have been strong to the end, that I should not vex you thus! It is the coward's part I play, perhaps, but I must speak! I cannot die without. I love you, I love you, I love you!"

His voice rose into a cry; in it rang long repressed passion, hopeless adoration, fierce joy in having broken the bonds of silence. He spoke rapidly, thickly, with a stammering tongue, now throwing out his hands in passionate appeal, now crushing between his fingers the dried moss and twigs with which the ground was strewn. "I loved you the day I first saw you. I have loved you ever since. I love you now. My God! how I love you! Die for you? I would die for you ten thousand times! I would *live* for you! Oh, the day I first saw you! I was in hell and I looked at you as lost Dives might have looked at the angel on the other side of the gulf.... I never thought to tell you this. I know that never, never, never.... But this is the day of our death. In a few hours we shall be gone. Do not leave the world in anger with me. Say that you pity, understand, forgive.... Speak to me, madam!"

The sun sank lower and the shadows lengthened and deepened, and still Patricia stood silent with uplifted and averted face, and fingers tightly locked together. With a moan of mortal weakness Landless dragged himself nearer until he touched with his forehead the low pedestal of rock upon which she stood. "I understand," he said quietly. "After all, there is nothing to be said, is there? Try to forget my—madness. Think of it, if you will, as the raving of one at death's door. Let it be as it was between us."

Patricia turned—her beautiful face transfigured. Roses bloomed in her cheeks, her eyes were fathomless wells of splendor, an exquisite smile played about her lips; with her nimbus of golden hair she looked a rapt mediæval saint. Her slender figure swayed towards Landless, and when she spoke her voice was like the tone of a violin, soft, rich, caressing, tremulous.

"There was no boat," she said.

"No boat!" he cried. "What do you mean?"

"The canoe going down the river. I told you that it held seven Indians and the mulatto. I lied to you. There were no Indians, no mulatto, no canoe. The shadows of the clouds have been upon the river, and the wild fowl, and once a fish-hawk plunged. I have seen nothing else."

Landless gazed at her with staring eyeballs. "You have thrown away your life," he said at last in a voice that did not seem his own.

"Yes, I have thrown away my life."

"But why—why—"

The rich color surged over her face and neck. She swayed towards him with the grace of a wind-bowed lily, her breath fanning his forehead, and her hand touching his, softly, flutteringly, like a young bird.

"Can you not guess why?" she said with an enchanting smile.

All the anguish of a little while back, all the terror of the fate that hung over her, all the white calm of despair was gone. The horror that moved nearer and nearer, moment by moment, through the painted forest, was forgotten. She looked at him shyly from under her long lashes and with another wonderful blush.

Landless gazed at her, comprehension slowly dawning in his eyes. For five minutes there was a silence as of the dead beneath the crags. Then with a great cry he caught her hands in his and drew her towards him. "Is it?" he cried.

"Yes," she answered with laughter trembling on her lips. "Death hath enfranchised us, you and me. Give me my betrothal kiss, my only love."

For them one moment of Paradise, of bliss ineffable and supreme. The next, the crags behind them rang to the sound of the war whoop.

CHAPTER XXXVI

THE LAST FIGHT

Out from the forest rushed the remnant of that band which had smoked the peace pipe with the Governor one sunny afternoon on the banks of the Pamunkey. Tall and large of limb, painted with all fantastic and ghastly devices, and decorated with hideous mementoes of nameless deeds; with the lust of blood written large in every fierce lineament and dark and rolling eye; with raised hands grasping knife and tomahawk, and lips uttering cries that seemed not of earth—a more appalling vision could not have issued from out the beautiful, treacherous forest, a more crashing discord have come into the music of the golden evening.

For the two in their rocky fortress beneath the crags the apparition had no terrors. All the pain, the anguish, the hopelessness of the world was passing from them—the cry that swelled through the forest was its knell. They smiled to hear it, and with raised faces looked beyond the many-tinted evening skies into clear spaces where Love was all. The intoxication of the moment when hidden and despairing love became love triumphant and acknowledged abode with them. In the very grasp of death ineffable bliss possessed them. Their countenances changed; the lines of care and pain, the marks of tears, were all gone and the beauty of the happy soul shone out. For that brief space of time transcendent youth and loveliness was theirs. About them, as about the sun now sinking behind the low hills, there breathed a glory, a dying splendor as bright as it was fleeting. They felt, too, a lightness and gaiety of spirit—they had drunk of the nectar of the gods, and no leaden weight of care, no heavy sorrow, could ever touch them, ever drag them down again to the sad earth.

"You are beautiful," said Landless, gazing at her, even in the act of raising his gun to his shoulder; "as beautiful as you were the day I first saw you. I hear the drone of the bees in the vines at Verney Manor. I smell the roses. I look up and see the Rose of the World. My eyes were dazzled then, are dazzled now, my Rose of the World."

"That day I wore brocade and lace, and there were pearls around my throat," she said with a laugh of pure delight. "There was rouge upon my cheeks, too, sir, and my eyes were darkened. To-day I go a beggar maid, in rags, burnt by the sun—-"

"The nut-brown maid," he said.

"Ay," she answered, "the nut-brown maid—'For in my mind of all mankind'—you may e'en finish it yourself, sir."

The Ricahecrians had paused at the foot of the ascent to hold a council. It was soon over. With another burst of cries they rushed up the steep and upon the rocks, behind which were hidden their victims. Landless, kneeling to one side of the gap between the boulders by which he and Patricia had entered, fired, and the foremost of the savages threw up his arms, uttered a dreadful cry, and fell across the path of his fellows. For one moment the rush was checked, the next on they came, yelling furiously and brandishing their weapons. Landless fired and missed, fired again and pierced the thigh of a gigantic warrior, bringing him crashing to the ground. The line wavered, paused, then turning, swept to one side and so passed out of sight.

"They have found this pass too formidable," said Landless. "They will try now to force an entrance from the side. Do you watch the front, my queen, while I face them, coming over the rocks."

"I looked only at the mulatto," she said. "The others are shadows to me."

"His time is come," said Landless. "Do not fear him, sweetheart."

"I fear not," she answered. "I have the perfect love."

Along the top of a tall boulder to their right appeared a dark red line—the arm of a savage, with clutching fingers. Above it, very slowly and cautiously, there rose first an eagle's feather, then a coarse black scalp lock, then a high forehead and fierce eyes. The echo of Landless's shot reverberated through the cliffs, and when the smoke cleared only the bare gray boulder faced him. But from behind it came a derisive yell.

"Thou wilt think me a poor marksman, my dear," he said, smiling, as he reloaded his musket. "I have missed again."

"It is because you are wounded," she said. "I would I had thy wounds."

"I had a wounded heart, but you have healed it," he said, and looked at her with shining eyes.

The sun sank and the long twilight of the hills set in. The evening star was brightening through the pale amethyst of the sky when Landless said quietly: "The last charge," and emptied it into an arm which for one incautious moment had waved above the rocks.

"It is the end, then," said Patricia.

"Yes, it is the end. We have beaten them back for the moment, but presently they will find that all we could do we have done, and then—"

She left her post beside the gap in the front, and came and knelt beside him, and he took her in his arms.

"It is not Death before us, but Life," she said in a low voice.

"It is God and Love, naught else," he answered. "But the river between will be bitter for you to cross, sweetheart."

"We cross it together," she said, "and so—" She raised her head that he might see her radiant smile, and their lips met.

"Hark!" she said directly with her hand on his. "What is that sound?"

He shook his head. "The wind has risen, and the forest rustles and sighs. There is nothing more."

"It is far off," she answered, "but it is like the dip of oars. Ah!"

Over against them, framed in the narrow opening between the rocks, his lithe, half-nude figure dark against the crimson west, and with a smile upon his evil lips and in his evil eyes, stood Luiz Sebastian. In the dead silence that succeeded he looked with a smiling; countenance from the musket, now useless and thrown aside, to his enemy, wounded and unarmed save for a knife, and to the woman in that enemy's arms; then, without turning, he said a few words in an Indian tongue. From the dusky mass behind him came one short, wild cry of savage triumph, followed by another dead silence.

Still holding Patricia in one arm, Landless rose from his knee, and stood confronting him.

"We are met again, Señor Landless," said Luiz Sebastian smoothly. Receiving no answer, he spoke again with a tigerish expansion of his thick lips. "You have had an accident, I see. Mother of God! that foot must pain you! But you will forget it presently in the pleasure of the pine splinters."

"I will forget it in the pleasure of this," said Landless, releasing Patricia, and springing upon the mulatto with a suddenness and violence that sent them both staggering through the opening between the rocks, out upon the narrow plateau and into the ring of Ricahecrians. Luiz Sebastian was strong, with the easy masked strength of the panther, but Landless had the strength of despair. The mulatto, thrown heavily to the ground, and pinned there by his adversary's knee, saw the gleam of the lifted knife, and would have seen nothing more in this life, but that a woman's cry rang out and saved him. Landless heard, turned, saw Patricia dragged from the shelter of the rocks, leaped to his feet, leaving his work undone, and rushed upon the knot of savages with whom she was struggling. A moment saw him beside her with the Indian who had held her dead at his feet. Behind them was the great boulder which had formed the front wall of their chamber of defense. He put his arm around her, and drew her back with him until they stood against this rock, then faced the advancing savages with uplifted knife.

So determined was his attitude, so terribly had they proved his power, so certain it was that before he should be taken one at least of their number would taste that knife, that the Ricahecrians paused, swaying to and fro, yelling, working themselves into a fury that should send them on like maddened brutes, blind and deaf to all things but their lust for blood.

"I hear a sound of footsteps over the leaves," said Patricia.

"The wind rustles in them, or the deer pass," answered Landless. "Oh, my life! are you content?"

She answered with a low, clear laugh. "I hold happiness fast," she said. "It cannot escape us now."

"They are coming," he said. "The last kiss, heart of my heart."

Their lips met, and their eyes with a smile in them met, and then he put her gently behind him, and turned to again face Luiz Sebastian.

With his eyes fixed upon the yellow face, he had raised his hand to strike at the yellow breast, spotted and barred with the black of the war paint, when an Indian, gliding between, struck up his arm, and sent the knife tinkling down upon the rocks. With a yell of triumph the savage snatched up the weapon, and brandished it, showing it to his fellows, who, seeing their work accomplished, and the two whom they had tracked so far actually in their hands, made the forest ring with their exultant shouts. A few closed in around the devoted pair, directing at them fiendish cries and no less fiendish laughter, and menacing them with knife and tomahawk, but the majority streamed down the steep and into the forest at its base.

"They go to gather wood," said the still smiling Luiz Sebastian. "By and by we are to have a bonfire. Señor Landless has often carried wood, I think, in those old times when he was a slave, and when the pretty mistress behind him there treated him as such—unless she gave him favors in secret. But, Mother of God! now that she has made him master, we must carry the wood for him!"

Landless, standing with folded arms, looked at him with quiet scorn. "It is the nature of the viper to use his venom," he said calmly. "Such a thing cannot anger me."

"At the same time it is as well to crush the viper," said a voice at his elbow.

The speaker, who was Sir Charles Carew, had come from behind the boulders which ran in a straggling line down the hillside toward the river.

He had his drawn sword in his hand, and as he spoke, he ran the mulatto through the body. The wretch, his oath of rage and astonishment still upon his lips, fell to the ground without a groan, writhed there a moment or two, and then lay still forever.

From the forest below rose a loud confusion of shouts and cries, followed by a volley of musketry. At the sound the half dozen savages upon the plateau turned and plunged down the hillside, to be met before they reached the bottom by the upward rush of a portion of the rescuing party. For a short while the twilight glades, low hills and frowning crags rang to the sound of a miniature battle, to the quick crack of muskets, the clear shouts of the whites, and the whoops of the savages. But by degrees these latter became fainter, further between, died away—a short ten minutes, and there were no warriors left to return to the village in the Blue Mountains. Fierce shedders of blood, they were paid in their own coin.

On the hilltop Sir Charles shot his rapier into its scabbard, and strode over to Patricia, standing white and still against the rock. "I was in time," he said. "Thank God!"

She made no motion to meet his extended hands, but stood looking past him at Landless. Her face was like marble, her eyes one dumb question. Landless met their gaze, and in his own she read despair, renunciation, strong resolve—and a long farewell.

"You are come in time, Sir Charles Carew," he said. "A little more, and we should have been beyond your reach. You will find the lady safe and well, though shaken, as you see, by this last alarm. She will speak for me, I trust, will tell you that I have used her with all respect, that I have done for her all that I could do.... Madam, all danger is past. Will you not collect yourself and speak to your kinsman and savior?"

He spoke with a certain calm stateliness of voice and manner, as of one who has passed beyond all emotion, whether of hope or fear, and in his eyes which he kept fixed upon her there was a command.

"Speak to me, my cousin; tell me that I am welcome," said Sir Charles, flinging himself upon his knee before her.

With a strong shudder she looked away from the still, white, and sternly composed face opposite to the darkening river and the evening star shining calmly down upon a waste world.

At length she spoke. "I was all but beyond this world, cousin, so pardon me if I seem to come back to it somewhat tardily. You have my thanks, of course—my dear thanks—for saving my life—my life which is so precious to me."

She gave him her hand with a strange smile, and he pressed his lips upon it. "Your father is below, dearest cousin. Shall we descend to meet him? As to this—gentleman," turning with a smile that was like a frown to Landless, "I regret that circumstances combine to prevent our rewarding him as the guardian (a trusty one, I am sure) of so precious a jewel should be rewarded. But Colonel Verney will do—I will do—all that is possible. In the mean time I observe with regret that he is wounded. If he will allow me, I will send him my valet, who is below, and is the best barber surgeon in the three kingdoms. Come, dearest madam."

He bowed low and ceremoniously to Landless, who returned the salute with grave courtesy, and gave his hand to Patricia. For one moment she looked at Landless with wide, dark eyes, then, her spirit obedient to his spirit, she turned and went from him without one word or backward look.

The color had quite faded from the west, and the stars were thickening when Landless became conscious that the overseer was standing beside him. "You are the hardest one to hold that ever I saw," said that worthy grimly, and yet with a certain appreciation of the qualities that made the man at his feet hard to hold showing in his tone, "but I fancy we've got you at last. You've gone and put yourself in bilboes."

Landless smiled. "This time you may keep me. I shall not interfere. But tell me how you come here. You were sent back to the Plantations."

"Ay," said the other, "and there was the devil to pay, I can tell you, when I had to report you missing to Sir William. But Major Carrington stood my friend, and I got off with a tongue-drubbing. Well, after about three weeks or so, during which time the dogs and the searchers brought back most all of the runaway niggers, and Mistress Lettice had hysterics every day, back comes the Colonel and Sir Charles with ten of the twenty men who had rowed them up the Pamunkey. The rest had fallen in a brush with the Monacans. They hadn't come up with the Ricahecrians, hadn't seen hair nor hide of them, had but one report from the Indian villages along the river, and that was that no Ricahecrians had passed that way. So after a while they were forced to believe that they were upon a false scent, and back they comes post haste to the Plantations to get more men, and go up the Rappahannock. Well, they went up the Rappahannock, and found nothing to their purpose, so back they came again to try the James and the country above the Falls. This time they found the Settlements, which had been before like an overturned hive, pretty quiet, the ringleaders of your precious plot having all been strung up, and the rest made as mild as sheep with branding and whipping and doubling of times. So, the tobacco being in and the plantation quiet, things were left to Haines, and I came along with the Colonel. Major Carrington, too, who they say is in the Governor's black books, though Lord knows he was active enough in stamping out this insurrection, asked to be allowed to join in the search for his old friend's daughter, and so he's down in the woods yonder. And Mr. Cary is there, and Mr. Peyton (Mistress Betty Carrington made *him* come) and Mr. Jaclyn Carter. Fegs! half the young gentry in the colony pressed their services on the Colonel. It got to be the fashion to volunteer to run their heads into the wolf's mouth for Mistress Patricia. But Sir Charles choked most of them off. 'Gentlemen,' he says, says he, 'despite the saying that there cannot be too much of a good thing, I beg to remind you that the disastrous fortunes of those who first struggled with the forest and the Indians in this western paradise are attributed to the fact that they were two thirds gentlemen. Wherefore let us shun the rock upon which they split'—"

"How many of my fellow conspirators were put to death?" interrupted Landless.

"All the principal ones—them that Trail denounced as leaders. The rest we pardoned after giving them a lesson they won't soon forget. We let bygones be bygones with the redemptioners and slaves—all but those devils who got away that night at Verney Manor, and with Trail at their head, made for Captain Laramore's ship which was going to turn pirate. Well, they got to the boats, and one lot got off safe to the ship which hoisted the black flag, and sailed away to the Indies, and is sailing there, murdering and ruining, to this day, I reckon. But the other boat was over full, and the steersman was drunken, and she capsized before she got to the middle of the channel. Some were drowned, and those that got ashore we hung next morning. But Trail was in the first boat."

"When do you—do we—start down the river?"

"At midnight. And it's the Colonel's orders that until then you stay here among the rocks and not show yourself to the men below. He'll see you before we start. In the mean time I'll keep you company." And the overseer took out his pipe and tobacco pouch, filled the former, lighted it, and leaning back against the rock fell to smoking in contented silence.

Landless too sat in silence, with his head thrown back against the rock and his face uplifted to the growing splendor of the skies. The night wind, blowing mournfully around the bare hill and the broken crag, struck upon his brow with a hint of winter in its touch. With it came the tide of forest sounds—the sough of the leaves, the dull creaking of branch against branch, the wash of the water in the reeds, the whirr of wings, the cries of night birds—all the low and stealthy notes of the earth chant which had become to him as old and tenderly familiar as the lullabies of his childhood. Below him, at the foot of the hill, a square of dark and stately pines was irradiated by a great fire which burnt redly, casting flickering shadows far across the smooth brown earth, and around which sat or moved many figures. Laughter and jest, oaths and scraps of song floated up to the lonely watcher upon the hilltop. He heeded them not—he was above that world—and no sound came from that other and smaller fire blazing at some distance from the first—and the tree trunks between were so many and so thick that he could see naught but the light.

CHAPTER XXXVII

VALE

The overseer knocked the ashes from his pipe and stuck it in his belt. "The master," he said curtly, getting to his feet as three cloaked figures, followed by a negro bearing a torch, came up the hillside and into the waste of stones beneath the crags. Advancing to meet them, he took the torch from Regulus's hand and fired a mass of dead and leafless vine depending from the cliff. In the bright light which sprang up, filling the rocky chamber and burnishing the face of the crags into the semblance of a cataract of fire, the parties to the interview gazed at one another in silence.

Colonel Verney was the first to speak. "I am sorry to see that you are wounded," he said gravely.

"I thank you, sir,—it is nothing."

The Colonel walked the length of the plateau twice, then came back to his prisoner's side. "My daughter has told me all," he said somewhat huskily. "That you and the Susquehannock sought for her and found her; that you fought for her bravely more than once; that after the Indian was slain you guided and protected her through the forest; that you have in all things borne yourself towards her faithfully and reverently, not injuring her by word, thought or deed. My daughter is very dear to me—dearer than life, I am not ungrateful. I thank you very heartily."

"Mistress Patricia Verney is dear to me also," said Sir Charles, coming forward to stand beside his kinsman. "I too thank the man who restores her to her friends—to her lover."

"And I would to God," said the third figure, advancing, "that we could save the brave man to whom so much is owed. If I were Governor of Virginia—"

"You could do naught, Carrington," broke in the Colonel impatiently. "The man is convict—outside the pale! A convict, and the head of an Oliverian plot! Scarce the King himself could pardon him! And if he did, how long d' ye think the walls of the gaol at Jamestown would keep him from the rabble—and the nearest tree? No, no, William Berkeley does but his duty. And yet—and yet—"

He began to pace the rocks again, frowning heavily, and pulling at the curls of his periwig. "You are a brave man," he said at last, stopping before Landless and speaking with energy, "and from my soul I wish I could save you. I would gladly overlook all that is over and done with, would gladly free you, aid you, help you, so far as might be, to retrieve your past—but I cannot. My hands are tied; it is impossible—you must see for yourself that it is impossible."

"None can see that so clearly as myself, Colonel Verney," Landless said steadily. "I thank you for the will none the less."

"To take you back with me," the other continued, beginning to stride up and down again, "is to take you back, bound, to certain death. And there is but one alternative—to leave you here in the wilderness. Your presence here is known only to those upon whose discretion I can depend. They would hold their tongues, and none need ever be the wiser. But the Settlements will be barred to you forever, and hundreds of leagues stretch between this spot and the Dutch or the New Englanders. Moreover, your description hath been sent to the authorities of each colony. And you are wounded, and winter is at hand. It may be but a choice of deaths! I would to God there were some other way—but there is none! You must choose."

In the dead silence that ensued the Colonel moved back to the side of the Surveyor-General, and the two stood, thoughtfully regardant of the prisoner. The light from the partially consumed vines beginning to wane, the overseer motioned to Regulus to collect and apply his torch to a quantity of the fagots with which the ground was strewn. The negro obeyed, and stood behind the light flame and curling smoke which he had evoked, like the genie of an Arabian tale. Sir Charles, left standing in the centre of the rocky chamber, hesitated a moment, then walked with his usual languid grace over to where Landless leaned against a boulder, his eyes, shaded by his hand, fixed upon the ground.

"Whichever you choose—Scylla or Charybdis—" said Sir Charles in his most dulcet tones, "this is probably the last time you and I will ever speak together. There have been passages between us in the past, which, in the light of after event, I cannot but regret. You have just rendered me an inestimable service. I have learnt, too, that you saved my life the night of the storming of the Manor House. I beg to apologize to you, sir, for any offense I may have given you by word or deed." And he held out his hand with his most courtly smile.

"It becomes a dying man to be in charity with the world he leaves," said Landless, somewhat coldly, but with a smile too, "and so I do that which I never thought to do," and he touched the other's fingers with his own.

Sir Charles looked at him curiously. "You make a good enemy," he said lightly. "Had it not been predestined that we were to hate each other, I could find it in my heart to desire you for a friend. You remain in the forest, I dare swear?"

"Yes," answered Landless, with his eyes upon the light in the glade below. "I choose the easier fate."

"The easier for all concerned," said the other with a peculiar intonation.

Landless glanced at him keenly, but the courtier face and the inscrutable smile told nothing. "The easier for myself, whom alone it concerneth," said Landless sternly.

Dragging himself up by the rock behind him, he turned to the two elder men. "I have decided, Colonel Verney," he said slowly, "I will stay here, an it please you."

"You shall have all that we can leave you," said the Colonel eagerly and with some emotion. "Ammunition in plenty, food, blankets, an axe—it's little enough I can do, God knows, but I do that little most willingly."

"Again I thank you," said Landless wearily.

Sir Charles caught the inflection. "You stand in need of rest," he said courteously, "and, this matter settled, our farther intrusion upon you is as unnecessary as it must be unwelcome. Had we not best descend, gentlemen?"

"Ay," said the Colonel. "We have done all we could." Then, to Landless, "With the moonrise we drop down the river—from out your sight forever. I have told you frankly there is no hope for you amongst your kind in the world to which we return. I believe there to be none. But have you thought of what we must needs leave you to? Humanly speaking, it is death, and death alone, in the winter forest."

"I have thought," said Landless.

"From my soul I wish that some miracle may occur to save you yet!"

"An ill wish!" said the other, smiling, "with but little chance, however, of its fulfillment."

"I fear not," said the Colonel with something like a groan, "but I wish it, nevertheless. Here is my hand, and with it my heartfelt thanks for your service to my daughter. And I wish you to believe that I deeply deplore your fate, and that I would have saved you if I could."

"I believe it," Landless said simply.

The Colonel took and wrung his hand, then turned sharply away, and beckoning the overseer to follow, strode out of the circle of rocks.

Sir Charles raised his feathered hat. "We have been foes," he said, "but the strife is over—and when all is said, we are both Englishmen. I trust we bear each other no ill will."

"I bear none," said Landless.

Sir Charles, his eyes still fixed upon the pale quiet of the other's face, passed out of the opening between the rocks, and his place was taken by the Surveyor-General.

"I would have saved you if I could," he said in a low and troubled voice. "I bow to a brave man and a gallant gentleman," and he too was gone.

In the glade below, the movement, the laughter and the song sank gradually into silence as the gentlemen adventurers, the rangers, Indian guides, and servants composing the rescuing party threw themselves down, one by one, beside the blazing fires for a short rest before moonrise and the long pull down the river.

Among the crags, high above the twinkling watch-fires and the wash of the dark river, there was the stillness of the stars, of the white frost and the bare cliffs. In the northern heavens played a soft light, and now and then a star shot. The man who marked its trail across the studded skies thought of himself as of one as far withdrawn as it from the world of lower lights in the forest at his feet. Already he felt a prescience of the loneliness of the morrow, and the morrow, and the morrow, of the slow drift of the days in the waning forest, the hopeless nights, the terror of that great solitude—and felt, too, a feverish desire to hasten that approach, to embrace that which was to be henceforth bone of his bone and flesh of his flesh. He wished for the dash of oars in the dark stream below and for the rise of the moon which was to shine coldly down upon him, companionless, immured in that vast fortress from which he might never hope to escape.

The sound of cautious footsteps among the rocks brought his sick and wandering fancy back to the present. Raising himself upon his elbow and peering intently into the darkness, he made out two figures, one tall and large, the other much slighter, advancing towards him. Presently the larger figure stopped short, and, seating itself upon a flat rock at the brink of the hill, turned its face towards the fires in the woods below. The other came on lightly and hurriedly—another moment, and rising to his knees, he clasped her in his arms and laid his head upon her bosom.

"I never thought to see you again," he said at last.

"I made Regulus bring me," she answered. "The others do not know—they think me asleep."

She spoke in a low, even, monotonous voice, and the hand which she laid upon his forehead was like marble. "My heart is dead, I think," she said. "I wish my body were so too."

He drew her closer to him and covered her face and hands with kisses. "My love, my lady," he said. "My white rose, my woodland dove!"

She clung to him, trembling. "Down there I was going mad," she whispered. "But now—now—I feel as though I could weep." He felt her tears upon his face, but in a moment she was calm again. "Do you remember the bird we found the other day, all numbed with cold?" she said. "It had been gay and free and light of heart, but it had not strength to flutter when I took it in my hands and tried to warm it—and could not. I am like that bird. The world is very gray and cold, and my heart—it will never be warm again."

"God comfort you," he said brokenly.

"They have told me that at moonrise we leave this place—and you. They say that it is all they can do for you—to leave you here. All!—Oh, my God!"

"They have done what they could," he said gravely. "I recognize that. And I wish you to do so too, sweetheart."

She looked at him wildly. "I have been silent," she said, pressing her clasped hands against her bosom. "I have not told them. I have obeyed what I read in your eyes. But was it well? Oh, my dear, let me speak!"

He took her hands from her breast and laid them against his own. "No," he said with a smile, "I love you too well for that."

From the woods across the river came the crying of wolves, then a silence as of the grave; then a whisper arose in the long dry grass and the leafless vines, and a cold breeze lifted the hair from their foreheads. The whisper grew into a murmur, prolonged and deep, a sound as of a distant cataract, or of the dash of surf upon a far away shore—the voice of the wind in the world of trees. A star shot, leaving a stream of white fire to fade out of the dark blue sky. From the forest came again the cry of the wolves. In the camp below there seemed some stir, and the figure seated on the rock turned its head towards them and lifted a warning hand.

"You must go," said Landless. "It was madness for you to venture here. See, the light is growing in the east."

With a low, desolate moaning sound she wrung the hands he released and raised her face to his. He kissed her upon the brow, the eyes and the mouth. "Good-by, my life, my love, my heart," he said. "We were happy for an hour. Good-by!"

"I will be brave," she answered. "I will live my life out. I will pray to God. And, Godfrey, I will be ever true to you. I shall never see you again, my dear, never hear of you more, never know till my latest day whether you are of this world still, or whether you have waited for me a long time, up there beyond those lights. If it—if death—should come Boon, wait for me—beyond—in perfect trust, my dear, for I will come to you—I will come to you as I am, Godfrey."

He bowed his face upon her hands.

The breeze freshened, and the sound of the surf became the sound of breakers. In the east the pale light strengthened. The figure below them stood up and beckoned.

"The moon is coming," said Patricia. "Once before I watched for it—in terror, with pride and anger in my heart. Then, when I thought of you, I hated you. It is strange to think of that now. Kiss me good-by."

"I too will be strong," he said. "I will await the pleasure of the Lord. Until His good time, my bride!"

Rising to his feet he held her in his arms, then kissed her upon the lips and put her gently from him. For a moment she stood like a statue, then with a lifted face and hands clasped at her bosom, she turned, and slowly, but without a backward look, left the circle of rocks. Through the opening he saw the slave come up to her, and saw her motion to him to fall behind—another moment, and both dark figures had sunk below the brow of the hill.

Stronger and stronger blew the wind, louder and louder swelled the voice of the forest. Below, the wash of the river in its reeds, the dull groaning of branch grating against branch, the fall of leaf and acorn, the loud sighing of the pines, the cries of the owl, the panther, and the wolf—above, the vast dome of the heavens and the fading stars. An effulgence in the east; a silver crest, like the white rim of a giant wave, upon the eastern hills; a pale splendor mounting slowly and calmly upward—a dead world,—all her passion, all her pain, all toil and strife over and done with,—shining down upon a sadder earth.

From beneath the shadowy banks there shot out into the middle of the broad moonlit stream a long canoe, followed by a second and a third, and turning, went swiftly down that long, bright, shimmering, rippling path.

In the last and smallest of the three boats a man rose from his seat in the stern, and with his eyes upon the line of moon-whitened cliffs above him, raised his plumed hat with a courteous gesture, then bent and spoke to a cloaked and hooded figure sitting, still and silent, between him and a burlier form. This canoe was rowed by negroes, and as they rowed they sang. The wild chant—half dirge, half frenzy—that they raised was suited to that waste which they were leaving.

The black lines upon the silver flood became mere dots, and the wailing notes came up the stream faintly and more faintly still. For a while the echoes rolled among the folded hills and the tall gray crags, but at length they died away forever.

Milton Keynes UK
Ingram Content Group UK Ltd.
UKHW030718041024
449263UK00004B/399

9 789362 518903